RECONCEPTUALIZING
THE STRENGTHS AND COMMON
HERITAGE OF BLACK FAMILIES

ABOUT THE EDITORS

Edith M. Freeman, Ph.D., MSW, is a Professor Emerita at the University of Kansas School of Social Welfare, Lawrence, Kansas, where she taught graduate practice courses at the doctoral and master's levels. Her writing and research interests include issues related to children and families (particularly families of color), substance abuse prevention and treatment, cultural competence, organizational change, community development, narrative approaches, and empowerment practice. She has published numerous books and articles in professional journals on these and other topics. Her consultation with community organizations and behavioral health agencies has also focused primarily on those topic areas.

Sadye L. Logan, DSW, MSW, holds the I. DeQuincy Newman Endowed Professorship in social work education with an emphasis in Social and Economic Justice at the University of South Carolina College of Social Work. She teaches practice methods courses and courses on family treatment. Her writing and research interests include social justice issues impacting upon families and children, culturally specific services for children and families of color, the psychospiritual dimensions of practice and education, addictive behaviors, and racial identity development. Dr. Logan has written and published extensively and provided consultation in these areas.

RECONCEPTUALIZING THE STRENGTHS AND COMMON HERITAGE OF BLACK FAMILIES

Practice, Research, and Policy Issues

Edited by

EDITH M. FREEMAN, Ph.D., MSW

and

SADYE L. LOGAN, DSW, ACSW

(With 14 Other Contributors)

CHARLES C THOMAS • PUBLISHER, LTD.
Springfield • Illinois • U.S.A.

Published and Distributed Throughout the World by

CHARLES C THOMAS • PUBLISHER, LTD.
2600 South First Street
Springfield, Illinois 62704

© 2004 by CHARLES C THOMAS • PUBLISHER, LTD.

ISBN 0-398-07488-7 (hard)
ISBN 0-398-07489-5 (paper)

Library of Congress Catalog Card Number: 2003071199

With THOMAS BOOKS *careful attention is given to all details of manufacturing and design. It is the Publisher's desire to present books that are satisfactory as to their physical qualities and artistic possibilities and appropriate for their particular use.* THOMAS BOOKS *will be true to those laws of quality that assure a good name and good will.*

Printed in the United States of America
GS-R-3

Library of Congress Cataloging-in-Publication Data

Reconceptualizing the strengths and common heriatge of Black families :
  practice, research, and social policy issues / edited by Edith M. Freeman
  and Sadye L. Logan ; with 14 other contributors.
     p. cm.
  Includes bibliographic references and index.
  ISBN 0-398-07488-7 – ISBN 0-398-07489-5 (pbk.)
    1. Social work with African Americans. 2. Family social work–United
States. 3. African American families–Social conditions. 4. African
American families–Research. I. Freeman, Edith M. II. Logan, Sadye
Louise, 1943–
HV3181.R43 2004
362.84'96073–dc22
                                                            2003071199

CONTRIBUTORS

Paula Allen-Meares, Ph.D. is a Professor and Dean of the University of Michigan School of Social Work, Ann Arbor, Michigan.

Brenda Crawley, Ph.D. is an Associate Professor at Loyola University School of Social Work, Chicago, Illinois.

Ramona Denby, Ph.D., ACSW is an Associate Professor and Associate Dean for Research at the University of Nevada-Las Vegas, Greenspun College of Urban Affairs, Las Vegas, Nevada.

Priscilla A. Gibson, Ph.D., ACSW is an Assistant Professor at the University of Minnesota School of Social Work, Saint Paul, Minnesota.

Shirley A. Hill, Ph.D. is an Associate Professor at the University of Kansas Department of Sociology, Lawrence, Kansas.

Norge W. Jerome, Ph.D. is a Professor Emerita, Department of Preventive Medicine and Public Health (Nutritional Anthropology), University of Kansas School of Medicine, Kansas City, Kansas.

Alice K. Johnson is a faculty member at the University of Illinois at Chicago, Jane Addams College of Social Work, Chicago, Illinois.

Bogart R. Leashore, Ph.D., ACSW is a Professor and Dean of Hunter College School of Social Work, New York, New York.

Ruth G. McRoy, Ph.D. is a Professor and Associate Dean for Research, University of Texas at Austin School of Social Work in Austin, Texas. She is also the Ruby Lee Piester Centennial Professor in Services to Children and Families.

Patricia O'Brien, Ph.D. is an Associate Professor at the University of Illinois at Chicago, Jane Addams College of Social Work, Chicago, Illinois.

Olga Osby is a faculty member and Director of the BSW Program for the Mississippi Valley State University School of Social Work, Itta Bena, Mississippi.

Sandra Owens-Kane, Ph.D., LCSW is an Assistant Professor at the University of Nevada Las Vegas School of Social Work, Las Vegas, Nevada.

Janice Matthews Rasheed, Ph.D. is an Associate Professor at Loyola University School of Social Work, Chicago, Illinois.

Cynthia Rocha, Ph.D. is an Associate Professor at the University of Tennessee at Knoxville College of Social Work, Knoxville, Tennessee.

I am,
Because you are,
And because you are,
I am.

–African Proverb

FOREWORD

This book, *Reconceptualizing the Strengths and Common Heritage of Black Families: Practice, Research, and Policy Issues,* is both inspirational and practical. It is appropriate for all individuals in service professions with black clientele-care managers; policy makers; social workers and other behavioral health professionals; health services and public health practitioners; commercial service providers; and municipal, county, and state employees, among others. Researchers who care about the quality of their data obtained on or from blacks also have good reason to add this resource to their research design and analysis bookshelf.

In particular, this book should serve as a reference guide to advocates and practitioners of "cultural tailoring" who fail to document the specific cultural group and cultural elements that are being "tailored." "Cultural tailoring" should include much more than hiring minority outreach workers or community people to assist in implementing research programs in diverse communities. At a minimum, it should document and include developing an understanding and application of the cultural norms and realities of the specific target population based on the culturally-centered principles laid out in this book.

Reflective readers will find this book to be an excellent resource for understanding why their professional practice involving human affairs and services should be grounded in the culture of their clients. To miss this fundamental point in the human service professions means misconstruing important elements of human behavior. It also means that the strengths and assets clients bring to the sociocultural encounter might not be captured by those professionals, thus causing them to miss opportunities for culturally appropriate and effective interventions.

After all, culture includes a group's design for living–its belief and value systems, its cherished ideals, treasured goals, its perspectives. Culture, also includes the thoughts and notions considered abhorrent to a group. These intangibles or nonmaterial aspects of culture define a people. Thus, if elements of culture are not incorporated into care and service programs, a people's strengths and weaknesses, assets and liabilities, and unique problem-solving abilities will be omitted from the intervention strategy, and an intervention failure will ensue.

Freeman and Logan (Chapter 1) document the case for a common cultural heritage of black families with differences based on the social context. They are convincing. As a black woman raised as a British "subject citizen" in colonial Grenada in the Caribbean in the 1930s and 1940s, acculturated in the United States of America with university classmates from West and Southern Africa in the 1950s and 1960s, and as a professional student of American culture with international development experiences in six African countries, the evidence in Chapter 1 is persuasive.

The common heritage or Africentric framework is presented in Chapter 1, and then is operationalized by Logan and Freeman in Chapter 2 to guide practitioners in their work with black families. Specific cultural strengths are not only identified and presented; they are put to work or applied to the benefit of the individual, family, community, and society.

Other chapters in Part II of the book serve the reader by providing historical data and cultural critiques of pivotal topics such as housing, mental health, crime and violence, labor, work and employment, substance abuse, youth, men, women, families, and the elderly. In each case, strengths and needs of black families are highlighted to exemplify a practice and research approach that is driven by cultural underpinnings and norms of experience.

To consider how to improve existing conceptual flaws and misdirected social programs, particularly for black families, study this book and refer to it often. It will help to shape your policies, programs, research, and practice in culturally significant ways.

NORGE W. JEROME, PH.D.

*Professor Emerita of Preventive Medicine
and Public Health (Nutritional Anthropology)
University of Kansas School of Medicine*

INTRODUCTION

The purpose of this book is twofold. First, it provides a comprehensive analysis and critique of the existing bodies of research literature on black families, children, and communities, and the effects of that literature on the status of this population today. Secondly, the book presents new and expanded practice and research frameworks with culturally sensitive guidelines for rebuilding and increasing the self- and collective sufficiency of this heterogeneous group. These frameworks are used to propose specific approaches to culturally meaningful research, practice, and policy development related to black families. Hence, the book's broad perspective is solution-focused, culturally specific (or emic), and strengths oriented.

The book's strengths orientation emphasizes the resourcefulness and natural resilience of African American families, both individually and collectively, in spite of numerous barriers with which they have been confronted. This orientation is important because much of the past and current literature on black families has been pathology-focused. That literature often uses a Eurocentric lens and related standards to frame discussions and make decisions about the life opportunities, health, viability, and well-being of African Americans. Further, this culturally biased lens and set of standards have been used in the development of public and social policy, leading to the many adverse economic, political, physical, and social conditions experienced by these families.

Fortunately, contemporary social work literature as well as some of the general social science literature now reflects many authors' and researchers' efforts to establish more positive perspectives about African Americans and other people of color. Some of this literature, however, still fails to acknowledge the strengths and resilience of these groups. This failure has had many negative consequences, most important has been a denial of the effects of institutional and policy barriers on the growth and survival of such families. Another gap in this literature is a failure to acknowledge the common heritage and struggles of black people who were brought to this country directly from Africa and enslaved, or who subsequently immigrated here from Europe, Canada, South America, and the Caribbean. Not recognizing these common cultural resources and problems, along with various environmental barriers, has no doubt, limited opportunities for identifying common approaches to planning and implementing family and community rebuilding.

Moreover, the current political climate has led to the development of many cost containment and social program reforms which have exacerbated existing resource inequities and negative media messages about black families and communities. Clearly, an expanded focus and new directions are needed in the literature to enable social work to actualize more effectively the strengths perspective and its' social justice priorities related to African American families and other groups of color. An equally important benefit of such a shift in the literature is that the profession, as illustrated in this book, can identify black stakeholder or consumer-involved dissemination and policy impact strategies for influencing the perspectives of policy developers and other decision-makers.

The book's contribution to this literature on black families includes its' discussions on practice, policy, and research issues at the micro, mezzo, and macro levels, which have seriously disrupted the well-being of African American families, currently and historically. This more integrative approach to systems analyses reflects these families' realities in which the effects of supports and barriers at all three levels often operate/influence each other simultaneously. While these common aspects exist in their realities and African origins, black families in the United States are from various countries and sociopolitical circumstances. They reflect a range of different lifestyles and ethnic identity orientations from the process of adapting to life in this country and in other countries. Hence, this book emphasizes that an understanding of black families must be derived from equally important knowledge areas regarding: (1) Their core African culture, values, and traditions (group commonalities); and (2) Their varied experiences and responses to a history of racism and oppression since the African diaspora (within group diversity). This dual perspective is essential for maintaining the strengths-focused and culture specific approaches that this book has used to address these important areas.

These two approaches are evident throughout the book, but particularly in Part One, which includes two chapters on the Conceptual, Theoretical, Research, and Practive Orientation of the Book. Chapter 1 by Freeman and Logan identifies common aspects of the heritage of black families: the common strengths, problems, and barriers that they have experienced from an Afrocentric cultural perspective. In that same chapter, the authors analyze how, in spite of these commonalities, such families are different, and the implications of those differences for a culturally sensitive research framework and policy reform process. The book also includes an analysis of the strengths perspective in Chapter 2 by Logan and Freeman, and some unique aspects of its' application to practice with black families and communities. Chapter 2 also discusses how the proposed Afrocentric model from Chapter 1 and the application of the strengths perspective and other spiritually-sensitive approaches can be integrated in assessing and intervening with African American families in their communities.

Part Two includes nine chapters on The Status and Quality of Research Literature on Black Families and Communities related to a number of cutting edge issues and special subgroups within this population. Those chapters provide an analysis and critique of research literature in each specified area in terms of the lens, methodology, and findings in this literature, and then each proposes topic or population specific guidelines for improving the cultural relevance of such research. Chapters 3 through 8 present critiques of black family research literature related to housing, mental health, crime and violence, employment and training, substance abuse, and education respectively. Chapters 8 through 11 address the research literature on African American children and youth within the education system as well as the literature on black women, men, and the elderly, in that order. The topic and population specific research frameworks proposed in these nine chapters provide guidelines that are consistent with the general research framework proposed by the editors in Chapter 1.

Finally, in Part Three, Chapters 12 through 14 focus on micro, mezzo, and macro practice approaches for helping black families and communities to build on their cultural strengths in the areas of cultural maintenance, social justice and political activism, and economic and social development. These family and community practice chapters include specific principles for systems changes and for improving the well-being of this population with an emphasis on including them as important stakeholders and collaborators based on knowledge summarized in the research chapters in Part II. Part III includes also the epilogue by Freeman, focused on the implications of such integrated strengths-oriented approaches for research, practice, and policy reforms.

This book is designed primarily as a direct practice-research text for graduate students in social work, psychology, mental health, case management, community planning, public health, public administration, and human resource programs that include a focus on practice with black families and communities. Hence, it is intended as an integrative text for graduate courses such as those focused on practice-research, participatory research, community empowerment/capacity building, and combined micro-mezzo-macro level practice. It should be useful as well to beginning and experienced helping professionals, administrators, consultants and trainers, researchers, policy makers, and community activists in a range of social science fields.

The intent of the editors is to provide the readers with an opportunity to rethink their approaches to research and micro, mezzo, and macro practice with African American families and communities. The use of more culturally relevant, stakeholder involved, and strengths focused approaches to research and practice with this population not only requires reconceptualizing this work, but it also requires changes in the readers' roles from expert professionals to the apprentices of key cultural informants. The goal of such changes is to improve the quality and outcomes of that work. We challenge the readers to undertake this essential long-term goal.

ACKNOWLEDGMENTS

The completion of this book represents a promising yet arduous journey for the editors. The idea for writing the book had its genesis during a Spring 1997 Institute on the Common Heritage of Black Families at the University of Kansas. The editors convened that invitational institute with a number of national scholars who had made significant contributions to the literature on black families and communities. The stimulating dialogue and rich exchange of knowledge among the institute participants served as a catalyst for the editors in conceiving and planning this book. As a result, many of the chapters in the book represent papers that were presented during the institute and subsequently revised, as well as other chapters that were added later to expand the list of topics.

Consequently, we wish to acknowledge the groundbreaking scholarship of our contributing authors in completing their chapters. Their work throughout this process has been both professional and collaborative. We also acknowledge and appreciate the work of Marian Abegg, support staff in the University of Kansas School of Social Welfare in Lawrence, Kansas, who typed parts of the manuscript. Finally, we thank our families for their enduring and nurturing support, and most of all, we are grateful for the spiritual and cultural inspiration that led us to write profoundly about the strengths, needs, and common heritage of African American families.

CONTENTS

PART THREE: MICRO-MEZZO-MACRO PRACTICE STRATEGIES FOR BUILDING ON THE STRENGTHS OF BLACK FAMILIES AND COMMUNITIES AND CHANGING LARGE SYSTEMS

RECONCEPTUALIZING
THE STRENGTHS AND COMMON
HERITAGE OF BLACK FAMILIES

PART ONE

CONCEPTUAL, THEORETICAL, RESEARCH, AND PRACTICE ORIENTATION OF THE BOOK

Chapter 1

COMMON HERITAGE AND DIVERSITY AMONG BLACK FAMILIES AND COMMUNITIES: AN AFROCENTRIC RESEARCH PARADIGM

EDITH M. FREEMAN AND SADYE L. LOGAN

General assumptions about black families in the media and professional literature have reinforced myths that such families are a homogeneous group. Contrary to these self-perpetuating myths, black families are from many different countries and sociopolitical circumstances. These assumptions and myths not only pathologize common aspects of black families and encourage gross generalizations about them (Barnes, 2001; Horton, 2002; Schiele, 1996), but they also ignore the importance of within group differences. Hence, they limit dominant society's understanding of and appreciation for variations in black families' cultural traditions, identities, experiences, values, beliefs, and lifestyles, as well as commonalities among them.

Black families' life opportunities and resources have been severely limited in a number of ways as a result. First, policy makers and those who influence them have used such assumptions as the basis for biased research and policy decisions, leading to and perpetuating a process of institutionalized racism and oppression toward black families, other families of color, and the poor. Biased research results and related social policy often lead to biased or culturally destructive service programs, another consequence of these assumptions (Freeman, 1996). Since service providers for these programs are not required to be culturally competent, the resulting services are often culturally insensitive and psychologically inaccessible to the target families and communities.

The purpose of this chapter is to present a common heritage framework that can increase service providers' and policy makers' understanding of the common strengths and needs of black families. The chapter also analyzes within group differences that are equally important for informing the development of culturally competent services that build upon the collective sufficiency of these families. A discussion is included on the implications for culturally competent research based on the commonalities and differences presented in the chapter, along with related policy issues. The term black families is used in this discussion to include all people of African descent and the African diaspora, a more inclusive concept than African Americans in this context. Before describing the common heritage framework, an analysis is presented of theoretical assumptions that support or dispute the concept of a common heritage among black people.

Theories about African Continuity and Discontinuity

Different theoretical concepts have been used to support or argue against direct linkages between the past and present culture of black families. These concepts, conclusions, and beliefs affect how the problems and strengths of black families are conceptualized. Moreover, they affect how services are organized and social policies are developed to address those problems, hence predisposing policies and programs to either acknowledge or ignore those strengths. Both continuity and discontinuity perspectives are grounded in assumptions about the African roots of black families.

African Discontinuity Perspective

This perspective assumes that although the cultural roots of black people are centered in Africa, vast differences existed among the African countries. Their different languages, religions, philosophies, customs, and values were assumed to be in conflict. Those assumed differences were used to infer the absence of a common culture among the various West African countries (Frazier, 1966), and to conclude that, collectively, those cultures were less valuable or valid than European cultures.

The fact that Africans quickly adapted to the cultures and demands of different countries after the diaspora, during slavery and colonization, is viewed as confirmation of the absence of a common valued culture rather than the existence of their culture as a strength (Sudarkasa, 1983). Some historians and researchers have labeled African adaptations as inferior versions of the European cultures of those who enslaved or colonized them. This argument ignores how those adaptations persisted in spite of enduring barriers, including American laws that prohibited the teaching of English, religion, and commerce to slaves (McRoy, 1990). Based on these assumptions, black families have often been called culturally deprived or ácultural.

The goal of policies and service programs based on these assumptions is to acculturate or socialize black families to Eurocentric traditions and values, including the "colorblind" myth perpetuated in America. Hence, the best progress is assumed to be that which makes black families blend in with other races and ethnic groups, an impossible and undesirable goal. Other programs based on these assumptions may imply that very little change in black families is possible, based on the intersection of social class and racial biases. This lack of belief in the possibility of change is implied by euphemisms such as "the poor will always be with us" and "why haven't black people done better given all the affirmative action and social programs being provided to them?"

The Continuity or Survival Perspective

In contrast to the discontinuity argument, the survival perspective assumes there *was* a common culture among Africans before the diaspora, particularly among West African countries. Some differences were acknowledged, however, those differences were assumed to be minor considering the degree of unity that Africans were able to develop in order to survive after the diaspora. During slavery and colonization, some historians and researchers believe the oral tradition allowed the blending of common aspects of the different countries' culture, traditions, language, and values (DeBois, 1969, Herskovits, 1958).

Dependence on a written language alone would have been a barrier to this blending process and to maintaining common aspects of language and traditions in spite of external efforts to eliminate all of these cultural attributes.

For example, the common lineage and kinship bonds of Africans helped them to transcend and cope with the family and clan disruptions caused by slavery or colonization, such as the need to care for orphan children across clan lines (Freeman, 1990). The forming of such new family arrangements was consistent with the common child-centered culture of each African country, thus insuring the survival of Africans beyond individual or clan continuity. The common organizational structure of religious, spiritual, marital, healing, agrarian, and socialization (e.g., rites of passage) institutions encouraged the transfer of those institutions in some form to all countries where Africans were taken during the diaspora. Many of those common institutions also endured throughout Africa during colonization when Europeans imposed new clan and geographical boundaries upon the inhabitants.

A Proposed Common Heritage Framework

Framework Overview

This African continuity perspective is at the heart of efforts to identify a common heritage framework for black families living in Africa, North America, Europe, South America and the Caribbean. Such a framework does not ignore important differences that existed among African countries centuries ago, or differences that developed from the various geographical, political, social, and economic conditions that confronted black families in the countries to which they were taken during the African diaspora. However, a failure to acknowledge common cultural resources and problems may impede efforts to address environmental barriers and utilize common planning and implementation strategies for helping black families and communities to strengthen themselves. The following Ethiopian proverb highlights the value of a common cause among black families based on their shared cultural heritage: "When spider webs unite, they can tie up a lion."

Using a framework for linking past and present cultural factors is not only a critical philosophical tenet, it is also an essential aspect of service delivery to black families. Logan, Freeman, and McRoy (1990) assert that:

> Social work practice with black families is a specialized area of practice that requires an understanding of the historical and cultural background of blacks in the United States and a consideration of the influences these factors have on the contemporary black family system. (p. 1)

Finally, self-pride in common ancestral origins and history is central to this framework. Africentricity is one of many tenets, such as collectiveness and mutual responsibility, spirituality, political and economic development, and indigenous leadership, that can help black families and communities to center their lives, depending on their cultural orientations. Africentricity is based on the teachings of Asante (1989) and Oliver (1989). Oliver defines Africentricity as:

> The internalization of values that emphasize love of self, awareness of traditional African heritage, and personal commitment to the economic and political power of African Americans and other people of African descent. (p. 26)

Using Africentricity as one exemplar for organizing the common heritage framework of black families leads to a focus on common roots, values, and traditions; diaspora and enslavement or colonization experiences; resettlement transitions; and current challenges.

Components of the Framework

Common Roots, Values, and Traditions. As illustrated by Figure 1.1, the core of the Common Heritage Framework for black families is their common roots, or essentially, their common African values and traditions. Those values and traditions are important because they help to explain the adaptations and maladaptations that black families made during and after the diaspora in response to various conditions in the countries to which they were taken. Examples of such values and traditions include use of the oral tradition for transmitting beliefs and ways of being, the importance of affective relationships, matrilineal kinship lines, group orientation or collectiveness, African spirituality and

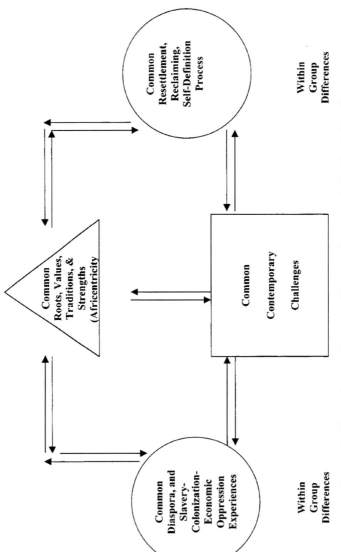

Figure 1.1 Example of a Common Heritage Framework for Black Families

philosophy, unity and harmony with nature, eldership, indigenous healing, and duality and balance (Schiele, 1996; Baldwin & Hopkins, 1990; Gyekye, 1992; Kambon, 1992; Crawley & Freeman, 1993).

Many of these values and traditions were closely interrelated in how they influenced Africans to maintain their culture and survival resources. For example, the healing tradition was often passed down across the generations within each tribe or clan, thus strengthening matrilineal kinship lines and reinforcing the value of strong kinship bonds. The storytelling or oral tradition was frequently the responsibility of tribal elders who expressed and passed on cultural wisdom through their stories. Those stories and proverbs became another source of significant cultural respect accorded to griots, consistent with the value of eldership across the different African tribes (Crawley & Freeman, 1993; McRoy, 1990).

Common Diaspora, Slavery-Colonization Experiences. During various periods of the diaspora, some Africans suffered geographical dispersal from their land and the cultural destruction of their meaningful and supportive traditions by white enslavers. They were taken through slavery, indentured service, apprenticeships, and extortion from their homeland and relocated to various parts of North and South America, Europe, Latin America, and Asia. Many of these relocated Africans died, or endured harrowing, often life-threatening experiences which eventually led to a life of slavery if they survived their middle passage. However, some Africans obtained freedom through completion of indentured service, running away through the underground railroad to Canada, and by other means. Slavery involved an all-encompassing oppression of the mind, body, and spirit, yet many survived these experiences through maintaining a common resilience and common values-traditions in spite of culturally destructive laws against the practice of those traditions (Figure 1.1).

It was possible for indentured servants and others who had served out a prescribed period of servitude to purchase their freedom through money they had earned. "Freedmen" enjoyed opportunities to prosper economically; to own land, slaves, or indentured servants; and to control their own destinies in other important ways. Among common challenges experienced by freed slaves and indentured servants was the possibility of whites destroying papers that documented their status, which they were required to carry at all times, and then selling them into slavery away from their families and ways of life. Many free persons, once sold or resold into slavery through such devious means, never achieved a free status again during their lifetimes, their fates and whereabouts often remaining unknown to their families.

Other Africans were not taken from their homeland, but suffered similar oppressive experiences through the institution of colonization by European invaders. African countries and tribes were conquered and then, geographically redistributed to decrease their opportunities to develop coalitions to reclaim their lands and freedom. Potentially strong clans without past hostilities were divided geographically, while those with traditional conflicts might be relocated to the same lands. A common aspect of European oppression through colonization was the seizing of African resources such as gold, iron, cattle, land, and diamonds, which was accomplished through war, relocations of Africans to crowded and less desirable areas, servitude, poverty, political and tribal disfranchisement, and various forms of apartheid.

In spite of these and other common challenges during the diaspora, for free persons of color, slaves, and colonized Africans alike, their mutual African values and traditions were used to sustain them, spiritually and culturally. And because they were spiritual and believed in the possibility of survival, many of them did survive their experiences, while others also were able to thrive (Sudarkasa, 1983). Many others, however, did not survive the brutality of those experiences, some choosing to end their lives and those of their children during the middle passage or colonization.

Common Post-Slavery/Colonization Resettlement Experiences. Although black people's experiences in various parts of the world were both similar and different prior to resettlement, there were common aspects of resettlement that many of them experienced. Those resettlement or reconstruction experiences included migration to urban areas from rural or village life; attempts to participate in local farming, business, or the informal economy; family reunification efforts; and the reestablishment of black cultural institutions (Figure 1.1). Whether in Africa, North America, or Latin America, a reconfigured form of economic and racial oppression was encountered by all black people (McRoy, 1990).

This oppression, supported by Jim Crow, segregation, or aparteid policies, was so pervasive that it infiltrated every aspect of life, including education, housing, health, employment, the legal system, and politics (Schiele, 1996). Poverty became the common mode of entrapment for black people intergenerationally. Its various forms included the sharecropping system across American farmlands and the diamond mining industry in South Africa. Similar black revolutionary movements developed in many parts of the world in response to this oppression. The range of strategies varied, from the Mau Mau's use of violence in Kenya, to Ghandi's use of passive resistance in South Africa and India. Separatists and Civil Rights activists in America later emulated each of those movements respectively during the 1960s and 1970s, often based on an africentric perspective (Asante, 1990; Kambon, 1992).

Common Contemporary Challenges. A review of common contemporary challenges to black families, as shown in Figure 1.1, is useful for two reasons. First, identifying common challenges can normalize black families' struggles to address and overcome those challenges, and help to pinpoint more accurately, the roles of the environment or society in reinforcing those challenges. Secondly, black individuals and families have coped with and reacted to these challenges differently, often based on their different belief systems, ways of coping, and post diaspora experiences in various countries. These challenges affect all black families, not only African Americans, including the following examples:

1. The gradual erosion and loss of roles assumed by the extended family and intergenerational support networks that are critical for cultural maintenance and for enhancing the strengths of black families.
2. An increasing use of legal systems worldwide to incarcerate black males in particular for economic- and social class-related crimes based on tougher policies for street versus white-collar crimes (e.g., drug use/sales and extortion versus the sale of junk bonds and use of insider trading on the stock market).
3. The dilution of black cultural values, traditions, beliefs, language, and ways of being through technological and political means via negative media messages.
4. The use of stereotypical black values/music/language/lifestyles for marketing consumer products, and the demonizing of black females as the primary rationale for establishing harsh welfare to work policies.
5. Denial or token efforts to acknowledge the value of black history and its contributions to the world's civilization in the fields of science, religion, architecture, the arts, and other nonstigmatized areas.

6. The devastating effects of multiple social ills, environmental risks, educational failure, poor decision-making and coping practices, oppression, other factors on contemporary black life around the world.
7. The absence of culturally viable political, social, and economic development resources to help black families rebuild their communities and sufficiency.
8. The gradual erosion of the black spiritual and religious heritage that has sustained African Americans over time as their cultural center.
9. Social class and other within-group barriers that prevent black people from various locations, national origins, educational levels and lifestyles, religions, and generations from developing a sense of cultural unity, common cause, collectivism, and cultural maintenance. (Bullock, Crawford & Tennstedt, 2003; Fitzpatrick & Tran, 2002; Horton, 2002; Mims & Biordi, 2001)

Within-Group Differences Among Black People

Differences noted in example #9 above may be due to dissimilar pre- and post-African diaspora experiences and cultural traditions, beliefs about or the meanings attributed to those experiences, the primary languages used (ways of thinking or conceptualizing ideas), educational opportunities, and to the subcultural coping abilities and practices involved. For instance, in Brazil and some other Caribbean countries, coping with differences has led to a social class system based on skin color and economic-education resources and social status (Allen, 1995). Members of the upper class in Brazil are mostly biracial or more fair-skinned, as well as economically and socially advantaged, compared to the skin color and disadvantaged status of many other Brazilians who live in poverty.

Other within-group differences may arise from variations in black people's access to tangible and intangible resources, including the availability of particular types of cultural coaches or models, for example, bicultural versus culturally-immersed and traditional models. Subcultural differences can also flow from the primary economic development strategies that are adopted by black communities and families globally. Those strategies range from economic and community development, to the use of cooperatives, mutual assets development methods, and individual entrepreneurial and leadership development approaches. Many Haitians who have immigrated to this country, for example, have effectively transferred their entrepreneurial and small business customs to their new homeland, based on a combination of African and Haitian cultural traditions (Allen, 1995).

Furthermore, black people around the world have adopted different social change philosophies and combinations of strategies, including violence, passive resistance, radical separatism, political/ social activism, and/or individual social mobility. Different outcomes from the use of these personal, economic, social, and political efforts toward change also have affected the life circumstances and outlooks of black people everywhere. Such influences are apparent in the broad range of roles, statuses, and functions they have fulfilled in their communities and in society as a whole in various parts of the world.

For example, African Americans who were born in this country have used social and political action to achieve varying levels of equity in education, housing, health resources, employment, and political power (Mosley-Howard & Evans, 2000; Wilson, 2000). In contrast, Ross-Sheriff (1995) notes that some recent African immigrants have tended to be highly skilled, unlike other African political refugees and illegal aliens. They often have become economically sufficient through individual upward mobility efforts in spite of the racial discrimination that they have frequently encountered in America (Apraku, 1991; Gozdziak, 1989; McSpadden, 1991).

Implications for Future Culturally Sensitive Research

This discussion on common and different aspects of black families worldwide has important implications for future research related to such families. Culturally sensitive research can identify indicators of those commonalities and differences, and help to establish principles for influencing programs and policies that lead to black families' empowerment. The definition of culturally sensitive research is discussed, along with underlying principles and challenges that are implicit in this type of research and effective methods. As a foundation for this discussion of future research, an overview of current and past research is summarized below.

Overview of Past and Current Research

As noted previously, much of past and current black family research is based on assumptions about this group's homogeneity and, consequently, it often addresses questions that are not culturally relevant to the broad range of black families. Clear biases exist in the theories, methods, findings, interpretations of findings, and policy and practice implications that have been drawn from some of this research. The following summary addresses the most serious gaps and biases in this research:

1. A lack of clarity exists about the population under study with participants often referred to as nonwhite, low income, single mothers, biracial, or African American (the latter term is often used by researchers to refer to all black people). Few references are made to specific social class, location, country of origin, lifestyle, cultural identity, and value differences among the study participants, or to the effects of such differences on the research outcomes.

2. Strengths and other individual, family, community, and cultural resources are ignored, stereotyped or generalized, reframed into negative characteristics, or attributed to external forces when they are deemed positive.

3. Individual, family, community, and cultural factors are viewed as evidence of pathology, and are emphasized as the main sources of black families' common *and* unique needs and problems. Researchers often fail to explore those factors within the context of participants' unique pre- and post-diaspora experiences (or within the context of *common* black pre- and post-diaspora experiences).

4. Little focus is placed on environmental and systemic barriers to black families' economic and political development or on the effects of oppression, resource inequities, and social justice issues on their needs and problems.

5. The black families and individuals under study are seldom involved in developing culturally relevant research questions, research designs, sampling methods, or study implementation procedures.

6. Services research frequently fails to clarify the providers' cultural and personal backgrounds, the effects of their backgrounds on the service process and outcomes, and the nature of or cultural appropriateness of the interventions for the particular black families or communities.

7. Research instruments that have been normed on white or culturally unspecified populations are often used without considering how that practice affects effective data collection, administration of instruments, or interpretation of data from black study participants.

8. Data analysis and interpretations are often based on the dominant culture's Eurocentric world views, values, priorities, and traditions without monitoring and analyzing how those biases affect the development, implementation, or outcomes of the research.

9. Researchers generally do not use other world views that could make research on black families more culturally sensitive (e.g., Africentric, bicultural, or social justice/equity perspectives).
10. Traditional quantitative research methods and paradigms are frequently used instead of, or in combination with, more culturally appropriate contextual or ethnographic methods. (Billingsley, 1992; Bowman, 1989; Dixon, 1976; Freeman, 1996; Longres & Scanlon, 2001; Piven & Cloward, 1971; Schiele, 1996; Sinclair, Hayes-Reams, Myers, Allen, Hawes-Dawson, & Kington, 2000)

A Culturally Sensitive Research Paradigm

Definition and Nature of this Paradigm. In contrast to the underlying but often unstated biases in some past black family research, culturally sensitive research has a *stated* political agenda. The latter is defined as research that explores the unique cultural context, experiences, beliefs, communication and language patterns, and meanings of black families related to the area of study, and the political, social justice, systems, and environmental factors that influence that context. Culturally sensitive research is based on empowerment theory, social constructivist theory, and the ecological and strengths perspectives. It uses strategies that encourage participants to tell their stories in their own words as experts on their life experiences (Freeman, 1999). Moreover, it involves black families and other participants actively in the research planning and implementation process. Related research concepts are: social inquiry, multicultural inquiry, narrative inquiry, participatory action research, anti-oppression research, critical dialogue research, and culturally competent research.

Research Challenges and Principles. Current and future researchers on black families are confronted with many challenges. A major challenge is for researchers to overcome the habit of oppression or control by the powerful few who are developing knowledge in this area. Researchers are trained traditionally to plan and implement their research without input from black families and other oppressed participants such as women, other groups of color, the elderly, children and youth, the poor, the sexually different, and those with disabilities.

Another major challenge is for researchers to encourage and support black families in not adopting a submissive role in the research process. Problem fatigue and past traumatic experiences with biased Eurocentric research can encourage black families to submit, or resist passively, rather than to assert themselves. Assertiveness may take several forms, including influencing researchers to engage in a more open inclusion process in return for community residents' active participation in the study; advocating with funding sources or university sponsors to require that the research process be more collaborative; or refusing to participate in a closed, predetermined, and often culturally-biased process. The following additional challenges and principles flow from these two main challenges, researchers should:

1. Acknowledge and address the effects of culturally-biased instruments on the process and outcomes of research with black families and individuals.
2. Include black families and individuals from represented, underrepresented, and typically unrepresented voices as study participants to reflect the full range of differences among the group in terms of social class, location, country of origin, age, language, family structure, communication patterns, lifestyles, cultural identities, sexual orientation, values/traditions, and needs.
3. Acknowledge and directly explore black participants' historical mistrust of researchers' motives and methods during initial contacts for planning and implementing the research and address that mistrust by actively involving participants in those processes.
4. Presume and explore black participants' common cultural strengths and resources as an integral part of the research in order to provide data for the development of culturally sensitive programs and policies and to prevent reinforcement of cultural stereotypes.
5. Explore black participants' needs, problems, and cultural realities by eliciting their experiences in their own words, along with their cultural meanings, goals, beliefs, dreams, values, traditions, rituals, and stories related to the phenomena under study.
6. Describe and measure the cultural relevance of program interventions from the participants' perspectives to allow opportunities for them to directly influence the research findings and outcomes, and the program revisions.
7. Avoid victim blaming through exploration of systems, environmental, and policy barriers and supports, including documenting the use or absence of informal and formal political action strategies to address social justice issues identified by black participants related to the research topic.
8. Use member checking (focus groups and critical dialogue groups) and creative dissemination strategies involving black participants and community members to continuously challenge the effects of the researchers' and policy makers' potential biases and Eurocentric cultural filters on the research. (Freeman, 1999)

Related Culturally Sensitive Research Methods. These research challenges and principles require the use of powerful and culturally sensitive methods for addressing the commonalities and differences among black families. Hence, the recommended methods in this discussion are directly linked to the eight challenges presented in the previous section. The challenge of culturally-biased instruments can be addressed by using combined qualitative and quantitative protocols that are self-developed for the particular research in consultation with black participants, and then pilot tested and revised based on their feedback (Challenge #1). The use of nonstandardized instruments such as self-anchored scales and self-developed ethnographic interview guides can allow participants to use their own language and cultural perspectives to describe their feelings, behaviors, and meanings (Bloom & Fischer, 1982). Debriefing sessions with participants can be used after pilot *and* ongoing instrument administrations to elicit feedback about the cultural relevance and sensitivity of protocols such as interview guides, focus group guides, surveys, self-anchored scales, narratives, and criteria for public testimonies (Hatchett, Holmes, Duran, & Davis, 2000; McNeilly, 2000).

Including a range of diverse black families and individuals in research means acknowledging within-group differences as part of the sampling process (Challenge #2). Key informants who help to develop a potentially diverse sample, through use of the snowball strategy, should be asked to identify participants who represent the range of cultural differences within the group(s) under study, and who can be recruited from diverse circumstances such as age-related, social class, religious, and cultural sites. Including French or Spanish-speaking black participants, for example, Haitians, Creoles, or black Puerto Ricans, requires the use of skilled interpreters and cultural coaches who can enhance sample development and recruitment, and decrease language and value barriers.

Methods used to address this challenge also involve culturally sensitive data collection once the sample has been identified and recruited. For example, data should be collected on participants' backgrounds, including country of origin and the effects of location on the phenomena under study, as well as the effects of their social class and cultural identity. These data can reflect the cultural context that clarifies within-group differences among black participants related to value priorities, strengths, and needs.

Mistrust of researchers' motives and methods by black participants, Challenge #3, requires methods that insure continuous monitoring and feedback prior to and during the research to avoid the use of culturally insensitive questions and interpretations. Black refugees, as well as legal and illegal immigrants, may react negatively to insensitive questions based on oppressive experiences involving police and political armies in Africa, Cuba, Haiti, and other countries (Ross-Sheriff, 1995). Moreover, they may have had similar culturally destructive experiences with INS officials in this country, often reminiscent of life-threatening encounters that African Americans have experienced with their local police.

Observations noted through monitoring and feedback require informal opportunities to explore the meanings involved with participants, as critical sources of information for planning and developing culturally sensitive methods. Once data collection begins, more formal opportunities should involve member-checking sessions with black participants to avoid biased analyses of data on their cultural experiences, meanings, traditions, values, strengths, and needs (Challenge #8). Multiple individual interviews with participants over time, focus groups with study participants, and critical dialogue groups are examples of member-checking procedures that can be used.

Presuming and exploring black participants' strengths (Challenge #4) involves using methods that encourage people's self-efficacy and voice, such as ethnographic interviews and survey instruments that elicit information about their strengths and resources. It also means focusing on participants' unique reactions to culturally universal life experiences such as developmental transitions, and on common black experiences such as coping with ethnic/social class oppression and exploring the cultural meaning of those experiences.

Exploration of supportive cultural traditions, rituals, social networks, values, and roles is equally important as the focus of survey items or focus group guides. This approach will enhance opportunities for researchers to identify key similarities and differences in black families' cultural attributes, for example, when analyzing the experiences of recent black immigrants versus black families born in this country. Furthermore, exploration of black participants' views about related large systems, environmental, and policy factors that enhance or limit these strengths is another important aspect of culturally relevant research (Challenge # 7). Meeting this challenge decreases the risk of victim blaming related to the negative effects of those factors on black study participants, and can highlight instances of adaptive coping among black families in response to structural barriers.

The long interview, continuous observation, and narrative inquiry are culturally sensitive methods that can be used to explore black participants' needs, problems, and cultural realities in their own words (Challenge #5). Narrative inquiry in particular is useful for helping participants to share stories about those needs and problems during several ethnographic interviews over time. This approach may be particularly supportive culturally in different types of research: studies on recent versus past black Caribbean immigrants to America, life review research on black elders, and research on black adolescents involved in rites of passage programs. The African oral tradition is consistent with the use of stories about the cultural context of black families' strengths, needs, problems, and meaningful experiences.

The member-checking method should be used so that black participants can further challenge and influence researchers' potentially biased interpretations of stories, observations, and experiences that are shared during multiple interviews. During services research, for example, on black single mothers involved in TANF welfare to work programs, qualitative process evaluation methods are useful for eliciting participants' views of the interventions' cultural relevance (Challenge #6). Researchers should have a genuine interest in those views and a commitment to revising interventions and research methods that are in conflict with or culturally destructive to the participants' life situations. Some interventions may conflict with black participants' cultural values related to particular work ethic, education, role, dietary, or child-rearing practices.

CONCLUSION

The black family common heritage framework in Figure 1.1 has served as a guide for this discussion on culturally sensitive research. The challenges that confront researchers and the methods that can be used to meet those challenges provide general guidelines for research with black individuals, families, and communities. These guidelines can be applied to research with these populations across research topics and with a diversity of black participants who have both common and different cultural traditions. Some research topics may require additional, more specific, guidelines that build upon the set of general guidelines presented in this chapter. Chapters 3 through 11 in Part Two of this book are designed to provide those more specific guidelines related to, for example, housing, health, education, and crime and violence related to black families and individuals.

The general research guidelines in this chapter are related also to Part Three of the book. Specific practice strategies and policy development-reforms are presented in that section, in Chapters 12 through 14, based on these guidelines. In those chapters, the community-building strategies and reforms under discussion are related to crosscutting issues for black families such as cultural maintenance and social justice.

REFERENCES

Allen, J.A. (1995). African Americans: Caribbean. In R.L. Edwards (Ed.), *Encyclopedia of social work* (19th edition) (121–129). Washington, DC: National Association of Social Workers.

Apraku, K.K. (1991). *African émigrés in the United States: A missing link in Africa's social and economic development.* New York: Praeger.

Asante, M. (1989). *Africentricity and knowledge.* Trenton, NJ: African World Press.

Baldwin, J. & Hopkins, R. (1990). African-American and European-American cultural differences as assessed by the worldviews paradigm: An empirical analysis. *The Western Journal of Black Studies, 14,* 38–52.

Barnes, S.L. (2001). Stressors and strengths: A theoretical and practical examination of nuclear, single-parent and augmented African American families. *Families in Society, 82*(5), 449–460.

Billingsley, A. (1992). *Climbing Jacob's ladder: The enduring legacy of African-American families.* New York: Simon and Schuster.

Bloom, M. and Fischer, J. (1982). Integrating research and practice. *Evaluating practice: Guidelines for the accountable professional* (pg. 3–10). Englewood Cliffs, NJ: Prentice-Hall.

Bowman, P.J. (1989). Research perspectives on Black men: Role strain and adaptation across the adult life cycle. In R.L. Jones (Ed.), *Black adult development and aging* (156–178). Los Angeles: Cobb & Henry.

Bullock, K., Crawford, S.L., & Tennstedt, S.L. (2003). Employment and caregiving: Exploration of African American caregivers. *Social Work, 48*(2), 150–162.

Crawley, B. & Freeman, E.M. (1993). Themes in the life views of older and younger African-American males. *Journal of African American Male Studies, 1,* 15–29.

DeBois, W.E.B. (1969). *The Negro American family.* New York: New American Library.

Dixon, V. (1976). World views and research methodology. In L. King, V. Dixon, and W. Nobles (Eds.), *African philosophy: Assumptions and paradigms for research on black persons* (51–93). Los Angeles: Fanon Center Publications.

Fitzpatrick, T.R. & Tran, T.V. (2002). Bereavement and health among different race and age groups. *Journal of Gerontological Social Work, 37*(2), 77–92.

Frazier, E.F. (1966). *The Negro family in the United States.* Chicago: University of Chicago Press.

Freeman, E.M. (1999). Culturally sensitive research on African Americans and culture specific programs. Paper presented at the Society for Social Work and Research Conference. Austin, Texas.

Freeman, E.M. (1996). Welfare reforms and services for children and families: Setting a new practice, research, and policy agenda. *Social Work, 41,* 421–432.

Freeman, E.M. (1990). The black family's life cycle: Operationalizing a strengths perspective. In S.M.L. Logan, E.M. Freeman, and R.G. McRoy (Eds.), *Social work practice with black families* (55–72). White Plains,NY: Longman.

Gozdziak, E. (1989). *New Americans: The economic adaptation of Eastern European, Afghan, and Ethiopian refugees.* Washington, DC: Refugee Policy Group.

Gyekye, K. (1992). Person and community in African thought. In K. Wiredu & K. Gykeye (Eds.), *Person and community: Ghanaian philosophical studies, I.,* (pp. 101–122). Washington, DC: The Council for Research in Values and Philosophy.

Hatchett, B.F., Holmes, K. Duran, D.A., & Davis, C. (2000). African Americans and research participation: The recruitment process. *Journal of Black Studies, 30*(5), 664–675.

Herskovits, M.J. (1958). *The myth of the negro past.* Boston: Beacon.

Horton, A. (2002). Violent crimes and racial profiling: What the evidence suggests. *Journal of Human Behavior in the Social Environment, 6*(4), 87–106.

Kambon, K. (1992). *The African personality in America: An African-centered framework.* Tallahassee, Fl: Nubian Nation Publication.

Logan, S.M.L, Freeman, E.M., and McRoy, R.G. (1990). *Social work practice with black families: A culturally specific perspective.* White Plains, NY: Longman.

Longres, J. & Scanlon, E. (2001). Social justice and research curriculum. *Journal of Social Work Education, 37*(3), 447–463.

McNeilly, M. (2000). Minority populations and psychophysiologic research: Challenges in trust building and recruitment. *Journal of Mental Health and Aging, 6*(1), 91–102.

McRoy, R.G. (1990). A historical overview of black families. In S.M.L. Logan, E.M. Freeman, and R.G. McRoy (Eds.), *Social work practice with black families: A culturally specific perspective* (3–17). White Plains, NY: Longman.

McSpadden, L. (1991). Cross-cultural understanding of independence and dependence: Conflict in the resettlement of single Ethiopian males. *Refuge, 10*(4), 21–25.

Mims, B. & Biordi, D.L. (2001). Communication patterns in African-American families with adolescent mothers of single or repeat pregnancies. *Journal of National Black Nurses Association, 12*(1), 34–41.

Mosley-Howard, G.S. & Evans, C.B. (2000). Relationships and contemporary experiences of the African American family: An ethnographic case study. *Journal of Black Studies, 30*(3), 428–452.

Oliver, W. (1989). Black males and social problems: Prevention through Africentric socialization. *Journal of Black Studies, 20,* 15–39.

Piven, F.F. & Cloward, R.A. (1971). *Regulating the poor: The functions of public welfare.* New York: Random House.

Ross-Sheriff, F. (1995). African Americans: Immigrants. In R.L. Edwards (Ed.), *Encyclopedia of social work (19th edition)* (130–136).

Schiele, J. (1996). Afrocentricity: An emerging paradigm in social work practice. *Social Work, 41,* 284–294.

Sinclair, S., Hayes-Reams, P., Myers, H.F., Allen, W., Hawes-Dawson, J., and Kington, R. (2000). Recruiting African Americans for health studies: Lessons from the Drew-RAND Center on Health and Aging. *Journal of Mental Health and Aging, 6*(1), 39–51.

Sudarkasa, N. (1983). Interpreting the African heritage in Afro-American family organization. In H.P. McAdoo (Ed.), *Black families* (37–53). Beverly Hills, CA: Sage.

Wilson, G. (2000). Race, class, and support for egalitarian statism among the African American middle class. *Journal of Sociology and Social Welfare, 27*(3), 75–91.

Chapter 2

AN ANALYSIS, INTEGRATION, AND APPLICATION OF AFRICENTRIC AND STRENGTHS APPROACHES TO BLACK FAMILIES AND COMMUNITIES

SADYE L. LOGAN AND EDITH M. FREEMAN

During the 1980s, practitioners used either generic or culturally sensitive approaches in working with black families and their communities. Traditional social work practice approaches are considered generic approaches (Turner, 1996; Allen-Meares & Garvin, 2000). Culturally sensitive approaches, in contrast, include culturally centered knowledge, skills, and awareness of the consumer's perspective. Such approaches are sufficiently expansive and flexible that their knowledge and skills can be used to assist with culturally specific needs and concerns (Logan, Freeman & McRoy, 1990; Chestang, 1972; Devore & Schlesinger, 1999; Martin, 2002; & Allen-Meares & Garvin, 2002).

From the early 1990s onward, the social work literature on black families and communities began utilizing a language and orientation that suggests a more holistic, uplifting perspective on practice. This change was evident in the reframing of traditional practice approaches, as well as in the concepts and principles from emergent approaches (Goldenberg & Goldenberg, 1996; Nicholas & Schwartz, 2002; Logan, 2001; Logan, Freeman & McRoy 1990). This chapter, therefore, provides a broad-based analysis of these emergent or spirituality-oriented approaches for understanding and working in the context of African

American families and communities. The chapter also provides a framework for integrating and applying a more holistic, strengths-oriented practice approach.

African American Families and Communities in Context

There are approximately 34.7 million African Americans in the United States. One half of these individuals are less than thirty years of age. The United States is in the midst of a major economic, techno-logical, political, demographic, cultural, and spiritual transformation, which suggests that the current generation of African Americans will impact and be impacted by this changing landscape in dramatic ways. According to Stafford (2001), to be successful in work and life in the twenty-first century, African Americans will be required to have more technological and conceptual skills, interact with diverse cultural and ethnic groups, stay abreast of cutting edge information and be able to incorporate this information into their professional and personal lives.

Juxtaposed against these multifaceted changes are major issues and concerns that are impacting the overall quality of life for all African Americans. Several polls have consistently identified major problem areas that are most important to African Americans: racism, racial dis-crimination in the workplace and in general, high rates of teenage preg-nancy, fewer jobs that pay decent wages, drugs and alcohol, crime, less commitment to moral and religious values, welfare dependency, pub-lic schools not providing an adequate education, and social program reforms and cost containment policies (Cose, 1999, Stafford, 2001).

These contextual factors impact upon all African American families and communities but in varying degrees, depending on the following factors: diverse qualities and characteristics of individual family mem-bers, unique dynamics of the immediate household, the qualities and characteristics of the extended family, the quality of community and social connections, and the unequal ways that families are situated in the larger society (Carter & McGoldrick, 1999). For all African Ameri-cans, regardless of gender, age, and education, racial discrimination continues to impact their lives (Boyd-Franklin 2003; McGoldrick, 1998).

This fluid life context in the larger society makes it imperative that African American families and communities find effective ways to influence the transformation of larger society to benefit all its citizens, in terms of social and economic justice. Concerned black leaders, the black church, and other community-based institutions will need to create the necessary impetus for sustained changes in this country's social and political structure. The most effective approach to keeping black leaders, families, institutions, and communities relevant is to adopt the African-centered world view presented in this chapter.

Integration and Application of Africentric, Strengths, and Other Spirituality-Sensitive Approaches

Africentric and strengths-based perspectives are conceptualized as evolving spirituality-sensitive approaches for work with black families and children (Logan, 2001). These approaches are also described as postmodern, because they focus on how families give meaning and purpose to their lives. An Africentric orientation draws upon the ethos and values of the people of Africa and the diaspora (Turner, 1996), which are shown in Figure 2.1, as conceptualized by several contemporary authors. While black families and children may vary in the extent to which they exemplify the African-centered values, characteristics, attitudes, and beliefs in Figure 2.1, this information can guide practitioners in their work with those clients.

According to Turner (1996), an Africentric orientation includes the history, culture and world views of black people and provides an expanded multilevel framework for understanding and working with them. Practice approaches that support an Africentric orientation include solution-focused brief therapy, solution-oriented therapy, collaborative language systems approaches, narrative therapy, gender-sensitive therapy and psychoeducational family therapy (Nicholas & Schwartz, 2002, Goldenberg & Goldenberg, 1996). Turner (1996) speaks of the Africentric orientation as holistic, and therefore, believes it underscores interconnectedness, equafinality, living in the moment, a consanguine family structure, consequential morality, and experiential spirituality. When people live in the awareness of these principles they live in harmony with the perfect flow of the universe, with all that is. The Africentric orientation describes a way of living that suggests spiritual wellness and balance.

The strengths perspective, not unlike the Africentric orientation, is

Some' 1998	Hill, 1997	Logan, 2001 Logan and Freeman 2000; Logan, Freeman, and McRoy, 1990	Martin and Martin, 2002	McAdoo, 1997 & 2003	Schiele, 2000
-Rituals of healing -Indigenous technologies -Healthy community -Spiritual world -Village community	-Strong kinship bonds -Strong work orientation -Strong achievement orientation -Strong religious orientation -Adaptability of family roles	-Inner (inherent) strengths -Unity -Wholeness -Self healing -Empowerment stance -Positive change -Loving and caring -Collectivism -Nurturance -Support -Perseverance	-Religious consciousness tradition -Fraternal orders - Unions -Ethnic -Women clubs -Race consciousness -Extension of extended families -Institution of black helping tradition -Pro socialization of children	-Kinship and mutual assistance -Extended family -More than provision of basic needs	-Afro-centricity -Human liberation -Spirituality -Collectivity -Self-Knowledge -Inclusiveness -Strong mother-child bond

Figure 2.1 Contemporary Black Families: Values, Characteristics, Attitudes, and Beliefs

also included among emergent approaches that are generally described as postmodern constructivism. In these approaches the emphasis is on collaboration and the language and meaning of given events. Change efforts are directed toward altering rigid and inflexible beliefs about self and the world and then replacing them with new, expanded explanations or alternatives. These alternative ways of being in the world may take the form of strengths, exceptions, problem resolution, unique outcomes, and generally, a greater emphasis on affirmations, self-determination, empowerment, and partnerships.

The following theoretical assumptions under-gird solution-oriented therapy, supporting a family helping process that shifts the focus from problems and pathology, to solutions:

1. **Change is inevitable.** Using language that emphasizes possibilities, builds hope and patience for the inevitable change.
2. **Families have resources to cope, change, and solve problems.** The helper supports the family's strengths in accessing and organizing these resources.
3. **Families must be the ones who decide what needs changing.** This is the source of their motivation for working toward change.

4. **Search for solutions.** To solve a problem you need to know more about possible solutions, not more about the problem.

5. **Focus on the here and now.** Focusing on past failures and problems decreases access to possible solutions. It is easier to develop positive behaviors instead of getting rid of negative behaviors.

6. **Search for exceptions or look for what is different.** Exceptions to problems involve strengths, abilities, resources, and clues to solutions.

7. **Small changes lead to other changes.** Greater changes are likely when families focus on small concrete, practical, doable and observable goals.

8. **Problems are unsuccessful attempts to resolve difficulties.** Families need support in getting "unstuck" from more of the same attempts to seek solutions.

9. **Multiple perspectives.** Realities are viewed from multiple points of view, thus there is no final or correct way of viewing behavior or of finding solutions. (Goldenberg & Goldenberg, 1996, p. 13; & Lipchik, 2002)

Drawing upon these nine theoretical assumptions, Table 2.1 is an African-centered visual depiction of the three broad areas of the social work process: assessment, intervention and evaluation. These broad areas of work are further refined through a multilevel analytical practice framework.

A Multilevel Analytical Practice Framework

This multilevel analytical practice framework includes: (1) the nine theoretical assumptions in the previous section regarding solutions, (2) a group of interrelated perspectives about people and how they change, and (3) a set of integrated practice principles that can be applied to practice with African Americans. As can be seen from the list of perspectives that follow, there is an emphasis on the strengths and spiritual-centeredness of the people involved:

1. **The view of people.** People are viewed as having inherent strengths, as interdependent and as partners in the helping encounter. (Logan, 2001)

2. **The view of change.** Change is viewed as inevitable. This level of change is both internal and external. Emphasis is placed on families and their environments and includes the spiritual, the emotional and the political. (This view of change is consistent with the African philosophy that all things and people are connected) (Some', 1998)

3. **The view of the family system.** The family system is reflected in the traditional African belief that it takes a village to raise children. "The village" includes fictive kin; numerous extended family members, and other available, reliable, and informal/indigenous community resources. (Some', 1998)

4. **The view of the community**. The community has physical, political, geographical, social, and cultural dimensions that interact with and influence each other. (Some', 1998)
5. **The view of diversity**. Identify and explore cultural elements of the family-helper relationship. Acknowledge relevant cultural differences and similarities and the impact of these factors on the helping process. (Logan, 2003)

**Table 2.1 An African-Centered Approach to Work
with Black Families and Communities**

Three Broad Areas of Work	Related Tasks:
Assessment Includes:	Individual, group, family and community history Religious/spiritual heritage Migration history Impact of racism and other forms of oppression Economic issues Cultural issues Environmental issues Self-image/ethnic identity issues
Intervention Focuses on:	What the client system wants to see changed/different Empowerment: Individual, family, community Strengths, self help, positive change, and collaborative partnerships Advocacy at the community level Schools & social services agencies: responsiveness to the needs of families and communities Action-oriented strategies
Evaluation includes:	Concrete measurable culturally relevant goals agreed on by the client system African-centered diagnoses Simple questionnaires and scaling questions Ongoing goal and task reviews

Building on these perspectives about people and change, and on the multilevel framework as a whole, the following set of integrated practice principles help to guide the work between practitioners and black families and children. The use of a collaborative partnership with the family system is necessary for finding solutions to the family's presenting concerns (Lipchik, 2002). The practitioner should:

1. Identify and understand the cultural identity of African American families and their unique history of enslavement and the continuing impact of living in an environment of oppression, racism, and gross inequalities.
2. Assume the existence of strengths for the family, search for exceptions, and support the family's strengths through the inclusion of significant others and through affirmations and an emphasis on solutions.
3. Walk and work side-by-side with client systems as partners.

An African-Centered Approach: Application and Analysis

A Case Presentation

The immediate family household consists of Mr. and Mrs. Davis (45 and 43 years old respectively), and Ms. Davis' nephew, fifteen-year-old Owen. The family was referred to the local mental health center after Owen had been suspended twice in one year from the middle school he attended. The presenting concerns were failing grades, "acting out behavior" in school and disrespectful behavior at home. This couple is childless and had been married for fourteen years when Owen came to live with them at nine years of age. They are now his legal guardians. Owen's parents never married, and then separated as a couple when he was two years old. Owen has one sibling, a twenty-five-year-old brother who is incarcerated for possession of an illegal substance. Owen has not had contact with his brother or his birth mother since he was removed from her home for neglect due to her drug abuse. Prior to coming to live with his mother's sister and her husband, Owen lived in a group home for six months and in foster care for three and one half years. It has been reported that Owens' mother used marijuana and crack during her pregnancy with him. Owen's biological father was killed when Owen was four years old. Since coming to live with Mr. And Ms. Davis, Owen was diagnosed by the local mental health center psychiatrist with Oppositional Deficit Disorder (ODD) and Attention

Deficit Hyperactivity Disorder (ADHD). He was prescribed Ritalin©
for those conditions. The Davises are committed to Owen's care and to
each other. There is a strong connection to the church and community
and extended family. The family has adequate income and is open to
working with the mental health center.

An African-Centered View of the Davis Family

The integrative multilevel conceptual framework from the previous
discussion is useful for understanding and working with this family.
Creating effective multilevel interventions and evaluating outcomes
requires a suspension of judgment and a nondoing for, nonknowing
stance on the part of the helper. Regardless of the family's ethnic background, this approach views families as being at the center of their existence; able to define whom they are and how they view and experience their world. In short, families are viewed with an Africentric lens.

Applying this framework to the Davises reveals that the family is between six and seven generations removed from slavery and the oppressive conditions associated with enslavement. All members of the
family were born and raised in the rural South. The Davis family currently resides in a small town that is between thirty minutes to an hour
from several larger towns. Mr. and Mrs. Davis are old enough to have
experienced and remembered the impact of the segregated south. They
remember riding in the back of public buses, attending segregated
schools and acknowledging "white only" signs when they used public
facilities. Headlines on the status of race relations within the state appeared sporadically in local newspapers. A recent headline reported
that the state still discriminates against women and people of color.

The Davis family dynamics reflect several African-centered family
values, including the assumption of parental care for young children
and close family ties. Essentially these values place the family at the
center of life processes, and support hope, growth, and change. The
members are extremely committed to each other, have a strong religious affiliation with their local church, and are very spiritual. All
members of the family appear to be in good health despite Mrs. Davis's
diabetes. The family has an open relationship with its friends in the
community, the church, with Owen's godmother, who is also his great
aunt, and with their extended family living in the same neighborhood.

They live in a small house with an adequate income and means of transportation.

The Davis' family draws upon its inner strengths for coping with the stresses and challenges of parenting a black male adolescent and handling day-to-day life events. Gurumayi Chidvilasanda (1998) defines inner strength as a gift from God. In a poem on this subject she speaks of inner strength as "holding everything in place, inside and out, as allowing both charged and the uncharged to take place . . . that inner strength isn't built with the power of clever words, nor does it come from the support of others . . . that it doesn't depend on a matching upbringing, nor does it lean on your accomplishment . . . that the Lord placed his own lustrous, tranquil energy within your being. . ." (p. 14–15).

Although their neighborhood is nicely kept, it exposes Owen to a number of people who model negative behavior, such as violence and crime, which are on the rise in the neighborhood. Owen is also dealing with a number of loss issues such as his mother's neglect and the lost of communication with his biological family. His older brother has been incarcerated for reckless homicide while driving under the influence of alcohol. Owen struggles with authority figures, sometimes creating stress at school and at home. The Davises have requested help with more effective ways of handling Owen's unacceptable behavior.

Africentric Needs Assessment and Intervention Strategies

The culturally relevant ecomap in Figure 2.2 and the African-centered family genogram in Figure 2.3 are used to gain a better understanding of the Davis family, but but these tools also serve as intervention strategies. Freeman (1992, 1993) and other authors have discussed the usefulness of the cultural ecomap for understanding and working with African American families. This map highlights the Davis family as a unit, and focuses on the family in both its immediate and larger extended environments. Its visual depiction brings immediate attention to the general quality and level of exchanges between the family and the various systems with which the family interacts. The following questions may be used to assist practitioners in effectively utilizing the map:

1. The Davises as a unit: Members' abilities to agree on and fulfill functional roles while also meeting individual needs (e.g., issues with school and respect for authority, family leisure time).

2. The African American ethnic group environment: The nature and quality of the relationship between this environment and the family: quality of family ties, intergenerational issues, the impact of substance abuse.
3. The broader, extended environment: Impact of privilege and power, sources of empowerment or powerlessness, the family's consensus or conflicts about how to cope with a racist environment. (Freeman, 1992, p. 32)

The Davis's African-centered family genogram in Figure 2.3 is based on two major assumptions about family relationships:

1. Kinship must be regarded and understood as it is construed by the ethnic/racial group of the particular family, and
2. Functional relationships are as important to represent in a genogram or diagram as biological relationships. (Watts-Jones, 1997, p. 96)

According to Watts-Jones (1997), both types of relationships need to be recognized in the genograms/diagrams of African American families. Outreach and the process of using the cultural ecomap and African-centered diagram/genogram to help the Davis family assess its strengths and problems provided the members with new insights and information about the family's heritage and ways of experiencing its world. Boyd-Franklin, 2000. The members told many cultural stories that produced information about three generations of the family. Owen was initially very tentative about participating. Eventually, he asked many questions related to his childhood experiences and his mother, father, and brother.

The Davises defined their presenting concerns as adjustment issues related to parenting a black adolescent male. They thought these issues were demanding a different kind of focus from them as a family and were causing a shift in their roles and expectations. They were aware of what appeared to be a negative trend in the way black children in general, and black male children in particular, were treated in the educational system, as well as in the mental health system.

The Davis's goals included wanting Owen to remain in school, improve his grades, decrease his anger, and develop respect for authority figures. Owen agreed with these expectations. Everyone was willing to work to realize these goals. As stated earlier, the African-centered approach is contextually based and is inclusive of a variety of different practice approaches. Given the Davis's concerns about parenting a black male teenager, and coping with the nonnurturing atmosphere in the school system, it was necessary to help the family articulate the

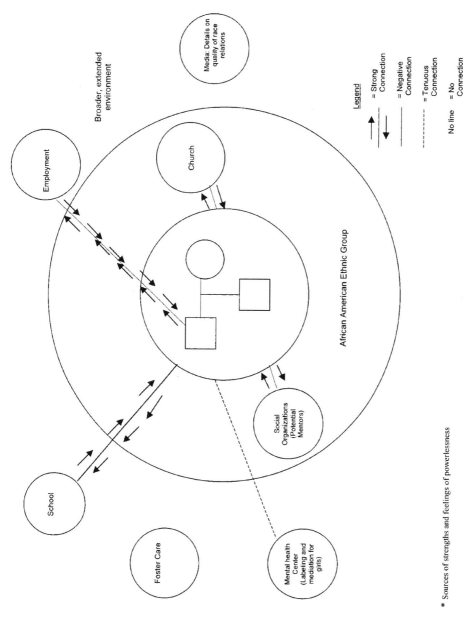

* Sources of strengths and feelings of powerlessness

Figure 2.2 The Davis Family's Culturally Relevant Ecomap*

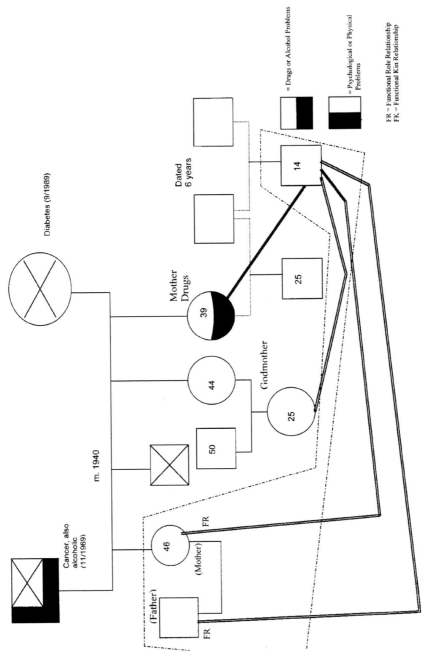

Figure 2.3 The Davis Family's African-Centered Diagram

larger system's impact on their lives. By giving voice and recognition to discrimination and racial hatred, the family was empowered to stand together as a team and support each other, and to search for creative ways to work toward change in the situation.

In addition to the African-centered family genogram, the cultural ecomap, culturally relevant readings, and family albums, individual and group cognitive-behavioral strategies were used in the sessions to focus on the kinds of messages the family was creating about interpersonal relationships and other experiences. The practitioner also initiated discussions with other mental health staff about the type of parent training they were using with the family.

Starting with the family's presenting concerns and goals as the baseline; the ecomap and simple questions were used to assess how the family was experiencing the change process. The couple began to feel less stressful and overwhelmed in their parental roles as well as in their relationship with each other. The family agreed that Owen could benefit from involvement with a male mentor and participation in activities at the local Boys Club. The Davises also agreed to participate in a community sponsored parenting class that they felt was more culturally relevant.

CONCLUSION

Practice approaches for work with African American families and communities should include more expansive and flexible paradigms. This recommended epistemology incorporates aspects of traditional practice approaches, integrated with an African-centered perspective, along with emergent or spiritually-oriented approaches. Operationalizing these approaches and perspectives requires a multilevel analytical framework. The use of such a practice framework requires, in turn, an emphasis on black families' strengths and on the commitment of practitioners to develop collaborative partnerships with these families.

REFERENCES

Allen-Meares, P., and Garvin, C. (2000). *The handbook of social work direct practice.* Thousand Oaks, CA.: Sage Publications. Inc.

Boyd-Franklin, N. & Hafer, B.B. (2000). *Reaching out in family therapy. Home-based, school, and community interventions.* New York: Guilford Publishers, Inc.

Boyd-Franklin, N., (2003). *Black families in therapy: Understanding the African American experience* (2nd ed.) New York: Guilford Publishers, Inc.

Carter, B. & McGoldrick, M. (Eds). (1999). *The changing life cycle. A framework for family therapy.* New York: Gardner.

Chestang, L. (1972). *Character development in a hostile environment. Occasional Paper No. 3.*

Chidvilasanda, G. (1998). *Smile, smile, smile.* New York: SYDA Foundation.

Cose, E. (1999, June 7). The good news about black America. *Newsweek,* Vol. CXXXIII, No. 23, 28–40.

Devore, W., & Schlesinger, E.G. (1999). *Ethnic-sensitive social work practice* (8th Edition). Boston: Allyn and Bacon.

Freeman, E.M. (1993.) *Family treatment: The sibling bond and other relationship issues.* Springfield, Il: Charles C Thomas.

Freeman, E.M. (Ed.) (1992). *The addiction process: Effective social work approaches.* New York: Longman.

Goldenberg, I. & Goldenberg, H. (1996). *Family therapy: An overview.* Pacific Grove, CA: Wadsworth, Inc.

Lipchik, E. (2002). *Beyond technique in solution-focused therapy: Working with emotions and the therapeutic relationship.* New York: Guilford Publications, Inc.

Logan, S.L.M. (Ed). (2001). *The black family: Strengths, self help and positive change (2nd. Ed.).* Boulder, CO: Westview Press, Inc.

Logan, S. (2003). Issues in multiculturalism: Multicultural practice, cultural diversity and competency. In R.A. English, (Ed.), *Encyclopedia of Social Work* (19th Edition), 2003 Supplement (pp. 95–106) Washington, DC: NASW Press.

Logan, S.L., and Freeman, E.M. (Eds.) (2000). *Health Care in the black community: Empowerment, Knowledge, Skills, and Collectivism.* Birmingham, AL: Haworth.

Logan, S.L., Freeman, E.M., & McRoy. R. (1990). *Social work practice with black Families: A culturally specific perspective.* New York: Longman.

Martin J.M., & Martin, E.P. (2002). *The helping tradition in the black family and community.* Washington, DC: NASW Press.

McGoldrick, M. (1998). *Re-visioning family therapy: Race, culture, and gender in clinical practice.* New York: Guilford Publishers, Inc.

Nicholas, M.P., & Schwartz, R.C. (2002). *Family therapy: Concepts and methods (3rd Edition).* Boston: Allyn and Bacon.

Some', M.P. (1998). *The healing wisdom of Africa: Finding life purpose through nature, ritual, and community.* New York: Jeremy P. Tacher/Putnam.

Stafford, W.W. (2001). The New York Urban League survey: Black New York on edge, but optimistic. In W. Spriggs (Ed.), *The state of black America 1999* (pp. 203–220). New York: The National Urban League.

Turner, R.J. (1996). Affirming consciousness: The Africentric perspective. In J.E. Everett, S.S. Chipungu, and B.R. Leashore (Eds.), *Child welfare: An Africentric perspective* (pp. 36–57). New Brunswick, N.J.: Rutgers University Press.

Watt–Jones, D. (1997). Toward an African American genogram. *Family Process, 36,* 375–383.

PART TWO

STATUS AND QUALITY OF RESEARCH LITERATURE ON BLACK FAMILIES AND COMMUNITIES: IMPLICATIONS FOR IMPROVED PRACTICE AND POLICY DEVELOPMENT

Chapter 3

MAINTAINING CONNECTIONS FOR FAMILY GROWTH AND HOUSING STABILITY IN BLACK COMMUNITIES: POLICY AND RESEARCH REFORMS

PATRICIA O'BRIEN, OLGA OSBY, AND ALICE K. JOHNSON

Adequate housing is an elemental need. It provides a foundation for health and well-being. When housing is inadequate, the result may be stress and conflict within the family and less than optimum development of its members (Harrison, Wilson, Pine, Chan & Buriel, 1990). However, for many black families, the American dream of home-ownership or affordable rental housing is elusive (McCarty, 2002).

Discussion and research on the issue of housing for black families reflects little consensus on the description of the problem, its explanations, or proposed policy and practice recommendations. On the one hand, attempts to arrive at satisfactory explanations of the nature of the problem have been ideologically driven either by liberal arguments of discrimination and social class subordination, or by conservative concerns with different group values and the labeling of family behavior as pathological, on the other hand. Nonetheless, there is convincing evidence that black families have not had fair access to safe, secure, and affordable housing. Despite the diversity that exists within black communities, black families continue to combat social, economic, and political hardships because of racial and economic discrimination. Racism has made it difficult for many black people to enter the economic mainstream and the long-lasting effects of poverty and oppression have caused many to feel broken by the system and hopeless (Bowie, 2001; West, 1991).

This chapter reviews the current debates and struggles in the research literature related to housing and its effect on black families. While recognizing the different strategies middle and upper-class black families have used to secure housing, this chapter focuses on what research has shown to be most effective for working and lower-income black families. We discuss the often-ignored reality of black families' resilience—the strength and flexibility of roles, the high value placed on religion and faith, education, and work that provide a framework for understanding their tenacity in the face of relocation, homelessness, and displacement. We argue that these strengths are building blocks that can be used to assist black families to find adequate, safe, and affordable housing. Finally, we argue that shifting and expanding the research lens is necessary for identifying factors that contribute to black families securing housing, and making a home out of the physical structure—that is, making an emotional anchor that establishes the foundation for healthy human development.

STRENGTHS OF BLACK FAMILIES AND COMMUNITIES

To understand the development and world view of African American individuals and families in this country, one must understand the negative social conditions that have historically existed for low-income black families and have so dominated the research and analysis of black communities. Black families in general, and low-income black families specifically, have been blamed for the worst of the social ills present in low-income communities. The "culture of poverty" framework was used to explain the state and circumstances in which black families lived. The 1965 study authored by Daniel P. Moynihan "attributed Black America's disadvantaged position in American society to structural defects in the black family, emphasizing the destructive legacy of slavery" (Moynihan, 1965).

While the report acknowledged the legacy of slavery, the historic discrimination against black Americans and the negative impact of urbanization on inner city blacks, it also stated that "the vast number of unskilled, poorly educated blacks had become enmeshed in a self-perpetuating cycle of poverty" (Moynihan, 1995). Hence, this report blamed the victims for the cycle of poverty confronting them without examining structural factors that contributed to that poverty. Years later William Julius Wilson provided a radically different view of this issue in research on the "Black underclass" (Wilson, 1987) which examined blocked opportunity structures that prevented low-income blacks from participating in mainstream America.

The controversy surrounding the Moynihan report led to responses from other authors and researchers that emphasized black families' strengths and resiliencies, in the face of overwhelming and adverse social conditions (Hill, 1997). Such responses signaled a new culturally validating rather than blaming or deficit perspective. In a sequel to his 1972 work, Hill states:

> I was concerned that most stories on the black community in the media or research studies were interested in explaining why blacks fail and underachieve, and not why the majority of low-income blacks are able to achieve against the odds. These analyses rarely seek answers to such questions as: why eight out of ten black families are not on welfare; why nine out of ten black adolescents do not have children out of wedlock; and why two out of three black males do not have contact with the criminal justice system. If one were truly interested in replicating successful inner-city achievement, I contend that greater attention would be given to identifying factors that make resilience possible. (1997, xii)

Hill notes there have been numerous studies over the past twenty-five years that have focused on the strengths, assets, and social capital of black families and that provide an alternative framework to the "culture of poverty." Although these studies and reports have been buried by the avalanche of research on the problems of low-income communities and the deficits of poor families, they contribute to the knowledge base on an expanding black middle class (Pattillo, 1998); effective family functioning across economic lines (Hill, 1997); a strong orientation toward academic and career achievement (Goings & Mohl, 1995); strong kinship ties with blood and nonblood relations (Hill, 1997); and strong spiritual and religious orientations (Goings & Mohl, 1995; Hill, 1997, Morris & Robinson, 1996).

For example, a defining characteristic of black families in the United States is their identification, membership, and association with specific communities. Rosewood in Florida, Harlem in New York City, Auburn Avenue in Atlanta, and Cabrini-Green in Chicago each tell the story of how such strengths have been reflected in those communities across several generations. Some of those communities, however, tell a story about a cycle of rise and fall, growth and decline, and stability and instability among black families, based on a combination of internal and external impinging conditions.

Formal and informal systems of support such as extended family members, fictive kinship ties, friends, and indigenous leaders, comprise the neighbors who black families turn to most for help in times of need. Formal systems of support, often cultural in nature, such as the church, the neighborhood school where generations of the same family have attended, community-based businesses, and civic and social organizations, help black families define community boundaries, provide a sense of community membership, and maintain cultural and community values and traditions.

Viewing black families and communities from a strengths perspective or framework facilitates an understanding of why, despite hostile environments or negative social problems, some families have survived continuously, and many have thrived. The strengths perspective has been used most often to assess the abilities, skills, knowledge, resources and desires of individuals (Saleebey, 1997). It can also be used to identify the ability of families to rebound from economic and social decline and employ strategies for securing housing (Early & GlenMaye, 2000; Hill, 1997). This perspective is useful too in exploring class and income differences among black families, factors that have affected these families' housing choices and aspirations.

SOCIAL CLASS DIVERSITY AMONG BLACK FAMILIES

A major stereotype about black Americans is the notion of cultural homogeneity that glosses over within-group differences related to social class, gender, religious beliefs, or sexual orientation. One of the more damaging of these beliefs is that all blacks have been raised or live in dangerous and poorly maintained neighborhoods (Harris, 1995). Although living in low-income and unstable communities is a reality for far too many black families (Beverly, 2001; Bowie, 2001), there have been many stable working and middle-class black communities (Harris, 1995).

In 1899, W.E.B. DuBois described the diversity attributed to social class within black communities (1969). DuBois identified four social classes of black Americans: "the well-to-do; the decent hard workers who were doing quite well; the 'worthy poor', who were working or trying to work but barely making ends meet; and, the 'submerged tenth,' who were beneath the surface of socioeconomic viability." Reed (1991) noted that today's black social class structure includes the black elite, the black middle class, and working or lower income blacks.

Black Elite Families

The black elite includes entertainers, athletes, and professionals, who often have a family legacy of education at historically black colleges and universities, along with doctors, lawyers, business owners and corporate executives, journalists and foundation heads. Many have been able to rise from low-income families and communities due to individual and community resources, civil rights legislation, affirmative action, and other equal opportunity policies. These black Americans are often bicultural. They live in affluent white communities and are comfortable in multicultural or primarily white social and professional circles, but frequently maintain their connections to the larger black community through attendance at all-black churches, beauty and barbershops, and membership in Greek or other black social organizations.

Black Middle-Class Families

Like the black elite, most members of the black middle class have also benefited from individual and community resources, as well as affirmative action and other equal opportunity programs and have become well educated, mostly at black colleges and universities generations ago. However, as higher education opportunities opened up over the past 30 years, more middle-class blacks are products of predominately white universities. Middle-class blacks tend to lead a dual life of working with white America, and returning home to either racially mixed or mostly black middle-class neighborhoods. Some black lower-middle-class neighborhoods are nestled next to or surrounded by low-income black communities, or by working class neighborhoods and public housing. Consequently, some of the social and economic problems that exist in lower income black communities are also present in some lower-middle-class communities. For example, some of those neighborhoods have higher rates of internal poverty and crime than their white counterparts (Pattillo, 1998).

In contrast, many black upper-middle-class families live in multicultural or predominantly white communities where such conditions are mostly not present. In general, however, black lower and upper-middle-class families rely heavily on black social, political, and religious institutions. Informal social networks of family, friends, and fictive kin keep them connected to both lower and middle income black communities, where those networks often exist for each family.

Black Working Class and Lower Income Families

Black working and lower income families generally live in racially segregated or predominantly black or minority neighborhoods, often with high concentrations of poverty. Generally, low-income minority communities have the highest levels of unemployment, poverty, one-parent households, school failure, crime and violence, and barriers to accessing government and private sector services (Franklin & Smith, 1995; Goldsmith, 1997; Hill, 1997). Very low-income communities, such as public housing developments have crime and homicide rates at three to four times the national average. Many of the social and economic problems that plague these communities are linked to structural problems such as decades of employment discrimination, residential segregation, redlining by banks and insurance companies, poorly funded and maintained public schools, and poorly managed public housing (Goldsmith, 1997; Gotham, 1998, Reed, 1991; Thompson, 1999).

Families who have moved out of public housing through vouchers or Section 8 housing certificates also live in these neighborhoods. Working and lower income communities struggle to create a stable economic and social balance in the community and to maintain the social fabric and traditional values of the black community. The black church, social service organizations, and strong community leaders are still present in these communities and have been leading factors in enhancing the quality of life for these community members (Staral, 2000). Other aspects of black families' quality of life have been affected by external factors, which have limited their access to adequate publicly funded housing in those low-income communities and throughout the cities in which they reside.

Social Conditions Affecting Black Families' Access to Housing Historically

Public Housing's Initial Role

The concept of publicly supported housing is rooted in the social reform or Settlement House movement. The intent of early reformers was to provide safe and sanitary housing for poor people. In return, adequate housing would function as a way up and out of poverty. Originally, the architectural design of public housing facilitated a sense of community among residents. For example, units designed by Frank Lloyd Wright in Chicago's immigrant neighborhoods included an inner courtyard. However, these early designs were never duplicated and the large-scale construction that followed lent itself to social isolation rather than community building. Still, in the early days of public housing before 1941, tenants represented a cross-section of black and white working class persons and the rents collected were sufficient to cover expenses and operating costs. By-and-large, public housing at that time reflected the social reformers' initial intent. O'Brien (1995).

After World War II, substandard housing conditions across much of America were the result of neglected domestic spending during the war effort. President Truman saw housing production as a way of meeting two objectives: building adequate housing and creating jobs for returning veterans (Klutznick, 1985). To operationalize these priorities, slum clearance was added to the original upward mobility mission of public housing. By the early 1950s, planning to develop the central core of cities was in motion. Families displaced by urban renewal were rehoused in new public housing developments. Schorr (1967).

The slum clearance objective led to the demise of viable public housing by requiring that new units be located in former slum areas and since land was expensive, high-rise units were designed to compromise cost with density. In Chicago, for example, old black tenements of the South and West Sides were replaced by new high-rise public housing

(Hirsch, 1983) with the "defacto purpose of . . . isolat(ing) the poor and especially the black population away from the white middle-class areas of the city." By removing the poor from interaction with other members of the community, their opportunities to learn from socially acceptable role models were limited. Public housing units isolated the poor and separated them from the strong social fabric of earlier immigrant communities.

The Expanded Role and Focus of Public Housing

By 1964, popular press and media attention focused on the growing number of blacks in public housing and on the "cycle of poverty" encouraged there (Schorr, 1967). Large-scale public housing developments had eliminated severe slum areas and replaced them with substantially better housing, but there was no evidence that the new housing had made the residents more self-sufficient. As a result, by the 1960s public housing had abandoned its historic notion of providing safe and affordable housing for families until they moved up the social income ladder and were able to achieve home ownership (Holzman, 1996).

In addition, public housing managers increasingly saw the problem family as the root of all evil in public housing. Public discussion linked the problems of public housing tenants to their personal histories of inadequate income, lack of education and skills, and psychological or social deprivation. In 1963, social services were included as part of the public housing package and public housing had evolved from a large-scale community-building program aimed at supplying safe and sanitary housing for upwardly mobile working-class families into a housing strategy emphasizing the delivery of welfare services to socially and psychologically demoralized tenants. President Johnson's Great Society program furthered this objective by actively placing Volunteers in Service to America (VISTA), Job Corps, Neighborhood Youth Corps, and Project Head Start programs within public housing projects.

By the time of the 1960s War on Poverty, poverty had taken center stage as the cause of problems in public housing (Schermer, 1968). With a low-income housing crisis at hand, HUD advised that tenant management be allowed. The Housing Act of 1968 mandated this approach along with a ten-year goal of developing twenty-six million new and rehabilitated housing units. Tenant management won the right over local housing authorities to raise rents and evict tenants, which had previously been done arbitrarily by those authorities. Tenant management was supported by important litigation on behalf of eight unwed mothers, which led to a suspension of housing authority control over moral standards in public housing. An unintended consequence of these progressive changes was the end to the concept of public housing as a way up and out of poverty as more and more tenants with only the barest means, including the homeless, were "warehoused" there.

Public outcry against public housing developments as seedbeds of crime caused new policy approaches to be undertaken. Section 8 housing was developed to allow the use of public subsidies for market rate units rather than the customary high-rise developments. By the end of the 1970s, existing public housing units were in a considerable state of disrepair. In general, public housing had become the housing stock of last resort. In 1981, the Reagan administration announced that the federal government was getting out of the housing business (Hartman, 1983).

RESEARCH ON CULTURALLY RELATED HOUSING ISSUES FOR BLACK FAMILIES

Housing Affordability Studies

According to Shinn and Gillespie (1994), the housing affordability gap is caused by a combination of two factors: the loss of housing that is affordable (in constant dollars) to poor renters and the erosion of incomes among poor households. In part, the shortage of affordable housing can be traced to massive cuts in federal funds for new housing construction. Between 1981 and 1988, federally subsidized housing appropriations plummeted from $30 billion to less than $8 billion, representing more than an eighty percent decline when adjusted for inflation. Gotham (1998).

During this same period, changes in tax laws made it more difficult for private investors to profit from low-income housing development. Waiting lists for housing subsidies grew dramatically throughout the 1980s and 1990s as the supply of low-income housing in the private market was also lost. Beginning in the 1980s, landlords began selling off low-income property at tremendous profits. A variety of other structural and market-driven forces such as undermaintenance, property tax delinquencies, mortgage foreclosures, eviction and eminent domain proceedings, arson, and demolition contributed both to the deterioration and destruction of housing stock. Gentrification, historic preservation, and the renovation and conversion of rental units to condominiums shifted these properties to high market values and made them unavailable to working and low-income black families.

Findings from the 1999 American Housing Survey show that despite the recent period of robust economic expansion, the housing stock affordable for struggling families (incomes at or less than thirty percent of the area median income) continues to shrink. The number of such affordable rental units decreased by 372,000 units, a five percent decline from 1991 to 1997. In 1997 for every 100 households, there were only thirty-six units both affordable and available for rent. Rents are rising at twice the rate of general inflation. As the affordable housing stock shrinks, the number of renters at or below thirty percent of median income (for example, $19,150 in Chicago) continues to grow. Between 1995 and 1997, the number of struggling renter households increased by three percent, from 8.61 million to 8.87 million—one of every four renter households in the United States (U.S. Department of HUD, 1999).

Based on the 30 percent of income rule for affordable rent set by the U. S. Department of Housing and Urban Development (HUD), the hourly wage required to afford a two-bedroom unit renting at fair market rate averaged more than twice the minimum wage. As of 1995, some 5.3 million very low-income renter households-including 2.4 million households with earnings as their primary income source; spent more than half of their income on housing or lived in severely substandard housing (HUD, 1998). Those households included disproportionate numbers of low income and working-class black families.

Research on Racial Segregation and Discrimination in Housing

Racial segregation in the United States has been created and is maintained by a complex web of private actions, market practices, and public policies. Despite the passage of the 1968 Fair Housing Act and other civil rights legislation, racial discrimination in housing remains a serious, albeit less acknowledged problem (Feins & Bratt, 1983; Goering, Kamely, & Richardson, 1997; Krivo, Peterson, & Rizzo, 1998; Ondrich, Stricker, & Yinger, 1990; Yinger, 1995). Using "dissimilarity indices" (used to quantify uneven residential patterns) and other indicators of segregation, Massey and Denton (1993) found that sixteen metropolitan areas, housing over a third of the nation's black population were "highly segregated," a condition they characterized as hypersegregation. Massey (1996) argues that the concentration of poverty observed during the 1970s and 1980s in U.S. urban areas reflects rising inequality caused by racial rather than class segregation so much so that "were black-white segregation to be eliminated, a principal force behind the spatial concentration of poverty in the United States would disappear" (405).

One of the few lines of research that explicitly addresses the effects of place and race on economic opportunities for inner-city blacks is the extensive body of scholarship related to the "spatial mismatch hypothesis." Kain (1992) first discussed this hypothesis in a paper published in 1968 in which he attempted to explain the eroding position of blacks in the metropolitan labor market. He argues that limitations on the residential choices of minorities, particularly the almost total exclusion of African Americans from white suburban areas, inhibit minority access to jobs (especially low-skill jobs), which have been steadily moving from central cities to the suburbs of most metropolitan areas for the past thirty years. Although there are gaps in data on key issues, the proximity of employment is important in youth employment, community costs for black workers, and unemployment rates among black males in metropolitan areas where jobs are most suburbanized and the minority population is most centralized (Jencks & Mater, 1990).

Housing discrimination affects the living conditions, education, and employment opportunities afforded to black and Hispanic families. Deprived of residential mobility and discouraged from owning their own homes, many minority families are unable to flee stagnant or unsafe neighborhoods. HUD's national Housing Discrimination Study found that blacks and Hispanics encounter discrimination including such explicitly segregation practices as steering in over half their encounters with sales and rental agents. Mortgage lenders are almost twice as likely to reject a loan application from an African American as from a white applicant with comparable income.

A racial differential in mortgage loan denial rates persists even after controlling for other underwriting criteria such as wealth and credit history. As a result, two thirds of black and Hispanic children are concentrated in high-poverty schools where educational achievement is low and dropout rates are high. Altogether, these effects of housing discrimination create a pernicious cycle–discrimination imposes social and economic barriers and the resulting hardships fuel the prejudice that leads whites and others to associate blacks and Hispanics with neighborhood deterioration (Yinger, 1995).

In summary, the isolation of black and other families of color in areas of concentrated urban poverty reflects the cumulative impact of persistent segregation and pervasive housing market discrimination. These practices have prevented black households from exercising free choice about where to live, constrained their pursuit of economic opportunities, and exacerbated the negative social consequences of this lack of opportunity.

Research on Residential Mobility

Residential mobility policies are promoted as means for overcoming some of the constraints imposed by place and race. They attempt to circumvent residential segregation and discrimination in the housing market by helping low-income minority families obtain rental housing in suburban areas that would otherwise be effectively inaccessible to them.

The Gautreaux Case. The first and best known mobility program designed to move low-income African Americans from inner-city neighborhoods to predominantly white suburbs came as a judicial remedy for public housing segregation. In 1966, Dorothy Gautreaux filed a class action suit alleging that the Chicago Housing Authority, with the full knowledge of HUD, employed discriminatory practices in determining the location of public housing developments and assigning tenants to them. More than ninety-nine percent of the public housing units in the city of Chicago were located in areas where the population was more than fifty percent black. Moreover, although black families comprised more than ninety percent of the families on the CHA's waiting list, they made up only seven percent of the residents of the four public housing developments in white neighborhoods.

In a controversial ruling that was upheld by the Supreme Court in 1976, the courts approved a remedial plan to give black families access to housing beyond the segregated areas where public housing was available. The plan encompassed the entire six-county Chicago metropolitan area in which HUD operated programs and was crucial in breaching the jurisdictional wall that historically insulated suburban communities from sharing responsibility for the urban poor's segregation. As a result, the Gautreaux program has enabled about 5,600 black families living in public housing developments or on the waiting list, to move to moderate and middle-income, mostly white, suburbs or to low-income black urban neighborhoods.

Although the consent decree excluded suburbs with more than thirty percent black populations and very high-rent suburbs were excluded by federally imposed rent ceilings, the relocation procedures created a quasi-experimental design that has allowed researchers to study the long-term effects of residential location on social isolation, employment, and education. Contrary to expectations, Rosenbaum (1993) found that most black families who moved to suburban areas were not socially isolated. Just over half encountered some initial racial harassment, but this quickly diminished. Suburban movers were more likely to be employed after the move than families who moved to other parts of Chicago.

After experiencing difficulty in adjusting to the different standards of the suburban schools, children generally did well in school. Suburban students were more likely to take a college-track curriculum and to attend a four-year college and only five percent of suburban movers dropped out of high school, compared with twenty percent of city movers. A major finding of studies of the Gautreaux program is the importance of counseling in enabling inner-city families to pursue housing opportunities outside their own neighborhoods. The constant involvement of a counselor eases fears of racial discrimination, and provides needed information about local resources.

Moving to Opportunity. In 1991, residential mobility reemerged on the national policy agenda when Congress authorized a five-year demonstration project called Moving to Opportunity (MTO) in Los Angeles, Boston, Chicago, Baltimore, and New York. MTO replicates many of the features of the Gautreaux program: very low-income residents of public and assisted housing are given Section 8 vouchers or certificates to aid them in obtaining housing in low-poverty areas. A cooperating nonprofit organization conducts landlord outreach to increase the availability of qualifying rental units and provides intensive pre- and post-move counseling to help participants access housing. A major difference between the Gautreaux program and MTO is that the former was explicitly designed to further racial integration whereas the latter focuses on the opportunity benefits reported by Rosenbaum.

Consequently, residency in a high-poverty area is the operative criterion and the communities to which MTO families relocate are defined by their low concentration of poverty rather than by racial composition as in the Gautreaux program. In practice however, the high correlation between race and concentrated poverty in large metropolitan areas makes it likely that participants' characteristics and destinations in the two programs will turn out the same.

This basic difference in programs' goals—one a program designed to further integration and the other designed to combat persistent poverty—gets at the heart of the ongoing debate about whether economics or race block black families from affordable rents or homeownership (Glazer, 1995; Nesiba, 1996). Glazer (1995), for example, argued in the 1960s that policies promoting residential integration are unnecessary because "Blacks would become residentially more integrated with whites as their economic circumstances improved" (p. 61). Thirty years later, he acknowledges that although the Gatreaux program has made an impact on the racial isolation of poor black families, "very little has been accomplished" for middle-class and higher-income black families toward the goal of integration (p. 77).

HELPING INDIVIDUAL FAMILIES SECURE AND MAINTAIN AFFORDABLE HOUSING

The following sections summarize some of the current programs implemented by nonprofit and government entities to enhance black families' housing stability. The Homeless Families Program, New Start/New Home, and Habitat for Humanity are all examples of creative efforts to provide individual families with affordable housing.

Research on the Homeless Families Program

A consequence of the affordability gap for renters is homelessness. In a multicity survey, Nunez and Fox (1999) found that families constitute the fastest growing segment of the homeless population and that blacks are heavily overrepresented among homeless families (58 percent as compared to twelve percent of whites in the homeless population). The Homeless Families Program, a joint demonstration effort of the Robert Wood Johnson Foundation and HUD, provides "service-enriched housing" in nine cities (Rog, 1999).

A cross-site evaluation of the program was designed to learn more about the needs of homeless families and about how services and systems might be better organized and delivered to meet those needs. Data collection included case studies of project sites, a review of key documents, on-site interviews with family members and staff, observations of program activities, and a collection of extensive survey data from the 1,300 families who participated in the program. In six of the nine sites, eighty-one percent of the families remained stably housed at least 18 months but the rates drop in some sites at thirty months. Although families accessed and made use of an array of services, particularly in mental heath and drug treatment, Rog (1999) concluded that the families remained vulnerable to housing instability due to other issues, especially psychological problems and domestic violence. In addition, she found that the program provided a small-scale fix to improve service delivery at a micro level, but did not affect broad-based system change at the macro level.

New Start/New Home Research

New Start/New Home began when a TANF (Temporary Assistance to Needy Families) client living at the Robert Taylor Homes in Chicago talked about the risk she felt in getting back and forth to work. This led to the recognition that inadequate or unsafe housing can be a barrier to residents moving from welfare to work. A pilot project funded with block grant monies from the Illinois Department of Human Services (IDHS) was one of the first nationwide to link welfare reform efforts to housing subsidy assistance (Mason, 2000). Billed as a partnership effort among IDHS, the Chicago Housing Authority, the Chicago Department of Housing, the Chicago Low-Income Housing Trust Fund, and several nonprofit social service agencies, the project is structured to include a variety of assistance and subsidies. The project also focuses on increasing the number of landlords who are willing to accept rent subsidies such as Section 8 certificates that pay the difference between the client's portion and the actual rent amount. Unlike other mobility programs, the rent vouchers under this program have enabled families to seek housing throughout the city limits of Chicago. Only families with earned income are eligible for the program.

Mason's (2000) evaluation of the program found that of the sixty-two families relocated, fifty-eight were African American families from public housing developments. Post-move interviews with these residents indicated that their level of satisfaction with their apartment, their buildings, and their neighborhoods had improved from the pre-move interview. One of the stated purposes of the project, to increase the availability of rental units was addressed through intensive recruitment of landlords to the program. Thirty landlords who were recruited for the program indicated they became committed to it in part because the partnering agencies provided brokerage functions (e.g., screening and tours of available properties). Mason also found that despite the improved level of satisfaction, many of the families reported "adjustment difficulties" related to personal or family issues and the general disruptions caused by moving such as the loss of dependable daycare.

Research on Home Ownership Programs: Habitat for Humanity

Low-incomes, combined with discrimination in housing and banking policies, have traditionally made home ownership out of reach for many black households. In view of the strong personal preference for homeownership over rental tenancy in the United States, Scanlon (1999) found that homeownership increased life satisfaction among African Americans. Using data from the National Survey of Black Americans with a random sample of 2,107 respondents, he documented that homeownership has a direct impact on life satisfaction and appears to have positive effects on respondents' perceptions of housing quality, neighborhood safety, social relations, and residential stability.

Millard Fuller's faith-inspired dream to end homelessness and bring adequate shelter to everyone who needed it was realized through the work of Habitat for Humanity. Founded in 1976 by Fuller and his wife, Habitat invites people to work together in partnership to help build houses with families in need. Using volunteer labor and donated materials as well as 500 hours of "sweat equity" contributed by the selected families, houses are built or renovated and then sold back to the new owners at no interest and no profit, thus making them affordable to low-income families. House mortgage payments are then used to finance other houses. Working through a structure of 1,900 affiliates in the United States and in more than sixty other countries around the world, Habitat has built more than 95,000 homes around the world. These homes have provided more than 475,000 people in more than 2,000 communities with safe, decent, affordable shelter (Habitat for Humanity Fact Sheet, 2000).

COMMUNITY EFFORTS TO INCREASE PRODUCTION OF AFFORDABLE HOUSING IN BLACK COMMUNITIES

Perhaps in response to the decreasing number of public housing, Section 8, and affordable market rate housing, three major community-based efforts have emerged to help fill some of the continuing gaps in low-income housing. Community efforts, unlike individual approaches, have helped black communities increase their stock of stable, affordable, and safe housing and to revitalize once deteriorated and abandoned neighborhoods. Three examples of these community efforts are: locally based Community Development Corporations, the revival of self-help movements by black Churches, and Community Development Financial Institutions (CDFI), such as Chicago's South Shore Bank. A common assumption of these efforts is that providing brick and mortar for low-income affordable housing is not enough to sustain community redevelopment. These programs typically provided a variety of support services, education and ongoing assistance based on the needs of the families and community. Some of these efforts have been researched to document their benefits to black community revitalization and housing development, while others have not been researched to date.

Community Development Corporations

Community Development Corporations (CDCs) have become one of the major community building organizations in the revitalization of low-income neighborhoods. As of 1999, there were over 2,000 CDCs around the country, working in urban communities and investing more than $275 million in the creation of affordable housing. A 1995 report

by the National Congress for Community Economic Development
(NCCED) found that by 1993, CDCs had created over 400,000 units of
affordable housing and another 30,000–40,000 units were established
in 1994 (NAHR, 1995). In recent years, CDCs have also developed as
community-based programs that provide more than just affordable
housing. They have initiated services to enhance economic development in neighborhoods in order to provide residents with job training
and placement programs, economic development activities, and neighborhood safety programs (Mulroy & Lauber, 2002).

Community Development Corporations have become such an established force in neighborhood redevelopment that they are now part
of federal legislation. The 1990 National Affordable Housing Act mandated that at least fifteen percent of funds in each participating jurisdic-
tion be set aside for nonprofit housing developers and that each state set
aside ten percent of its low-income housing tax credits for use by nonprofit organizations (Vidal, 1997). These mandates have ensured a
stable economic base for CDCs and non-profit organizations focused
on housing and community development.

Fredericksen and London's (2000) study of eighteen CDCs in EI
Paso, Texas focused on their organizational structures in an attempt to
assess the long-term ability of these organizations to sustain themselves.
The study found that these groups offered a number of services in addition to affordable housing. All of them offered services and programs
identified as needed by the families in their respective areas, such as
child care, substance abuse referral, job training, and so on. However,
the study highlighted a need for more research on participants' satisfaction regarding redevelopment efforts and the effectiveness of these
organizations in meeting the needs of program participants and in redeveloping communities. Despite the tremendous success of community development housing groups in producing thousands of affordable
housing units and in attracting federal, state and local government attention to the need for community revitalization, there is little research
on the long-term viability of these organizations.

Programs Sponsored by the Black Church

The black church has traditionally been a stabilizing influence in
black communities and a major social support system for black families,

attending to their spiritual needs and at times, daily survival. The black church has been the one institution that all black families could turn to without social stigma or threats of being denied services.

Historically, the church's role has been to enhance the social, political and economic base of the black family and community. During the social activism of the 1950s and 1960s, the black church was a major player in the advancement of the civil rights movement. However, the church experienced a shift in its role following the social and economic changes in the 1970–80s. As middle-class blacks moved away from traditional black communities, and headed for the suburbs, the church was also faced with the growing needs of its working and lower income residents surrounding the church property. As many churches witnessed the decay of once strong and vibrant communities, the church began to reexamine its role in the economic base of the black community.

Today, churches across the country have revived the self-help movement and become catalysts for assisting in the creation of affordable housing, the establishment of black-owned businesses, and the education of communities on financial investments and economic development. Examples of these initiatives include the Wheat Street Baptist Church in the historical district of Auburn Avenue in Atlanta and the Hartford Memorial Baptist Church in Detroit (Gite, 1993).

One of the most successful efforts toward housing production and community revitalization can be found in the Nehemiah Housing Plan started by a coalition of black churches in New York City's East Brooklyn and South Bronx neighborhoods. The Nehemiah Plan is a home loan program that reduces the mortgage costs of home buyers instead of investing in scattered site housing around certain neighborhoods or communities (Pare & Bordwin, 1993). This plan differs from other community-based home ownership programs in that it develops a community by redeveloping rows of houses at a time.

In addition to producing a thousand new homes in Brooklyn, campaigns sponsored by the coalition were successful in getting street signs replaced, improving conditions in local supermarkets, demolishing abandoned buildings, getting smoke shops (places for selling illegal narcotics) closed, and registering new voters. As part of the 1987 Housing and Community Development Act, the Nehemiah plan became part of a federal initiative program to fund other nonprofit organizations in making loans to moderate-income families purchasing homes through these organizations. This and other church-sponsored community housing and revitalization programs can benefit from research that explores how they work and their outcomes.

Community Development Financial Institutions: South Shore Bank

South Shore Bank, or Shore Bank as it is often called, is the oldest and best-known community development bank in the country (Lutton, 1998). Based in Chicago, the bank also has affiliate branches in Cleveland, Detroit, and Astoria, Oregon and expects to expand into Europe, including some former communist countries (Shore Bank Annual Report, 1999). The bank was created in Chicago almost thirty years ago to prove that financial institutions can have positive effects in declining neighborhoods, revitalize poor communities, and remain viable institutions.

Over the years, the bank has expanded across the south side of Chicago, and into low-income communities on the west side of Chicago, with over $840 million in assets. The bank has focused on community revitalization in two areas. It provides loans to small, minority businesses and black churches that traditionally were denied loans from larger, more established banking institutions and it works with developers who are rehabilitating decaying properties in their target areas and with low-income families who want to become first-time homeowners (Shore Bank Annual Report, 1999; Lutton, 1998). Shore Bank's philosophy is to create programs and services that educate community residents about investing, saving, and working toward purchasing a home.

Since its inception, the bank has rehabilitated over 22,000 apartments. In 1999, it financed $58.2 million for the purchase and rehabilitation of over 3,300 apartments, mostly on the south side of Chicago (Shore Bank Annual Report, 1999). In the 1980s, Shore bank started a peer support group called Sisters Building Bridges for women living in subsidized housing rehabilitated by the bank in Chicago. One of the bank's newest initiatives has been to provide building loans to churches for community child care centers and educational buildings for programs focused on children and youth. In 1999, the bank made over $20 million in loans to churches (Veenker, 1999). South Shore Bank has changed how banking institutions view, and are viewed by, the community. It is one of a few examples of a banking institution that has successfully invested in poor, undercapitalized communities and yet remained financially competitive. Because many of the Shore Banks' successes have been described in formal reports and other documents, research is needed to support those conclusions and to provide opportunities for replication by other institutions.

FEDERAL POLICIES FOR CREATING BLACK FAMILIES' ACCESS TO AFFORDABLE HOUSING

Federal policies are needed to radically change the possibilities for black families' housing in the future. Two examples of still-evolving strategies are Hope VI and Individual Development Accounts.

Early Research on Hope VI

In 1992, Congress created the Urban Revitalization Demonstration known as HOPE VI to tear down severely distressed public housing developments and to create mixed-income, affordable housing units. Hope VI will raze 100,000 apartments in the nation's worst public housing projects and relocate the mostly African American residents living there. In Chicago, for example, fifty-two public housing high-rise buildings that make up nearly forty percent of the city's public housing (11,000 units), will be torn down over the next fifteen years. Of the families who will leave Robert Taylor Homes, the nation's largest public housing development, 99 percent are black and nearly half of the adults live on less than $5,000 a year.

A part of the relocation plan is to replace these high-rise buildings with smaller developments that mix families of different income levels. However, a recent article in the *Chicago Tribune* reported that only a third of the new housing will be publicly subsidized (Gezari, 2000). Thousands of public housing tenants will receive housing subsidies that will allow them to move into market-rate and scattered site units throughout the metropolitan area. The goal is to relocate families out of the concentrated poverty area surrounding public housing developments. Similar relocation efforts in the past have replicated the segregation patterns of traditional public housing-that is, black families using Section 8 certificates and vouchers often move to neighborhoods similar to those surrounding public housing (Fischer, 1999; Mason, 2000). Many fear that tearing down public housing will continue to concentrate Chicago's poor in neighborhoods that are just as bad as the areas from which they were relocated.

To evaluate the long-term effectiveness of HOPE VI, HUD is examining local plans and identifying outcomes at each of the fifteen project sites. Salama (1999) has identified six major goals from the legislative history of appropriations for the program. Those goals include lessening the concentration of low-income households; leveraging private resources; limiting project costs; helping residents to achieve economic self-sufficiency (particularly for persons enrolled in welfare-to-work programs); designing projects that blend into the community; and ensuring meaningful resident participation in project planning.

In comparing the initial years of implementation to the listed goals, Salama (1999) found that in three sites (Atlanta, Chicago, and San Antonio), complex economic and community tradeoffs were necessary to begin full implementation of the program. For example, at Cabrini Green, a public housing development in Chicago, residents were actively resistant to the redevelopment plan. Since ninety-three percent of Cabrini-Green residents did not have earned income, they feared that the proposed seventy-nine percent reduction of public units on site would result in massive displacement. To address this concern, a compromise was reached by developing an additional 423 public housing units in an adjacent area and authorizing the use of twenty percent of the grant funds for supportive services designed to increase the earned income of residents.

Individual Development Accounts (IDAs) Studies

IDAs are matched savings accounts designed to help low-income and low-wealth families accumulate funds for education or job training, homeownership and micro-enterprise. Community organizations (usually nonprofit organizations) counsel and monitor participants, provide money management training, control the matching funds (from funders), and authorize participants' withdrawals. Johnson and Sherraden (1992) argue that asset accumulation provides a tangible means for working poor and welfare poor households to have an equitable opportunity for homeownership as compared to middle and upper-class families who receive tax benefits for purchasing a house.

With support from ten foundations, the *American Dream Policy Demonstration* (ADD) (Sherraden, Page-Adams, & Johnson, 1999) is the first large test of the potential that IDAs have as a route to economic independence for low-income Americans. The ADD is a nationwide demonstration of individual development accounts and is scheduled to run for four years (1997–2001) with an additional two years of evaluation. The research plan for the ADD calls for multiple research methods including implementation assessment, participation data collection, experimental design surveys, in-depth interviews to supplement the experimental survey, community level evaluation and cost-benefit analysis. The initial report on the start-up data (Sherraden et al., 1999) indicates that of the 453 participants (37 percent African Americans) who have accounts, the most common intended use of IDAs is home purchase (51 percent), followed by micro-enterprise (13 percent), and postsecondary education (12 percent).

EXPANDING THE LENS FOR RESEARCH ON BLACK FAMILIES AND HOUSING

The programs and policies outlined in this chapter provide a multi-faceted blend of approaches for making housing more accessible to black families. At the same time, research and formal reports on these programs document and describe the linkage between livable housing and the health and well-being of the black community and culture. However, this brief review does not provide a full picture of the web of interrelated issues that enable black residents to be safe in their homes and a part of a healthy community. The framework outlined in Figure 3.1 suggests areas of needed research on multiple system levels.

Micro Level Research: Individuals and Families

Micro approaches to housing for individual families have provided a limited response to the crisis of homelessness or inadequate housing, therefore failing to account for the importance of community linkages in establishing a home. The Homeless Families Program (Rog, 1999), New Start/New Home (Mason, 2000), and Habitat for Humanity *(Fact*

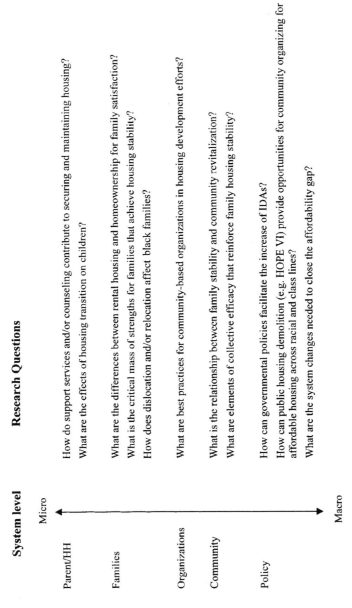

Figure 3.1 Housing Opportunities for Black Families–Implications for Future Research

Sheet, 2000) are approaches that create or move families into affordable housing. In the first two rental programs, counseling is a necessary component for assisting families in making this transition. Although neither research delineated the type or duration of effective counseling, Rog (1999) reports that the families continued to be vulnerable to homelessness due to personal and family problems. There is no evidence that Habitat participants receive any counseling or social services as they assume first time homeownership. Research is needed to show how families access resources and social supports in new communities where they have found housing or purchased a home. Particularly, research is needed to show how access to services benefits the healthy development of children.

Also at the micro family level, research is needed to help us understand how the strengths of black families interacts with and impacts upon their housing situations. O'Brien (1995) identified some crucial attributes among long-term residents in public housing. However, in that review, she found little information describing how individual families used their strengths to deal with housing dislocation or relocation in a new community. Although Glazer (1995) argues that it is on a one-by-one or family-by-family basis that racial inequality is broken down, there is little data to support this position. Future research should focus on the characteristics of black families who are able to successfully manage the biculturality necessary for living in a multicultural neighborhood or predominantly white suburb.

The Mezzo or Community Level Studies

At the community level, efforts to provide affordable housing for individual families have advanced community revitalization efforts. Community Development Corporations, financial institutions, and black churches have all played a role in developing programs that address both housing needs and the neighborhood environment for maintaining housing. There are, however, few evaluations of these programs, which provide little more than anecdotal or descriptive findings about the effects of housing programs with a focus on the production of housing units.

Moreover, since community empowerment requires that neighborhood development involve residents and other local stakeholders in identifying problems and designing solutions, the voices of community members about their perspectives on these programs and the linkage between individual family stability and community revitalization are missing in the research. Kreutziger, Ager, Lewis, & England (2001) provide some ideas for implementing participatory research within a low-income neighborhood that enables community members to assume the role of knowledge producers for prioritizing community needs. In this example, community members owned the process as well as the goals for the action plan that emerged from examining their community's needs and assets.

Another important area of future research at the community level is the role and contribution of black churches. Black churches have expanded their role in providing housing and related social services since the early 1980s, but the full extent of these services and the difference they make have yet to be addressed. Research that examines how churches develop and implement community-wide initiatives may produce practice and policy models, which in turn, may stimulate additional support. Research is also needed regarding the types of organizations best suited for community revitalization efforts. This line of research should examine the dynamics, attributes, and resources that foster long-term success, along with definitions and indicators of success.

Macro or Policy Level Research

W.E.B. DuBois's century-old research is one of the most comprehensive studies on race. Recently, however, research has begun to link labor market dynamics, racial attitudes, and residential segregation. Despite apparent gains for minorities during the last several decades, a five-year, multicity inquiry indicates that racial segregation persists, particularly at the structural and institutional level (O'Connor, Tilly, & Bobo, 2000). In addition, Wilson (1999) presents compelling arguments for locating the current racial inequality within social class and property or economic domains. Assets-based strategies suggested by the IDA demonstration projects are an example of policy development in this direction. IDAs provide the mechanisms for low-income families to accumulate assets similar to what has traditionally been provided to the nonpoor through the tax system. Changing the policies that encourage and reinforce savings and investments normalizes and expands the transitions that families negotiate as they move from rental housing to homeownership.

In view of the growing income gap between the poor and working poor and the wealthy in the United States, Wilson (1999) suggests that people of all racial and ethnic groups form class-based, rather than race-based alliances to pursue new policies "to bridge the racial divide." This line of thinking falls within the traditional purview of social work. Thus, broad-based coalitions and class-based alliances for affordable housing and improvement of neighborhood social conditions is an important area for further research.

As part of macro level research, the federal government's solution to the housing needs of black families requires building more affordable housing units and ensuring that discrimination and segregation do not prevent them from living in such housing. Historically, however, housing programs in the United States are often underfunded, fragmented, and lack clearly focused goals (Wong, 2002). HOPE VI is an effort to change the look of public housing and revitalize access to scattered site, subsidized housing. Further program evaluations are needed to show how the massive relocation of public housing residents affects access to social services and the improvement of neighborhood and community conditions in concentrated areas of poverty.

The Moving to Opportunity program also represents a shift in federal policy from investing in vast public housing projects to the use of vouchers to relocate black families in less segregated areas of the city. There is some indication that families moving to the suburbs have found jobs and their children have done better in school than those who stayed in high-poverty areas in the city. Research is needed on the extent to which these families maintain linkages with the community they left behind and how these linkages facilitate or inhibit stability in suburban relocation programs.

CONCLUSION

In the same way that becoming homeless or being inadequately housed results from a chain of events and circumstances (Johnson, 1999; Rosenthal, 1994), this review of the literature indicates that there are multiple issues in the process of becoming sufficiently housed. Future research on black families–especially focusing on homelessness, subsidized housing, and homeownership programs–should include measures and methods for studying their use of personal and social strengths in accessing and maintaining housing. Future research should also focus on the role that assets play in providing upward mobility for black families to homeownership or in securing tenure in rental housing within neighborhoods of their choice.

REFERENCES

Beverly, S.G. (2001). Material hardship in the United States: Evidence from the survey of income and program participation. *Social Work Research, 25*(3), 143–151.

Bowie, S.L. (2001). The impact of privatized management in urban public housing communities: A comparative analysis of perceived crime, neighborhood problems, and personal safety. *Journal of Sociology and Social Welfare, 28*(4), 67–87.

Dubois, W.E.B. (1969). *The Negro American family.* NY: New American Library.

Early, T.J. & GlenMaye, L.F. (2000). Valuing families: Social work practice with families from a strengths perspective. *Social Work, 45,* 118–131.

Feins, J. D., & Bratt, R. G. (1983). Barred in Boston: Racial discrimination in housing. *Journal of the American Planning Association, 49*(3), 344–355.

Fischer, P. (1999). *Section 8 and the public housing revolution: Where will the families go?* Chicago: Woods Fund of Chicago.

Franklin, D. L. & Smith, S.E. (1995). Correlates of marital status among African American mothers in Chicago neighborhoods of concentrated poverty. *Journal of Marriage and the Family, 57,* 141–153.

Fredericksen, P. & London, R. (2000). Disconnect in the hollow state: The pivotal role of organizational capacity in community-based development organizations. *Public Administration Review, 60*(2), 230–240.

Gezari, V. (2000). CHA tearing down last symbol of troubled complex. *Chicago Tribune,* Section 2, 3.

Gite, L. (1993). The new agenda of the Black church: Economic development for Black America. *Black Enterprise, 5:* 54–60.

Glazer, N. (1995). Black and white after thirty years. *Public Interest, 121,* 61–79.

Goering, J., Kamely, A., & Richardson, T. (1997). Recent research on racial segregation and poverty concentration in public housing in the United States. *Urban Affairs Review, 32,* 723–745.

Goings, K. W., & Mohl, R. A. (1995). Toward a new Mexican American urban history. *Journal of Urban History, 95,* 283–296.

Goldsmith, W. W. (1997). Who cares about the inner city? *Journal of the American Planning Association, 63,* 154.

Gotham, K.F. (1998). Blind faith in the free market: Urban poverty, residential segregation, and federal housing retrenchment. *Sociological Inquiry, 68*(1), 1–31.

Habitat for Humanity Fact Sheet. (2000). Americus, GA: Author.

Harris, E. (1995). How do we measure progress? *National Minority Politics, 7,* 22–29.

Harrison, A., Wilson, M., Pine, C., Chan, *S.,* & Buriel, R. (1990). Family ecologies of ethnic minority children. *Child Development, 61,* 347–362.

Hartman, C. W. (1983). *America's housing crisis: What is to be done?* Boston: Routledge & Kegan Paul.

Hill, R.B. (1997). *The strengths of African American families: Twenty-five years later.* Baltimore: R & B Publishers.

Holzman, H.R. (1996). Criminological research on public housing: Toward a better understanding of people, places, and spaces. *Crime & Delinquency, 42,* 361–378.

Jencks, C., & Mater, S. E. (1990). Residential segregation, job proximity, and black job opportunities. In L. E. Lynn & M. G. H. McGeary (Eds.), Inner-city poverty in the United States. Washington, DC: National Academy Press.

Johnson, A. K., & Sherraden, M. (1992). Asset-based social welfare policy: Home-ownership for the poor. *Journal of Sociology & Social Welfare, 19*(3), 65–83.

Johnson, A. K. (1999). Working and non-working women: Becoming homeless in the context of their lives. *AFFILIA: Journal of Women and Social Work, 14*(1), 42–77.

Kain, J. F. (1992). The spatial mismatch hypothesis: Three decades later. *Housing Policy Debate 3,* 371–460.

Klutznick, P.M. (1985). Poverty and politics: the challenge of public housing. *Journal of Housing, 42,* 9–10.

Kreutziger, S.S., Ager, R., Lewis, J.S., & England, S. (2001). A critical look at a contemporary welfare-to-work program in light of the historic settlement ideal. *Journal of Community Practice, 9*(2), 49–69.

Krivo, L. J., Peterson, R. D., & Rizzo, H. (1998). Race, segregation, and the concentration of disadvantage: 1980–1990. *Social Problems, 45*(1), 61–80.

Lutton, L. (1998). Chicago's South Shore says buyout of Black bank has paid off for community. *American Banker, 163,* 11–12.

Mason, M. (2000). *New Start/New Home evaluation report.* Chicago: Mid-America Institute on Poverty.

Massey, D. *S.,* & Denton, N. A. (1993). *American apartheid: Segregation and the making of the underclass.* Cambridge, MA: Harvard University Press.

Massey, D. S. (1996). The age of extremes: Concentrated affluence and poverty in the twenty-first century. *Demography, 33,* 395–412.

McCarty, D.A. (2002). Concentration of poverty and social isolation of African American public housing residents in east and southeast Texas. *Dissertation Abstracts.*

Morris, J. R. & Robinson, D. T. (1996). Community and Christianity in the Black church. *Counseling and Values, 41,* 59–70.

Moynihan, D. (1965). *The Negro family: The case for national action.* Washington, DC: U.S. Government Printing Office.

Mulroy, E.A. & Lauber, H. (2002). Community building in hard times: A post-welfare view from the streets. *Journal of Community Practice, 10*(1), 1–16.

National Association of Housing and Redevelopment (1995). Report finds CDC's produced over 400,000 housing units. *Journal of Housing and Community Development, 95*(3).

Nesiba, R. F. (1996). Racial discrimination in residential lending markets: Why empirical researchers always see it and economic theorists never do. *Journal of Economic Issues, 30*(1), 51–78.

Nunez, R., & Fox, C. (1999). A snapshot of family homelessness across America. *Political Science Quarterly, 114*(2), 289–308.

O'Brien, P. (1995). From surviving to thriving: The complex experience of living in public housing. *AFFILIA: Journal of Women and Social Work, 10*(2), 155–178.

O'Connor, A., Tilly, C., & Bobo, L. (2000). *Urban inequality: Evidence from four cities.* New York: Russell Sage Foundation.

Ondrich, J., Stricker, A., & Yinger, J. (1990). Do real estate brokers choose to discriminate? Evidence from the 1989 housing discrimination study. *Southern Economic Journal, 64*(4), 880–901.

Pare, T., & Bordwin, A. (1993). Buy a home downtown. *Fortune, 128,* 93–95.

Pattillo, M.E. (1998). Sweet mothers and gangbangers: Managing crime in a Black middle-class neighborhood. *Social Forces, 76,* 747–775.

Reed, V.M. (1991). Civil rights legislation and the housing status of Black Americans: Evidence from fair housing audits and segregation indices. *Review of Black Political Economy, 19,* 29–43.

Report finds that CDC's produced over 400,000 housing units. (1995). *Journal of Housing & Community Development, 52*(5), 3–12. Author.

Rog, D. J. (1999). The evaluation of the homeless families program. *American Journal of Evaluation, 20*(3), 558–562.

Rosenbaum, J.E. (1993). Closing the gap: Does residential integration improve the employment and education of low-income blacks? In L. B. Joseph (Ed.), *Affordable housing and public policy: Strategies for metropolitan Chicago.* Chicago: Center for Urban Research and Policy Studies.

Rosenthal, R. (1994). *Homeless in paradise: A map of the terrain.* Philadelphia: Temple University Press.

Salama, J. J. (1999). The redevelopment of distressed public housing: Early results form HOPE VI Projects in Atlanta, Chicago, and San Antonio. *Housing Policy Debate, 10*(1), 95–142.

Saleebey, D. (Ed.) (1997). *The strengths perspective in social work practice* (2nd Edition). New York: Longman.

Scanlon, E. (1999). *The impact of homeownership on the life satisfaction of African-Americans.* St. Louis: Washington University-George Warren Brown School of Social Work.

Schermer, G. (1968). *More than shelter: Social need in low and moderate-income housing.* Washington, DC: U.S. Government Printing Office.

Schorr, A. L. (1967). Slums and social security. In J. Bellush & M. Hausknecht (Eds.), *Urban renewal: People, politics, and controversy.* Cambridge, MA: M.I. T. Press.

Sherraden, M., Page-Adams, D. & Johnson, L. (1999). *Down payments on the American dream policy demonstration: Startup evaluation report.* St. Louis: Center for Social Development, Washington University.

Shore Bank Annual Report. (1999). Chicago: The South Shore Bank. Author.

Shinn, M. & Gillespie, C. (1994). The role of housing and poverty in the origins of homelessness. *American Behavioral Scientist, 37,* 505–521.

Staral, J. M. (2000). Building on mutual goals: The intersection of community practice & church based organizations. *Journal of Community Practice, 7*(3), 85–95.

Thompson, H. A. (1999). Rethinking the politics of white flight in the postwar city. *Journal of Urban History, 25,* 163–199.

U.S. Department of Housing and Urban Development. (1995). *Evaluation of the HOPE 3 program: Final report.* Washington, DC: U.S. Government Printing Office. Author.

U.S. Department of Housing and Urban Development. (1998). *Rental Housing Assistance–The Crisis Continues: The 1997 Report to Congress on worst case housing needs.* Washington, DC: U.S. Government Printing Office. Author.

U.S. Department of Housing and Urban Development. (1999). *Widening the gap: New findings on housing affordability in America.* Washington, DC: U.S. Government Printing Office. Author.

Veenker, J. (1999). Chicago bank has new faith in credit-poor churches. *Christianity Today, 43,* 23–28.

Vidal, A.C. (1997). Can community development re-invent itself? *Journal of the American Planning Association, 63*(4), 429–439.

West, C. (1991). *Race matters.* New York: Vintage Books.

Wilson, W. J. (1987). *The truly disadvantaged.* Chicago: University of Chicago Press.

Wilson, W. J. (1999). *The bridge over the racial divide: Rising inequality and coalition politics.* Berkeley, CA: University of California Press.

Wong, Y.L. (2002). Tracking change in psychological distress among homeless adults: An examination of the effect of housing status. *Health and Social Work, 27*(4), 262–273.

Yinger, J. (1995). *Closed doors, opportunities lost: The continuing cost of housing discrimination.* New York: Russell Sage Foundation.

Chapter 4

AFRICAN AMERICAN FAMILIES, MENTAL HEALTH, AND LIVING COOPERATIVES: A PROGRAM AND RESEARCH ANALYSIS

RAMONA DENBY, CYNTHIA ROCHA, AND SANDRA OWENS-KANE

African Americans encounter a great number of tenuous circumstances that serve as obstacles to their optimal physical health, mental health, and general well-being. Experiences that pose potential threats to African Americans' mental health include, but are not limited to, poverty, discrimination, cultural bias, impaired physical health, substance abuse, environmental warfare, unemployment, the portrayal of negative black images in the media, and generalized stress (Clark, Anderson, Clark & Williams, 1999; U.S. Department of HHS, 2001). Among the myriad factors that produce these problem situations are environmental conditions borne of large societal structures and perpetuated by smaller organized entities that propose to remedy the problems. Individuals who find they cannot withstand these adverse conditions may develop diverse and complex mental health and social support needs. For example, they may need parenting resources, skill strengthening, emotional support and validation, and spiritual rebirth.

African Americans who need assistance and/or mental health support should be able to seek solace in the mental health service system, which operates to alleviate stress and suffering. However, many of them are unable to find the resources they need within existing formal support structures. Traditional service delivery structures often fall short of meeting the needs of African American families, because there is a mismatch between what these service entities provide and what African Americans need (Ramirez, 1999; Whaley, 2001). This phenomenon of service mismatch is a legacy that dates back to the first establishment of formal welfare, mental health, and social support service, therefore, it is not new. Its impact on African Americans may be more pronounced now, because they have seemingly abandoned many early cultural practices that previously sustained them.

For example, at the turn of the century, mental health provisions for African Americans were virtually nonexistent, and at best they were minimal and segregated. However, during that era, indigenous African American benevolent groups and programs, fraternal orders, church-based programs, and mutual-aid societies acted as cultural buffers. Although such supports were not formal, government-supported, or legitimized among the larger society, they did meet a crucial need for African Americans (Logan, 1996; Martin & Martin, 1985). With the growing recognition of civil rights and the push for social reform, formal mental health systems was forced to serve the mental health needs of African Americans. These mandates opened the doors of eligibility to African Americans, but unfortunately, they did not meet their needs. Another unintended consequence was the decreased recognition of, and reliance on, African-American sponsored groups and programs that had previously proven successful in aiding African Americans.

There is a dire need for African Americans to rediscover these earlier, more culturally defined and self-sustaining traditions. Not only have such traditions proved more compatible to their unique mental health needs, but also some reforms in the formal service system have become barriers to African Americans' access to services. The justification for culturally defined programming is also evident due to the prevalence and complexity of African Americans' mental health needs (Baker, 2001; Lindsey, 2002).

By critically probing the research literature on mental health services to African Americans, this chapter identifies best practices in this area based on their cultural values, and highlights the mismatch between current service provisions offered by formal mental health agencies and the mental health needs of African Americans. The research analysis also provides a rationale for the more culturally compatible mental health program and research model that is discussed in the chapter.

Feasibility issues are addressed related to potential barriers and sources of success for the model. In conclusion, the impact of this proposed model on African American individuals, families, groups, and communities is described within the context of social work roles and skills that are required for implementing the model.

BEST PRACTICES IN AFRICAN AMERICAN MENTAL HEALTH SERVICES: AN ANALYSIS OF THE RESEARCH LITERATURE

Underlying Philosophy

The research literature on mental health services to African Americans has been analyzed to identify best practices. Such practices can only be culturally relevant to the extent that they conceptualize African American mental health and social support needs broadly, from an environmental rather than a presumptive disease model. The focus should not be on mental disease and illness, but on those factors that contribute to impaired positive mental well-being. For decades some researchers have used an environmental perspective to effectively guide their studies on black mental health (Clark, 1965; Gary, 1978; Grier & Cobbs, 1968; Jones & Korchin, 1982; Pettigrew, 1964; Poussaint, 1990; Willie, Kramer, & Brown, 1973). Environmental threats to African Americans' mental well-being include poverty, discrimination, cultural bias, suicide, depression, physical health problems, substance abuse, and other more general factors that create stress.

Hence, the unique needs of African Americans require mental health service programming that is undergirded by several fundamental practice philosophies intrinsically related to their cultural value base (Billingsley, 1968, 1990, 1992; Denby, 1996; Martin & Martin, 1985; McAdoo, 1981). That value base has been integrated into each section of the following discussion about best practices in mental health services to African Americans.

Historical and Contemporary African American Value Base

What is the ideological base? African Americans embrace a value system whereby they believe that individuals, just by the mere fact that they have life, should be afforded services and assistance in times of need. A time-honored cliché within the African American culture is as follows, "if you haven't experienced trouble yet, you just keep on livin'." Captured in this statement is the notion that at some point in everyone's life, he or she will need support for problems currently being experienced. Given this belief, a culturally compatible support and mental health program should not transmit a message that only those who are "deserving" will be assisted. Within an African American value base, everyone is deserving of help. Research has documented that such ideological premises must be embraced and respected to decrease the shame, stigma, prejudice, and other psychological barriers that many African Americans experience when they seek mental health services (Diala, Muntaner, Walrath, Nickerson, LaVeist, & Leaf, 2000; Gary, 1978; Jones & Korchin, 1982; Poussaint, 1990; U.S. Department of HHS, 2001).

Individuals and Their Service Needs

How is the need for assistance viewed? Given the many stressors that African Americans face, the need for assistance and help should not be viewed as a weakness but rather as a health coping response to adverse social conditions. African Americans have a long-standing tradition of using mutual assistance in times of need. Informal reciprocal helping is offered as a means to prevent problems and sustain individuals during times of need (Colarossi & Eccles, 2003). Borman (1984) characterizes effective mutual assistance programs as possessing the following characteristics: (1) self-responsibility; (2) continuity over time; and (3) solidarity. These core features are particularly relevant for the mental health framework needed for African Americans.

Programming that cultivates a sense of power, richness, and dedication among social network members can foster member responsibility. Likewise, programming that remains continuous over time and withstands changing funding patterns and political agendas can best meet the special support needs of African American clients through the use of mutual assistance. Martin and Martin (1985) noted that the legacy of mutual assistance among African Americans began in traditional African life, continued through slavery and reconstruction, and remains as part of current urban America. It emanates from factors such as the need to remain united under adverse conditions, race consciousness, and religious or spiritual centeredness. Mutual reliance and assistance are cultural strengths to be valued. Program solidarity can be harnessed by attention to these African American traditions.

How are individuals in need of services viewed? To ensure optimal mental health outcomes for African Americans, service participants must be viewed as citizens, as opposed to patients. For African Americans to receive maximum program benefit, research findings indicate that they need first to be viewed in the context of normalization (Levkoff, Prohaska, Weitzman, & Ory, 2000; McNeilly, Musick, Efland, Baughman, Toth, Saulter, Sumner, Sherwood, Weitzman, Levkoff, Williams, & Anderson, 2000; U.S. Department of HHS, 1999). In keeping with African American values, individuals must be embraced, accepted, and given participatory citizenship status within service programs. Such a status requires that African American program participants act upon unfolding events instead of being acted upon by practitioners, through active involvement in treatment decisions and in providing meaningful feedback about the cultural relevance of services.

How are problems viewed? To establish mental health service programming that has the potential to yield the greatest success in African American outcomes, it is paramount that planners take into account the role of political, economic, and familial systems. As a general practice principle, it is widely acknowledged that problem identification cannot rest solely at an individual level. This principle is even more critical where African Americans are concerned. Mental health service programs must plan for the circular and consequential relationship that often exists between African American program participants and their overtaxed family network, depleted economic resources, and disempowered sociopolitical base. Thus, a culturally congruent, multisystemic perspective must be used and then documented through research in its effects on desired outcomes: the identification and amelioration of micro, mezzo, and macro problems (Sue, Fijino, Hu, Takeuchi, & Zane, 1991; Sue & Sue, 1999).

What assumptions are made about human nature? Mental health service programs that create a sense of positive regard and are guided by a strengths-oriented perspective toward African Americans stand to create the most optimal service environment. African Americans have a fundamental belief in the inherent worth and value of people. This belief and value should be the reigning sentiment that is espoused in order to best serve their mental health needs. Studies have shown that the absence of such a perspective, or a lack of cultural responsiveness, increases dropout rates and decreases the accessibility of mental health programs for African Americans and other people of color (Clark, Anderson, Clark, & Williams, 1999; Keith, 2000; Sue, Fujino, Hu, Takeuchi, & Zane, 1991).

Issues of Authority and Power

What is the structure of program authority? Despite the adversities endured by African Americans, many maintain a positive self-regard, a sense of fairness and equity, and a cooperative nature (U.S. Department of HHS, 2001; Keith, 2000). In appreciation of such values, best practices in mental health services to black clients involve democratic decision making as an intervention, as opposed to hierarchical decision making (Clark et al., 1999).

What is the role of authority? Many African Americans have had little if any participation in the decision making and planning of public social services that they differentially utilize, therefore, they seldom identify with those programs. Research supports the use of indigenous persons in key leadership and decision-making roles as culturally relevant interventions in mental health service programming. For example, in discussing mutual aid in immigrant populations, Borman (1984) contrasts traditional social service agencies with social services by indigenous groups. He notes that the traditional distinction that exists between professionals, board members, and policy makers and the members, clients, and consumers who utilize services, is absent in indigenous group social service systems. Therefore, mental health programming suitable to the needs of African Americans should follow a similar course, whereby program participants also function as the directors, experts, and planners. Borman writes that, "One is an expert or leader largely because of one's experiences with the focal concern or heritage of the group" (p. 53).

Thus, optimal programming should have at its very core a plan for the inclusion of self-regulating mechanisms. Such mechanisms do not exclude the use of outside professionals. In fact, outside professionals can be skillfully used as consultants, special assistants, and task leaders.

Researchers have found that social workers are able to successfully assume a nonintrusive role in self-regulating groups and programs (Belton, 1993). In a study of social group work that mobilized citizens who were dealing with issues of unemployment, debilitating physical conditions, and mental illness, Glasser and Suroviak (1989) noted that outside, community professionals were pivotal to the program's success through their regular presentation of material and resources of relevance to the program participants' needs. However, successful work of outside professionals must be continuously driven by the principles of client self-determination.

Collaborative Relationships/Views About Knowledge

What is the nature of the worker-client relationship? Given African Americans' "people-centeredness" and belief in the sharing of roles and responsibilities, it is paramount that the worker-client relationship be egalitarian. Such relationships are not only consistent with African Americans' value base, but they foster needed feelings of empowerment and ownership in the support process. Another important component of the worker-client relationship is the need for outside professionals to expand their view of the African American participant to include the influence of the larger cultural system. Other research documents that professionals need to establish a client relationship that encapsulates the need to assist in crucial impending sociocultural conditions in order to better serve African Americans (Clark et al., 1999). Recognition of issues of acculturation and biculturalism are also crucial in the worker-client relationship. The role of advocate must be fostered in the collaborative relationship between worker and client.

What is the role of professional and local expertise? Although African Americans highly regard formal education, they also give significant credence to age-old wisdom, mother wit, "common sense," life experience, and what social constructivists value as local knowledge (Hill, 1971; Billingsley & Caldwell, 1991). African Americans believe that people in general, and especially elders, have a great deal of knowledge to contribute to effective problem-solving. In keeping with this value, mental health services should provide opportunities for peer-level linking, as a part of culturally meaningful interventions, whereby problems are solved collectively, and each person's life experiences and knowledge are embraced and appreciated.

Effects of Program Diagnostic Procedures

What is the purpose of classification? Labeling program participants with *a priori* categories satisfies a practical reality related to organizational survival: it ensures a diagnosable, reimbursable, perhaps treatable, and separable condition for programs. Kirk and Kutchins (1988) conclude that classification schemes such as the Diagnostic Statistical Manual of Mental Disorders also have a disadvantage for clients, especially clients who are more vulnerable to environmental conditions that affect their responses to services. For example, such classification schemes can lead to misdiagnosis, detrimental labeling, and compromised social worker-client relations. There is no evidence to suggest that professional, pre-assumed labels increase participants' understanding of the problems they face or how they cope with or resolve those problems. Moreover, there are no research findings to suggest that a label prods a client toward a positive outcome. In fact, labeling may lead to outcomes that hamper clients' self-disclosure and problem identification if they have fears about being tracked or grouped with similar others.

What other approaches support client empowerment? In addition to the use of required pre-established imposed labels, a more empowering approach may be to afford program participants the opportunity to identify with one another through the mutual recognition of need and background. Such systems of membership have been recognized through research as being pivotal in establishing program success and member adaptation (Borman, 1984). It is more empowering if an African American client can identify with someone who shares similar plights, struggles, or life circumstances rather than diagnostic labels (Whaley, 2001).

A More Culturally Compatible Mental Health Programming and Research Model: The Use of Cooperative Living

Definition of Cooperative Living Programs

From the above analysis of best practices and important shortcomings of traditional mental health programs for African Americans, it is clearly advisable to explore alternative service frameworks that provide these clients with both preventive and sustaining services. Cooperative living programs are one of several promising culturally compatible mental health service models that have emerged recently in the practice and research literature. According to the University of Wisconsin Center for Cooperatives (1997), a cooperative is an autonomous association of persons united voluntarily to meet their common economic, social, and cultural needs and aspirations through a jointly owned and democratically controlled enterprise.

Tuller (1990) defines cooperative living as households of five or more sharing a common kitchen and household expenses, and defining themselves in collective terms (p. 14). According to Starak (1986), the objective of the cooperative community of students in his study was to establish, develop, and maintain a society based on cooperation as an alternative to competition, on sharing as an alternative to individual property, on pacifism as an alternative to aggression, and on equality as an alternative to discrimination (p. 53).

Rationale for Cooperative Living Programs

There are many types of cooperative arrangements, but as a therapeutic intervention, these programs commonly provide a means for people with similar conditions to solve problems and receive support. Support is achieved through the workings of the program and with the assistance of various consultants. Cooperative living programs enhance living standards, provide social support, strengthen individuals' ability to gain access to mental health and other key resources, provide connection, and are generally therapeutic. Typically, the most effective among these programs consist of interrelated programmatic and research components.

A Cooperative Living Program Model for African American Families

The Model's Benefits. Given the African American tradition of self-help and mutual assistance, and considering that social work's early professional identity centered on work within communities, it is surprising that cooperative living has not been pursued as a viable alternative to current mental health services for this group. Cooperative living may enhance the living standards of African American families in particular, increase their opportunities for social support, and strengthen their ability to gain access to needed resources and build assets. The accumulation of assets leads to attitudes and choices that promote employment, . . . [increase] . . . confidence about the future . . . and promote the creation of social capital through connectedness with the community (Coulton, 1996, p. 516). Cooperative housing promotes the positive attributes associated with home ownership (Leavitt & Saegert, 1984). Moreover, the participants can share concrete and practical resources such as baby-sitting and transportation. In addition, therapeutic interventions can take place through peer counseling/accountability, mentoring, and support groups that are created through the residents' own interests.

Examples of the Model's Implementation. There are examples of cooperative movements in many countries, including the United States. Farm cooperatives, food cooperatives, housing cooperatives, worker cooperatives, and child care cooperatives all have been tried with varying degrees of success in the United States (Soifer & Resnick, 1993; Lichtenstein, 1986; Martineau & Smith, 1986; Leavitt & Saegert, 1984). Although student cooperative living is probably one of the most well-known examples of housing co-ops, they are not the only example of cooperative living in the United States.

In fact, between 1979 and 1982, the federal government funded rural housing cooperatives through the Rural Cooperative Housing Demonstration Project (Martineau & Smith, 1986). This project was funded by the Small Community and Rural Development Policy of the Carter Administration; it had three objectives: (1) to test the viability of small, self-managed, limited-equity cooperatives in rural areas; (2) to create a consortium of technical service organizations to help organize, support, and sustain individual housing cooperatives; and (3) to develop an integrated delivery system for cooperative housing in rural areas (p. 341).

The state of New York has also experimented with limited-equity housing cooperatives in poor communities through the Tenant Interim Lease (TIL) Program (Leavitt & Saegert, 1984). This program has continued to receive funding and is seen as a viable alternative to retaining low-and moderate-cost housing in communities that have suffered from landlord abandonment. Once a building is abandoned, the city must take over the cost of maintaining it. Tenants in the TIL program are required to manage their own building under annual leases, and ultimately, to own those buildings. They must have agreement from seventy-five percent of the current residents to participate in this program, and then establish a board of directors, and demonstrate the ability to get insurance and run the building.

A Related Research Framework/Component

This research framework for cooperative living programs can provide guidelines for documenting the extent to which such programs are effective with African American clients in culturally meaningful ways. The framework includes three main tasks: exploration of how well programs integrate the values and principles of cooperatives into their implementation process, examples of viable intervention outcomes for African American participants, and the social work roles and skills that are required to support the combined program and research model.

Task: Exploring How the Model's Values and Principles are Applied. Cooperatives are based on the values of self-help, self-responsibility, democracy, equality, equity, and solidarity. A set of related principles of cooperative ownership are very important to the empowerment and strengths perspectives in social work. Those principles complement the African American value base and have great potential for building assets and developing resources. Researchers can explore the benefits, challenges, and outcomes that programs experience in integrating those principles into their services through a combination of quantitative-qualitative, participatory, and culturally relevant procedures. The principles include voluntary and open membership, democratic member control, member economic control, autonomy and independence, education, training and information, cooperation among co-ops, and concern for community (Castro & Rice, 2003; Gellis, 2001; International Cooperative Alliance, 1995).

Voluntary and Open Membership: Cooperatives are voluntary organizations, open to all persons who are able and willing to use their services and willing to accept the responsibilities of membership without gender, social, racial, political, or religious discrimination.

Democratic and Member Control: Cooperatives are democratic organizations controlled by their members who actively participate in setting their policies and making decisions. The members serving as elected representatives are accountable to the membership. In most cooperatives, members have equal voting rights, for example, one member, one vote.

Member Economic Participation: Members contribute equitably to the capital of their cooperative. Members democratically allocate surpluses for any or all of the following purposes: developing their cooperative, setting up reserves, part of which at least would be indivisible; benefiting members in proportion to their transactions with the cooperative; and supporting other activities approved by the membership.

Autonomy and Independence: Cooperatives are autonomous, self-help organizations controlled by their members. If they enter into agreements with other organizations, including governments, or raise capital from external sources, they do so on terms that ensure democratic control by their members and maintain their cooperative autonomy.

Education, Training, and Information: Cooperatives provide education and training for their members, elected representatives, managers, and employees so they can contribute effectively to the development of their cooperatives. They inform the general public, particularly young people and opinion leaders, about the nature and benefits of cooperation.

Cooperation among Cooperatives: Cooperatives serve their members most effectively and strengthen the cooperative movement by working together through local, national, regional, and international structures.

Concern for Community: Cooperatives work for the sustainable development of their communities through policies approved by their members.

Task: Documenting Relevant Program Outcomes. In addition to the outcomes implied in the above description of cooperative living principles, this research framework emphasizes and guides researchers to examine other relevant outcomes. This process requires that researchers remain current about information in the research literature that can inform improvements in such programs and in related research procedures. For example, in a study of one of the New York TIL program cooperatives, Leavitt and Saegert (1984) found that residents who were committed to the cooperative developed a shared sense of identity in the building and in their own apartments, as one important outcome. The cooperative facilitated other relevant outcomes such as child care arrangements, social relationships, and a future orientation among residents. Some outcomes may have had interactional effects. For example, residents' beliefs in their own efficacy, in building something for their community, in hope for the community itself, were tied up in their commitment to the housing co-op (p. 36).

This study is of particular significance for low-income African American populations. Stegman (1982) found that for city-owned buildings in New York, fifty-four percent were African American households, and twenty-four percent were Hispanic households. The median income of residents was only $6,865, while thirty percent of residents received public assistance, and forty-six percent were below the poverty level. Female-headed households made up fifty-eight percent of the households. The likelihood of this population obtaining home ownership on their own without the program's support would be dismal at best.

Task: Analysis of Required Social Work Roles and Competencies. Social workers may not be adequately prepared to work in a cooperative environment, although many of the roles required are familiar to them. However, the required competencies for performing these roles in a cooperative and democratic format by a community-based agency differ from the traditional control-oriented policies of the medical model under which social workers have traditionally practiced. Although little is written on social work roles in cooperatives, social work roles in community-based organizations have been delineated in the literature and are consistent with the proposed cooperative model. Johnson (1998) describes key community-based, micropractice roles as network developer, broker, resource developer, advocate, and consultant. Brody and Nair (1995) add to this list community roles such as mobilizer and enabler.

Gutierrez (1995) also discusses the roles of facilitator and consultant. She warns that in community work, in order to empower and strengthen families, social workers must act as facilitators instead of leaders and as consultants instead of instructors. Social workers must be able to accept the client's definition of the problem, identify and build upon existing family strengths, and engage in power analyses with the client. Researchers can develop monitoring procedures for analyzing the transition period when social workers shift from traditional to cooperative living roles, and for gathering stories about the challenges practitioners encounter in the process.

Given these roles and the focus on client strengths and empowerment, the following competencies, skills, and techniques are advocated in the research literature. Hanna and Robinson (1994) emphasize that social workers need to be educated in the small-group-work orientation, self-directed (nonhierarchical) learning, and a collective approach to group awareness and decision making. Hanna and Robinson (1994) describe the important strategies of the adult model of learning, which require strict adherence to the rules of democracy by social workers. Johnson describes the competencies needed by social workers in community-based agencies. To practice effectively, social workers must develop skills in cultural awareness and cross-cultural practice, client participation, assessment, negotiation, and networking (Harper & Lantz, 1996; Lipford-Sanders & Bradley, 2002).

Equally important cooperative living skills include providing opportunities for clients to pursue a goal, which is as important as the accomplishment of the goal. Van Den Bergh and Cooper (1986) contend that this skill can be conceptualized as an enabling and facilitative force akin to an empowering experience. In cooperative housing, facilitating the process of sharing work, experiences, and resources; of self-help and support groups; of developing relationships and programs within the household; and the experience of having control and power over their environment are skills that will strengthen families and give them a sense of competence in their ability to take control of their own lives.

Teaching and coaching African Americans through the process of sharing resources and building assets in housing stock is as important as the outcome of a stable living environment, shared baby-sitting, therapeutic groups, or any other programs that residents may devise. The goal of the cooperative living research framework is to examine and document social workers' use of such competencies in facilitating these community building processes with African American clients, while also exploring related client outcomes.

Historically Supportive Traditions in Social Work

Tradition of Group Work, Community Practice, and Settlement Houses in Social Work

The previous focus on community building and cooperative living programs with African American families is not new in terms of broad-based approaches to mental health. In fact, the roots of social group work in communities across the United States began with Jane Addams and the settlement house movement in the late 1800s (Lee, 1989). The settlement house or neighborhood movement was an attempt to remediate the social ills that came from urban industrialization (Karger, 1987). Group life was seen as a cure for excessive individualism and social instability; it was based on strengthening the family, school, and neighborhood. Since then, social work has increased its understanding of the importance of group empowerment and advanced the concepts of mutual aid and social support networks as a way to enhance families' mental health and well-being (Lee, 1989). The concept of neighborhood-based social group work is rooted in the settlement house spirit and embodies the movement's core values of mutual aid, democratic functioning, and civic responsibility.

While social work has had a long tradition of work with communities and groups, the settlement house movement was not effective in meeting the needs of many African Americans due to its urban, northeastern orientation and to the racist assumptions of settlement workers (Lasch-Quinn, 1993). In spite of these earlier failures, the profession's current more culturally sensitive interest in social group work in communities has great potential for the African American population.

Mutual Assistance, the Cooperative Movement, and Social Work Practice

The cultural gap between the professional world's goals and the world of human services consumers' needs continues to require bridging (Glasser & Suroviak, 1989). For example, mutual aid groups are often skeptical about the intentions of professionals. Consequently, the mutual aid movement has frequently been perceived as threatening to mental health workers (Coplon & Strull, 1983). However, when mental health workers are responsive to group members' needs and allow the members to maintain some control over the problem-solving process, the result can be increased trust and an eagerness to cooperate (p. 261), particularly among African Americans and other clients of color. This process provides clients with a new sense of self, allowing self-help and mutual assistance to take place in a cooperative atmosphere by using the social worker as a consultant who offers suggestions and helps group members to decide on their agenda.

Table 4.1 depicts the core value base that is shared by African Americans, cooperative living programs, and the social work profession. These core values are acceptance, democracy, collective economics, self-regulation, a high value on education, and communalism.

Table 4.1 Compatibility Between African Americans, Cooperative Living, and Social Work

Core Value Base	African Americans	Cooperative Living	Social Work
Acceptance	Appreciation for each other	Voluntary and open membership	Natural environmental service Provisions/family-focused
Democracy	Cooperative politics and social goals	Democratic and member-controlled	Balanced power relationships
Collective economics	Cooperative economics	Member economic participation	Expanding capacity/account-ability to the community
Self-regulation	Quest for self-governance	Autonomy and independence	Community self-reliance as an alternative to welfare state, empowerment-oriented
High value on education	Strong achievement orientation	Provisions made for education, training, and information	Multicultural competency/leadership skills/reciprocal learning
Communalism	Mutual aid and reciprocity	Cooperation among cooperatives and concern for the community	Collaborative partnership

Although historically social work has not organized most social programs to be consistent with these values, the profession has always espoused them in practice and in its code of ethics. For example, the community practice literature in social work has long advanced the core value base described in Figure 1(Johnson, 1998; Weil, 1996; Specht & Courtney, 1994). Establishing cooperative living programs for African American families could expand opportunities to integrate these values, because cooperatives share that same value base.

For African Americans, the first value, acceptance, is represented in their appreciation for each other and in their inherent belief in individual worth. Likewise, social work is family-focused, and its representatives hold a belief in providing services in the natural environment. Cooperatives embrace the core value of acceptance through voluntary and open membership. For African Americans, the core value of democracy is maintained through cooperative politics and social goals; social work strives for balanced-power relationships; and cooperatives exist through democratic and member-controlled structures. The core value of collective economics is evidenced in all three through the provision of cooperation, participation, and accountability. Self-regulation is encompassed in the concepts of self-governance, autonomy, and empowerment, which lead to community self-reliance. All three concepts place a high value on education through a strong achievement orientation, training, leadership skills, and reciprocal learning. Finally, communalism encompasses the principles of mutual aid and reciprocity, collaborative partnerships, cooperation, and concern for the community.

The contrast between cooperative living programs and most traditional mental health and social service programs is remarkable. However, the compatibility between cooperative programs and the African American value base is ideal. Given this compatibility and social work's previous failures in the delivery of traditional mental health services to African Americans, new social work intervention programs should strongly consider the use of cooperatives.

Feasibility of Housing Cooperatives as a Social Work Alternative

Analysis of Potential Barriers

In a discussion of cooperatives for social workers, Soifer and Resnick (1993) outline several potential obstacles to the success of these practitioner coops. These barriers can be generalized to social workers' interventions within cooperatives in general. First, Soifer and Resnick point out that our free enterprise economic system discourages cooperatives in several ways. The economic system promotes individualism and competition, while cooperatives strive for cooperation and participation. There is little understanding of, or research on the positive aspects of cooperation. People are not socialized to know much about cooperatives, and therefore, may have negative images of this concept.

This philosophical/political barrier has often led to inadequate funding for cooperatives, a second barrier. For example, the federal government has provided very little funding support for the concept of cooperation, as documented by Martineau and Smith's (1986) discussion of the Rural Cooperative Housing Demonstration Project. Funding was allocated for the first three years of this project, but only for the demonstration project itself. Funding for financing the building of cooperatives and the mortgages for purchasing them had to be obtained from other sources. Martineau and Smith (1986) point out yet another barrier, that rural people in particular often perceive the concept of cooperative housing differently from normal home ownership. Therefore, their objections to efforts to obtain financing were based primarily on a lack of understanding of the proposal (p. 347).

A final major obstacle that Soifer and Resnick (1993) identified for cooperatives was the social work profession itself. Social work's history, professional models, ideology, and orientation are not compatible with the formation of client and practitioner cooperatives. Generally speaking, historically, the profession has helped to maintain systems instead of challenging or changing systems. Too often, the focus has been on advising or changing the individual rather than the system (Soifer & Resnick, p. 110). In the past, social workers have defined success as individual achievement or independent living, rather than individual well-being (Price, 1987). This past failure to work toward systems changes is consistent with a failure to address the cultural mismatch of service provisions for African Americans. Current theories, however, such as the Multicutural Person-Environment-Fit Worldview, assume that maladjustment problems are the result of a mismatch between people, or between people and their environments. Such theories reject or refute the assumption that problems develop because people or groups are culturally inferior (Ramirez, 1999).

Potential Supports

Cooperatives that result from the rehabilitation of abandoned housing, such as in the New York example, are often dismissed as not viable, because they are perceived as noncost-effective and disruptive. However, this urban strategy prevents homelessness and helps to retain the building stock in low-income communities. The lack of existing development packages for families near or below the poverty level and the demand for low-income housing suggest that cooperatives may be a very feasible alternative to single family home ownership for these families (Leavitt & Saegert, 1984).

Because state housing authorities do not have to maintain these buildings or look for other alternatives for the residents, most of whom are eligible for housing subsidies anyway, cooperatives can lead to financial savings for state housing departments. Furthermore, funding for the necessary start-up capital may not be as difficult to obtain as some may think. Funding for community-based programs and services has increased in the 1990s as the federal government prepares for devolution of funding to the state and local governments through the mechanism of block grants (Coulton, 1996).

If financing issues can be resolved, the positive outcomes from cooperative housing can work very well in conjunction with social work interventions. Meeting the survival needs of African American families through cooperatives can allow social workers to differentiate between which client behaviors are due to mental health issues, which behaviors are due to the stress of resource deprivation, and which may result from a combination of these factors. Furthermore, the supportive atmosphere of cooperative communities can help to create a more therapeutic environment for clients as well as practitioners.

CONCLUSION

Social work has a unique opportunity to assist families through the development of cooperatives which provide a mutually supportive environment where families' participation in social work interventions is experienced as positive and encouraging. More specifically, a mental health program model such as cooperative living can prove beneficial in meeting the social support needs of African Americans because it is so closely aligned with their mutual assistance tradition. This tradition has historically sustained African Americans and met their needs when formal structures turned a blind eye. Hence, the use of cooperatives as a social work intervention is very fitting for African Americans, because they promote unity, self-determination, collective work and responsibility, cooperative economics, purpose, creativity, and faith. These long-standing African ideals and principles, these Nguzo Saba, are goals toward which African Americans strive. The use of cooperative arrangements in addressing their social support needs is offered as a next step on the grand stairway toward the achievement of optimal mental, physical and financial health for African American families.

REFERENCES

Baker, F.M. (2001). Diagnosing depression in African Americans. *Community Mental Health Journal, 37*(1), 31–38.

Belton, W. J. (1993). Mutual aid-support groups: A study of the roles social workers assume with this informal system of care. Doctoral dissertation. New York: Columbia University.

Billingsley, A. (1968). *Black families in white America.* Englewood Cliffs, NJ: Prentice-Hall.

Billingsley, A. (1990). Understanding African American family diversity. In J. Deward (Ed.), *The state of Black America* (pp. 85–108). New York: National Urban League.

Billingsley, A. (1992). *Climbing Jacob's ladder: The enduring legacy of African American families.* New York: Simon and Schuster.

Billingsley, A., & Caldwell, C. H. (1991). The church, the family, and the school in the African American community. *Journal of Negro Education, 60*(3), 427 – 440.

Borman, L. D. (1984, Summer). Self-help/mutual aid in changing communities. *Social Thought,* 49–62.

Brody, R. & Nair, M. (1995). *Macro practice: A generalist approach* (3rd Edition). Wheaton, IL: Gregory Publisher.

Castro, J.R. & Rice, K.G. (2003). Perfectionism and ethnicity: Implications for depressive symptoms and self-reported academic achievement. *Cultural Diversity and Ethnic Minority Psychology, 9*(1), 64–78.

Clark, K. B. (1965). *Dark ghetto: Dilemmas of social power.* New York: Harper and Row.

Clark, R., Anderson, N. B., Clark, V. R., & Williams, D.R. (1999). Racism as a stressor for African Americans. *American Psychologist, 54,* 805–816.

Colarossi, L.G. & Eccles, J.S. (2003). Differential effects of support providers on adolescents' mental health. *Social Work Research, 27*(1), 19–30.

Coplon, J. & Strull, J. (1983). Roles of the professional in mutual aid groups. *Social Casework: Journal of Contemporary Social Work,* 259–266.

Coulton, C.J. (1996). Poverty, work and community: A research agenda for an era of diminishing federal responsibility. *Social Work, 41*(5), 509–520.

Denby, R. W. (1996). Resiliency and the African American family: A model of family preservation. In S. L. Logan (Ed.), *The black family: Strengths, self-help, and positive change* (pp. 144–163). Boulder, CO: Westview Press.

Diala, C., Muntaner, C., Walrath, C., Nickerson, K.J., LaVeist, T.A., & Leaf, P.J. (2000). Racial differences in attitudes toward professional mental health care and in the use of services. *American Journal of Orthopsychiatry, 70*(4), 455–464.

Gary, L. E. (Ed.). (1978). *Mental health: A challenge to the black community.* Philadelphia: Dorrance and Company.

Gellis, Z.D. (2001). Using a participatory research approach to mobilize immigrant minority family caregivers. *Journal of Social Work Research and Evaluation, 2*(2), 267–282.

Glasser, I. & Suroviak, J. (1989). Social group work in a soup kitchen: Mobilizing the strengths of guests. *Group Work with the Poor and Oppressed* (95–107). New York: The Free Press.

Grier, W. H., & Cobbs, P. M. (1968). *Black rage.* New York: Basic Books.

Gutierrez, L. (1995). Working with women of color: An empowerment perspective. In J. Rothman, J. Erlich & J. Tropman (Eds.), *Strategies of community intervention* (5th Edition). Itaska, IL: Peacock Publishing.

Hanna, M. & Robinson, B. (1994). *Strategies for community empowerment.* Lewiston, NY: Edwin Mellen Press.

Harper, K. V., & Lantz, J. (1996). *Cross-cultural practice: Social work with diverse populations.* Chicago, IL: Lyceum.

Hill, R. (1971). *The strength of black families.* New York: Emerson Hall.

International Cooperative Alliance (1995). Cooperative definition, history, and general information. http://www.coop.org/

Johnson, A. K. (1998). The revitalization of community practice: Characteristics, competencies and curricula for community based services. *Journal of Community Practice, 5*(3), 37–62.

Jones, E. E., & Korchin, S. J. (Eds.) (1982). *Minority mental health.* New York: Praeger Publishers.

Karger, J. J. (1987). Minneapolis settlement houses in the not so roaring 20s. *Americanization, morality and the revolt against popular culture.* New York: Greenwood Press.

Keith, V. M. (2000). A profile of African Americans' health care. In C. Hogue, M. A. Hargreaves, & K. S. Collins (Eds.), *Minority health in America* (pp. 47 –76). Baltimore: Johns Hopkins University Press.

Kirk, S., & Kutchins, H. (1988). Deliberate misdiagnosis in mental health practice. *Social Service Review, 62,* 225–237.

Lasch-Quinn, E. (1993). *Black neighbors: Race and the limits of reform in the American Settlement House Movement, 1890–1945.* Chapel Hill, N.C.: University of North Carolina Press.

Leavitt, J. & Saegert, S. (1984). Women and abandoned buildings. *Social Policy, 15*(1), 32–39.

Lee, J. (1989). Introduction: Return to our roots. *Group work with the poor and oppressed* (5–9). New York: Columbia University Press.

Levkoff, S.E., Prohaska, T.R., Weitzman, P.F., & Ory, M.G. (2000). Recruitment and retention in minority populations: Lessons learned in conducting research on health promotion and minority aging. *Journal of Mental Health and Aging, 6*(1), 5–7.

Lichtenstein, P. (1986). The U.S. experience with worker cooperation. *Social Science Journal, 23*(1), 1–15.

Lindsey, M.A. (2002). Social network influences on African-American adolescents' use of mental health services. *Doctoral Dissertation*. Pittsburgh, PA: University of Pittsburgh.

Lipford-Sanders, J. A., & Bradley, C. (2002). *Counseling African American families.* Alexandria, VA: American Counseling Association.

Logan, S. L. (1996). *The black family: Strengths, self-help, and positive change.* Boulder, CO: Westview Press.

Martin, J. M., & Martin, E. P. (1985). *The helping tradition in the black family and community.* Washington, DC: National Association of Social Workers.

Martineau, T. & Smith, M. (1986). Cooperative housing as an approach to rural housing problems. *Policy Studies Journal, 15*(2), 337–350.

McAdoo, H. P. (1981). *Black families.* Beverly Hills, CA: Sage Publications.

McNeilly, M., Musick, M., Efland, J.R., Baughman, J.T., Toth, P.S., Saulter, T.D., Sumner, L., Sherwood, A., Weitzman, P.F., Levkoff, S.E., Williams, R.D., & Anderson, N.B. (2000). Minority populations and psychophysiologic research: Challenges in trust building and recruitment. *Journal of Mental Health and Aging, 6*(1), 91–102.

Pettigrew, T. F. (1964). *A profile of the Negro American.* Princeton, NJ: D. Van Nostrand Company.

Poussaint, A. F. (1990). The mental health status of black Americans:1983. In D. S. Ruiz and J. P. Comer (Eds.), *Handbook of mental health and mental disorders among black Americans* (pp. 17–52). New York: Greenwood Press.

Price, L. (1987). Global neighborhoods. *Social Development Issues, 11*(1), 49–55.

Rabinowitz, H. N. (1974). From exclusion to segregation: Health and welfare services for southern blacks, 1865–1890. *Social Service Review, 48,* 327–354.

Ramirez, M. (1999). *Multicultural psychotherapy: An approach to individual and cultural differences* (2nd edition). Boston, MA: Allyn and Bacon.

Siegel, J.M. (1974). A brief review of the effects of race in clinical service interactions. *American Journal of Orthopsychiatry, 44,* 555–562.

Soifer, S. & Resnick, H. (1993). Prospects for social work cooperatives in the 1990s. *Administration in Social Work, 17*(3), 99–116.

Specht, H., & Courtney, M. (1994). *Unfaithful angels: How social work has abandoned its mission.* New York: The Free Press.

Starak, Y. (1986). Alternative communities: Living prototypes for a future society. *Social Development Issues,10*(1), 50–57.

Stegman, M. (1982). *The dynamics of rental housing in New York City.* New Brunswick, NJ: Center for Urban Policy Research.

Sue, D. W., & Sue, D. (1999). *Counseling the culturally different: Theory and practice* (3rd edition). New York: Wiley.

Sue, S., Fujino, D., Hu, L. T., Takeuchi, D. T., & Zane, N. W. (1991). Community mental health services for ethnic minority groups: A test of the cultural responsiveness hypothesis. *Journal of Consulting and Clinical Psychology, 59,* 533–540.

Thomas, S. L, (1995). Exchanging welfare checks for wedding rings: Welfare reform in New Jersey and Wisconsin. *Affilia, 10*(2), 120–137.

Tuller, J.L. (1990). Making cooperative houses work: Participants' views of group processes in urban communes. Dissertation #9100916. Ann Arbor, MI: UMI.

U. S. Department of Health and Human Services (1999). *Mental health: A report of the surgeon general.* Rockville, MD: Author.

U. S. Department of Health and Human Services (2001). *Mental health: Culture, race, and ethnicity: A supplement to mental health: A report of the surgeon general.* Rockville, MD: U. S. Department of Health and Human Services, Substance Abuse and Mental Health Services Administration, Center for Mental Health Services.

University of Wisconsin Center for Cooperatives (1997). (www.wisc.edu:/uwcl).

Van Den Bergh, N. & Cooper, L.B. (Eds.) (1986). *Feminist visions for social work.* Silver Springs: MD: National Association of Social Workers.

Weil, M.(1996). Community building: Building community practice. *Social Work, 41,* (5), 481–499.

Whaley, A.L. (2001). Cultural mistrust of white mental health clinicians among African Americans with severe mental illness. *American Journal of Orthopsychiatry, 71*(2), 252–256.

Williams, D. R. (1998). African American health: The role of the social environment. *Journal of Urban Health: Bulletin of the New York Academy of Sciences, 75,* 300–321.

Willie, C. V., Kramer, B. M., & Brown, B. S. (1973). *Racism and mental health.* Pittsburgh: University of Pittsburgh Press.

Chapter 5

ANALYSIS OF RESEARCH ON CRIME AND VIOLENCE: IMPACT ON THE AFRICAN AMERICAN FAMILY

Violence is often viewed as an anathema in American society–a moral error to be punished or a psychiatric aberration to be treated. Within this framework, violence is also seen as a form of social deviance; it is usually associated with those who are poor, inadequately socialized, or members of racial minority groups. However, the notion of violence as uncommon or confined to certain categories of people is clearly contradicted by both historical and contemporary data. Violence played a major role in the founding of America, the extraction of land, exploitation of labor, implementation of slavery, maintenance of racial segregation, subjugation of women, and the quelling of worker protests.

Violence is widespread in American society, and even today, it is highly touted as a means for reaching social, economic, and political objectives. Coercive and illegal tactics used by police officers are applauded, efforts to control gun ownership routinely fail, tough guys are idolized in the media, and the popularity of politicians soars when military troops are activated. The use of violence by public officials is paralleled by high rates of violence in the general population: the National Research Council (1993) found America to be more violent than any other industrialized nation, with notably higher rates of homicide, serious sexual assault, and threats of physical harm.

Families are microcosms of the larger society, so it is no surprise that they also engage in high rates of violence, especially toward their more vulnerable members: children, women, and the elderly. After the official discovery of child abuse in the early 1960s, rates of reported family violence and abuse skyrocketed, yet researchers agree that these reports vastly understate the actual level of family violence. A mind-boggling array of causes and consequences of child abuse and family violence have been identified, and teachers, medical professionals, neighbors, and friends have now been encouraged to report what was once seen as the private, if sad, business of families. Despite the high profile family violence has garnered in the media and public mind, it seems that little has been done to diminish its prevalence. Such failure undoubtly stems from blaming individuals for their troubles rather than focusing on the broader social context and policies that foster violence. In 1994, John McKinlay shared the following metaphor on the futility of trying to save victims while ignoring the larger social forces that cause victimization:

> There I am standing by the shore of a swiftly flowing river and I hear the cry of a drowning man. So I jump into the river, put my arms around him, pull him to shore and apply artificial respiration. Just when he begins to breathe, there is another cry for help. So I jump into the river, reach him, pull him to shore, apply artificial respiration, and then just as he begins to breath, another cry for help. So back in the river again, reaching, pulling, applying, breathing, and then another yell. . . . I am so busy jumping in, pulling them to shore, applying artificial respiration, that I have no time to see who the hell is upstream pushing them all in. (pp. 509–510)

Speaking primarily to health care professionals, McKinlay suggests the need to "focus upstream"–to solve the crisis by getting at the source of the problem. In this chapter, the same metaphor is applied to the problem of violence by pointing out how "upstream," factors–namely persistent patterns of race, social class, and gender inequality–produce, promote, and perpetuate violence. These inequalities have increased in recent decades, eroding the traditional cultural resources that once strengthened black families and ensured their survival. This chapter begins with a look at the literature on the prevalence of violence against children, women, and the elderly, then explains how violence is a social and political construct based on gender and family ideologies that evolved historically within the dominant culture as a result of industrialization and modernization. The unique development of African American families and the relevance of major theories of violence to their experiences are described, based on an analysis of the research literature. The chapter concludes with a description of a more culture and gender sensitive research framework for exploring and elucidating the problem of family violence among African Americans.

Literature Review: The (Re)Discovery of Family Violence

Early Conceptualizations of Family Violence

In 1962, Dr. Kempe and his associates published their seminal article in the *Journal of the American Medical Society* documenting the existence of the "battered child syndrome"—a phenomenon that shocked many Americans given the dominant portrayal of families as middle-class, happy, child-centered, and successful. In the ensuing decades, the revelation of family violence against children was broadened to include the abuse of women, the elderly, and even husbands. This initial report on the battered child syndrome in a leading medical journal suggested that such behavior was rare, and perhaps even inflicted by parents who were suffering from some type of mental illness. Since then, researchers have found that the abuse of children is neither rare nor the result of mental illness. Moreover, the concept of child abuse has been broadened to include neglect as well as the physical, emotional, and sexual maltreatment of children (Behl et al., 2003).

Violence Prevalence Rates

Violence Against Children. Current figures reveal that more than 3.1 million cases of child maltreatment are reported each year (Zinn & Eitzen, 2002), yet the gap between reported and actual rates of child abuse is undoubtedly significant. Child abuse most often occurs in the the privacy of the home, goes unobserved and unreported, and is sometimes so habitual that family members see it as normal. States also vary in how they collect and report data on child abuse, making information about its prevalence difficult to interpret (Mash & Wolfe, 1991). Based on national reports of child maltreatment, the most common type is child neglect: parental failure to adequately feed, clothe, shelter, supervise or provide for the basic needs of children. Neglect constitutes nearly half of all reported cases of child abuse. Emotional abuse (being verbally harsh, overly critical, or rejecting of children) is much more difficult to document, but it makes up about five percent of all reported cases of child abuse. Sexual abuse or incest accounts for ten–twelve percent of child abuse, and physical abuse for more than one-third of reported cases of abuse (Adams, Harper, Knudson & Revilla, 1994; Benokraitis, 1996).

Spousal Abuse. As a result of the feminist movement, studies of family violence during the 1970s shifted significantly toward the exploration of spousal and intimate family violence. The first national study of family violence was conducted during the 1970s; in it Straus, Gelles, and Steinmetz (1980) interviewed a random sample of more than 2,000 married people and found that twenty-eight percent of all couples had engaged in violence at least once during the course of their marriage. Spousal abuse is found in every social class and ethnic group, but this study reported that it was 400 percent more common among African Americans, without examining the interactional effects of ethnicity and poverty on those rates. More recently, a National Crime Survey published by the Justice Department in 1996 reported 960,000 cases of intimate partner violence, for example, murder, rape, and assault, leading to 1,842 deaths (Lamana & Riedmann, 2000). Women who were young (20–34 years of age), poor, and uneducated were the most likely victims (Bennice, Resick, Mechanic & Astin, 2003). Moreover, research has found a connection between intimate partner abuse and child abuse: about seventy percent of wife beaters also are physically violent to their children (Kurz, 1993). The concept of wife rape was also articulated during the late 1970s, challenging historic laws that entitled husbands to have sex with their wives whenever they wanted to. Diana Russell's (1986) pioneering work on marital (or wife) rape, based on a random survey of 930 women, found that fourteen percent of women had been raped by their husbands or ex-husbands. A significant proportion of these women, about one-third of them, had been raped twenty times or more, making rape a constant threat in their lives. Since this seminal study, nearly all states have passed laws against rape in marriage (Siegel, 1998).

Violence Against Elders. Finally, elder abuse became the violence issue of the 1980s. The number of elderly people in the country grew dramatically during the twentieth century, and they now constitute more than twelve percent of the American population. As is the case with other forms of violence, family members are the most likely perpetrators of violence against the elderly, and much of that abuse goes unreported (Block & Sinnot, 1979; Filinson, 1989; Lau & Kosberg, 1979). Researchers suggest that from one to ten percent of the elderly are victims of abuse: Tataro and Blumerman (1996) found that of reported cases of abuse, fifty-nine percent were neglect, sixteen percent were physical abuse, twelve percent were material or economic abuse, and seven percent were emotional abuse. Women, because of their longer life spans and thus increased probability of needing family caregiving, are the most common victims of elder abuse. More specifically, the typical victim of elder abuse is a white female with health challenges that require her to rely on her spouse or other family members for care, and most of such abuse is associated with caregiver burden and stress (Zinn & Eitzen, 2002).

The Emergence of Family Violence Historically

Religious and Social Roots of Family Violence

The prominence of research and media attention devoted to family violence suggests that what consitiues violence can be clearly defined and objectively measured, and that there exists a consensus on its inappropriateness. Yet, in reality, notions of violence, abuse, and maltreatment are socially and politically defined based on prevailing family norms and values; thus they vary both historically and cross-culturally. The focus on child abuse that began in the 1960s made family violence sound like a new phenomenon, yet since then historians have refuted that myth by pointing out that child abuse and neglect date back to prehistoric times, when parents murdered, mutilated, or deformed their children for a variety of religious or cultural reasons (Tower, 1996). In the Jewish culture, for example, parents could sell, abandon, or kill a child with few if any legal ramifications, as seen in the biblical account of Abraham's near sacrifice of his son, Isaac. In a number of religions, beatings were seen as vital to the salvation of children; Proverbs 23:14 instructs: "Thou shalt beat him with a rod, and shalt deliver his soul from hell." DeMause (1974) has argued that, prior to the

1800s, nearly half the European population died in infancy due to abuse and/or neglect.

Violence Patterns in Colonial America

Legal Sanctions: White Families. Statistics on the historical prevalence of family violence in the United States are not available, yet the potential for it is deeply embedded in patriarchal and religious ideologies that support the subordination of women and children. In early America, white women and children were viewed as the property of their husbands and fathers and subject to their control. The traditional marriage contract, based on the doctrine of coverture, declared that a woman ceased to exist as a legal entity once she married; thus, married women often had no rights, and their bodies, sexuality, labor, and property legally belonged their husbands. They were expected to live under their husband's rule and could be whipped or fined for failing to do so. Children fared little better: They were the economic assets of their fathers and were often described as being ruled by religion, repression, and respect (Hill, 1999). The influence of Christianity led parents to focus on what was assumed to be the innate wickedness of children, and to use strict physical and emotional discipline to break their wills.

The Institution of Slavery and Violence. Even less is known about violence in African American families during the colonia era but, again, the potential for it was enormous. Africans brought to the United States were from strong patriarchal cultures where polygyny, or multiple wives, was often the cultural norm. These family practices suggest a tradition of male domination and privilege, although some authors argue that in West African societies women's important economic and childbearing roles, their reliance on female-centered networks, and the priority of blood relations over marital relations mitigated the adverse impact of patriarchy (Nobles, 1985).

Chattel slavery was founded on the denial of the basic humanity of black people, and therefore, was saturated with mental, physical, and emotional violence against African Americans. The system paradoxically reinforced and distorted African traditions by rewarding high rates of childbirth, forcing women to prioritize work over their family roles, disrupting their reliance on extended family networks or clans, separating families, and usurping the role of men in their families. Slave owners ran and controlled black families to their own advantage, resorting to violence to strip men of their status, sexually exploit women, determine the fate of their children, and enforce and exploit their labor.

Given these circumstances during slavery, it would seem unlikely that black males would, in turn, treat family members violently; but D.G. White (1999) has found evidence of wife abuse in enslaved families. Similarly, historians have described black parents as strong and even harsh disciplinarians who understood that the unintentional and careless behaviors of children could bring great harm to the entire family. Still, evidence suggests that slave parents valued and loved their children (Blassingame, 1972).

America's Industrial Period and Economic Changes

From Labor Unit to a Gender Division of Labor. Family life for white and African American families changed radically during the final decades of the nineteenth century, as the emerging industrial economy undermined the Southern agricultural economy and its system of slavery. Entire white families, including husbands, wives, and children, were drawn into the industrial labor force initially, but by the late 1800s urbanization, the granting of a family wage to men and the growth of technology, negated the need for women's and children's labor. The exclusion of white women and children from the labor market led to new family ideologies: Rather than being seen essentially as work units, families were increasingly defined in emotional and sentimental terms. With modernization, the emphasis was placed on romantic love, companionship and a gender-determined division of labor.

The doctrine of separate spheres, the belief that women belonged in the home and men in the labor market, led family researchers to argue that the breadwinner-homemaker family model was ideally suited for the new industrial economy. Through this model, men achieved success and status by becoming good economic providers for their families, while women devoted their time to caring for the home and children. Thus, the family came to be defined as a loving refuge from the harsh realities of industrial life, as a haven in a heartless world. Children were defined as emotional rather than economic assets, and more attention was paid to protecting their well-being.

From Slavery to New Forms of Economic Exploitation. For African Americans, the emergence of the modern industrial economy during this period signaled the end of slavery, but it did not make the breadwinner-homemaker family model more accessible to them. Black sharecroppers who tried to emulate this family model were often criticized for their efforts (Dill, 1988). For the most part, emancipation initially meant that African Americans were thrown into a society where no one would hire, house, marry, or feed them. Many black parents lost custody of their children when some states passed laws allowing former slave owners to indenture or re-enslave and abuse the children of ex-slaves who were not married or employed (Scott, 1985). Blacks struggled to reunite with spouses, children, and other relatives who had been lost or sold during slavery. Rates of illegitimacy among blacks declined sharply (Frazier, 1966) and by the late 1800s the two-parent nuclear family was the norm (Gutman, 1976).

Their assimilation into mainstream society, however, continued to be thwarted by economic exploitation and racial exclusion, and prior to the twentieth century, most blacks remained in the Southern agricultural system which demanded the labor of entire families. This system involved continuous violence toward black families by farm owners who enforced oppressive sharecropping agreements and by hate groups that terrorized blacks throughout the South. In 1896, economic exclusion of African Americans was legitimized by the *Plessy vs. Ferguson* decision of the U.S. Supreme Court, which made racial segregation the law of the land.

Twentieth Century Trends in Families and Violence

The Social-Deficit View. This view held that slavery had destroyed the morality, self-esteem, and family life of African Americans (Kardiner & Ovesey, 1951), and that northward migration had undermined whatever stability they had achieved after emancipation (Frazier, 1966). While the social-deficit view acknowledges slavery as the root cause of these problems, ironically, it does not address the culpability of white slave owners who perpetuated slavery, and thus, the development of those problems. From this deficit perspective, black women were characterized as inappropriately heading families, black men as emasculated, and black children as disrespectful and delinquent. The childrearing strategies of black parents were described as inferior to those of white middle-class families. In 1951, Kardiner and Ovesey described black mothers as harsh, arbitrary, and authoritarian in dealing with their children, and black fathers as taciturn, violent, and overly punitive.

The Structural-Functionalist Perspective. Family studies blossomed during the early- to mid-1900s, with most researchers heralding the modern white nuclear family as the pinnacle of family organization. Such ideas were embedded in structural-functionalism, the dominant sociological theory of the day, which equated the structure of families (breadwinner-homemaker roles) with their ability to function properly. Researchers rarely acknowledged the existence of African American families, and those who did often labeled their matriarchal structure as disfunctional and disorganized (Frazier, 1966).

Among white families during the 1950s, an era of affluence, prosperity, and familism was being experienced. Millions of veterans had returned home victoriously following World War II and reassumed the position of economic providers for their families. The majority of white women, no longer needed as workers in defense and manufacturing industries, were again able to devote their full-time energies to being wives and mothers. The postwar industrial economy produced a seemingly endless supply of jobs for white men, with escalating wages and a higher standard of living for many of their families, and suburban homes, automobiles, and televisions became a reality for millions. Families were characterized as white, middle-class, nuclear, and composed of a successful male wage earner and female homemaker.

During the 1960s, however, such family ideals stood in sharp contrast to the emergent understanding of families as violent institutions. Feminist critiques of the ideal nuclear family exposed child and wife abuse as major problems during this period. Massive numbers of women entered the labor force in order to maintain the middle-class lifestyles they were accustomed to as the postwar prosperity ended. This change in women's roles shifted the gender balance of power in the home and threatened male dominance, conditions that generally foster stress and family violence in patriarchal societies such as America.

Analysis of Research on African American Family Violence

The Role of Poverty

Poverty Dynamics. Researchers have devoted considerable efforts to explain factors that contribute to family violence, enumerating various economic, social, and psychological factors associated with abuse and neglect. While family violence can be linked to a web of social factors, poverty is most often at the center of that web. For many black families and poor families in other ethnic groups, hunger, unpaid debts, unemployment, poor health, unsafe neighborhoods, homelessness, and lack of access to medical care are everyday stressors. Thus, while family violence is found among all races and social classes, poor people, regardless of their ethnic group, are more likely than affluent people to become involved in violence as a perpetrator or victim. In *Violence and youth: Psychology's response* the American Psychological Association stated emphatically:

> Many social science disciplines, in addition to psychology, have firmly established that poverty and its contextual life circumstances are major determinants of violence . . . Violence is most prevalent among the poor, regardless of race . . . Few differences among races are found in rates of violence when people at the same income level are compared. But beyond mere income level, it is the socioeconomic inequality of the poor—their sense of relative deprivation and their lack of opportunity to ameliorate their life circumstances—that facilitates higher rates of violence. (Quoted in Sherman, 1994, p. 38)

Related Factors and Consequences. Poverty is the key social structural—or upstream—factor that causes and perpetuates family and societal violence. It is linked to having an inadequate education, poor parenting skills, unrealistic expectations of children, high levels of stress and social isolation, poor health, and low levels of self- and ethnic-esteem (Brown et al., 1998; Erickson, 1991; Gelles & Conte, 1990; Tower, 1996). Certain characteristics of children, such as premature birth, mental retardation, illnesses, failure to bond with mothers, prenatal exposure to drugs, and rebelliousness exacerbate the risk of violence in poor families (Tower, 1996; National Research Council, 1993). Poverty, stress, and depression diminish the ability of poor mothers and fathers to parent. Sherman (1994) has pointed out that mothers who are depressed are less verbal, affectionate, and spontaneous in their interactions with children, and therefore, more likely to have children with behavioral and developmental problems.

Parents who are poor are also less able to be nurturing, kind, patient, and warm toward their children, and more likely to punish them with increased frequency, severity, and inconsistency than affluent parents (Nam & Tolman, 2002; Sherman, 1994). Coercive discipline and physical abuse may undermine the ability of children to perform well in school, thus creating more problems for parents to manage. Overall, rates of physical and sexual abuse are six times higher for children in poor families than for other children (National Research Council, 1993), and rates of intimate partner violence are also higher among the poor. African Americans remain overrepresented among those living in poverty; nearly twenty-five percent of all black adults and half of all black children are poor. This elevates their risk for violence, yet there is no consensus over whether actual rates of child abuse are higher in black families in particular (Zinn & Eitzen, 2002). There is a lack of good research on family violence among people of color (Hampton, 1991), which is at least partially the result of assumptions that associating ethnicity with family violence is politically contentious.

Gender Inequality Issues

Rationale for Gender Focus. Feminist scholars have argued that gender inequality is the linchpin of family violence, as it upholds male privilege and the subordination of women (Dobash & Dobash, 1979; Goetting, 1991; Kurz, 1989, 1993). African American women, as members of a devalued ethnic and gender group, suffer a dual subordination and oppression from family violence in this regard. Although some researchers contend that mutual battering between men and women is the norm, others make a distinction between common everyday episodes of minor abuse and patriarchal terrorism, a cycle of often severe and escalating abuse based on men's need to exert absolute control over women (Johnson, 1995). Further, they note that reported cases of intimate partner violence are highly gendered: more than ninety percent of victims are women and more than ninety percent of victimizers are men (Kurz, 1989; Zinn & Eitzen, 2002). Men are also disproportionately implicated in child abuse, given the fact that generally, they spend less time with children and invest less energy in caring for them, yet are responsible for as much child abuse as women (Whaley, 2000).

Similarly, cases of sexual abuse and marital rape are shaped by gender, with male perpetrators and female victims (Kurz, 1993; McGruder-Johnson, Davidson, Gleaves, Stock & Finch, 2000; Russell, 1986; Walker, 2000). The root of gendered violence lies in the socialization of boys and girls; boys are socialized into masculine norms that prize sexuality, aggression, and control, while girls are socialized to assume roles of passivity and dependence. Black men in particular, have fewer socially sanctioned opportunities to apply these gender norms than white men, and consequently, experience culturally-based stressors that may be contributing factors in family violence. There may be a tendency among some African American women to tolerate the abuse of their male partners because they believe it results from the marginalization, mistreatment, and frustration black men experience in the dominant society. As a result, many are reluctant to bring negative attention to their men, families, and communities by reporting and exposing episodes of family violence (Richie, 1995; E. White, 1985).

Interaction of Gender and Ethnicity. These assumptions about women assuming roles of passivity and dependence pose an interesting issue for African Americans, since some research shows a greater gender equality in black families. Richie (1995) argues that black women are taught to be strong and self-reliant, while other researchers contend that gender socialization of black children is less rigid than that of white children (Lewis, 1975; Scott, 1993). Yet Straus and his collegues (1980) found spouse abuse to be 400 percent more likely among African Americans than whites. Richie (1995) and White (1985) have broken the silence about black women's victimization at the hands of their intimate male partners. Hine (1995) argued that rape and violence against black women by their male counterparts has never garnered much research attention, yet it was a major factor in motivating northward migration in the early twentieth century.

Some studies suggest African American women fight back physically; Hampton (1991), for example, found that while severe violence by black husbands declined between 1975 and 1985, that violence by black women toward men increased by thirty-three percent. Although the pattern reversed itself during the early 1990s, African American women were more likely in the mid-1970s to be the perpetrators of murder against intimate partners than the victims of it (Lamana & Riedmann, 2000). Collective protest has also been used to reject the notion that black men have the right to abuse or rape women, as detailed in A. White's (1999) study of efforts to educate black women about rape.

Gender-Role Perspective. Intimate partner violence among African Americans reflects their higher levels of poverty, but also a tension that has always existed between black men and women over their respective roles. Ideological support for traditonal gender roles in families runs high among African Americans (Hill, 1999; hooks, 2001), yet in their lived experiences many women too often find themselves not only responsible for economically supporting their families, but also for most of the housework and child care. Although role flexibility and role sharing have been identified as important cultural strengths for these families, involving spouses, children, and extended family members (Hill, 1972), the gap between ideology and reality has made this issue even more complex. Black men have never escaped the stigma of being unable to adequately provide for their families due to racial discrimination, nor have some women worked through the resentment of having to perform or share in this task. Researchers have found that a lack of economic success, status, and power among men in general is correlated with higher rates of violence (Anderson, 1997; Lamana & Riedmann, 2000).

Racial-Ethnic and Social Class Considerations

Race-Ethnicity as an Independent Factor. Another issue is whether race-ethnicity, independent of poverty and gender inequality, affects rates of abuse and violence within African American families. This issue remains a matter of some debate (Hampton & Gelles, 1991; Hampton, Gelles, & Harrop, 1991). As previously noted, this issue is a politically volatile one, given African American family scholars' efforts to refute long-standing myths of dysfunctional black families. Some early research suggested that medical and public authorities were simply more likely to suspect and report child abuse in black families than in white families (Turbett & O'Toole, 1980), while others have pointed out that ethnic differences in violence rates are really a result of socioeconomic factors (Johnson & Ferraro, 2001).

A third perspective is that African Americans have cultural patterns and beliefs that differ from those of the mainstream culture, and are being stereotyped and penalized for those differences. The issue of what constitutes child abuse and violence provides an example of such differences, as these definitions are politically and socially constructed on the basis of the prevailing values and culture of white America. Straus (1994) has defined violence as "an act carried out with the *intention, or perceived intention,* of causing physical pain or injury to another person" (p. 7) (emphasis added), a definition that makes intent and pain central issues, and which includes spanking as abusive and violent. Even the definition of child maltreatment offered by the 1974 Federal Child Abuse Prevention and Treatment Act leaves room for some interpretation: "The physical or mental injury, sexual abuse, negligent treatment, or maltreatment of a child under the age of eighteen by a person who is responsible for the child's welfare under circumstances that indicate that the child's health or welfare is harmed or threatened thereby" (Tower, 1996).

Many African American parents agree that spanking children is acceptable (Hill, 1999), based on a cultural belief that is tied to their religious ideologies as well as to the practicalities of raising children in often unsafe neighborhoods. Black children, especially those from poor and working class familes, frequently grow up in environments that have alarmingly high rates of violence, and their parents justify harsh discipline as necessary for teaching them to be tough and protect themselves. Their living conditions may also be conducive to neglect, when children have to fend for themselves at an early age, often sharing in housework and the care of younger siblings (Hill & Zimmerson, 1995). Black parents sometimes view and treat their children as being older than they are, as was true for white Americans before their women and children became exempt from the labor force and family life was romanticized. To some extent, however, having children assume parental roles may be more social class rather than ethnic group-based, as when middle income blacks become bicultural by adjusting their behavior and beliefs to accommodate childrearing customs in dominant society and in their ethnic group (Hill, 1999).

If ethnicity has a specific influence on family violence, it would operate through cultural behaviors and beliefs, as skin color clearly does not predispose people to violence. The notion that a unique African American culture exists with its own values and norms is quite appealing, as it bestows a sense of cohesion, solidarity, continuity, and peoplehood. It also validates the shared history of African Americans, before and since the African diaspora, and their unique contributions to art, literature, music, dance, science, social science, religion, and myriad other areas. Afrocentric theorists argue that African Americans have retained a world view and family traditions that are essentially West African in orientation; however, such perspectives should consider the ongoing influences on those world views and traditions, otherwise, they present culture as static and monolithic.

Interaction of Race-Ethnicity and Social Class. A view of culture or ethnicity as a sole independent factor in family violence fails to address the effects of social class on this and other behaviors, and the effects of economic factors in shaping values that contribute to violence. Social class affects every aspect of family life, as well as childrearing and gender ideologies. For example, a 1946 study by Davis and Havighurst pointed out that black and white middle-income families were quite similar in their childrearing practices.

The ethnicity/culture versus social class debate has deep roots in studies of African American life. Some scholars have long debated whether the black culture is anything more than a set of adaptive (or maladaptive) behaviors that grew out of poverty. Others describe black people as having a unique culture that is both African and African-American oriented, as well as a set of common responses to their common history of oppression. Understanding this ethnic group in terms of its culture *and* these adaptive/maladaptive responses is essential (Butler, Lewis, & Sunderland, 1998) for addressing violence and other issues.

For example, the meaning and experience of culture, and thus violence, differ for African Americans across social classes; many poor blacks are different from middle income blacks in their lifestyles and values. They may cope with oppression differently based on those values and on the resources they believe are viable, that is, whether they use violence or systemic solutions such as equal opportunity agencies. Culture differs, too, across the age divide regarding the risk of violence and the underlying philosophy. Some younger African Americans embrace the hip hop culture which glorifies violence and the denigration of women while others immerse themselves in an African-centered value system which emphasizes family loyalty, a global humanistic philosophy rather than violence, respect for the elderly, and a collective responsibility for children and the black community.

Race-Ethnicity as a Strength and Vulnerability. Finally, an emphasis on African American cultural stengths must be balanced with an understanding about how such resources can become cultural vulnerabilities. Focusing only on those strengths as buffers to violence may ignore the paradoxical role they can play in the risk of violence. For example, a spiritual orientation and religion have often been seen as stengths within black families (R. Hill, 1972; S. A. Hill, 1999), yet the underlying ideologies can often justify patriarchal families and harsh physical discipline of children.

Extended families often provide opportunities for greater support and the sharing of material resources; but they may also lead to tension and role confusion as the members negotiate personal space, power, housework, child care, and monetary considerations. Young mothers and the children in such families may be confronted with the authority of several adults who do not always agree on childrearing issues, thus giving rise to conflicts and the potential for child abuse or other forms of violence. Respect for the elderly and a reluctance to institutionalize them may suggest that black families have the resources to care for them without assistance, thus giving and contributing to the stress and caregiver burden most often associated with elder abuse.

Effects of Social Policies on African American Violence

Policies in General. The cultural resources that once served poor African American families well, such as extended families, female-centered kinship networks, shared childrearing, and respect for the elderly have waned in the face of economic recessions, social class polarization among blacks, and neighborhood decline due to economic restructuring and the loss of middle-income blacks in inner city areas (Wilson, 1987). These factors have placed black men, women, and children living in poor neighborhoods at a greater risk for violence, and various social policies have reduced their access to services for addressing that risk. Wiese and Dar (1995), for example, found that substance abuse was the most important factor contributing to child abuse and the placement of black children in foster care, even while numerous studies documented significantly higher rates of violence in African

American communities (National Research Council, 1993; Bell, 1991; Goetting, 1991). Recent policies on substance abuse treatment, however, have significantly limited poor people's access to those services, as health care costs have escalated and public and private insurance coverage has decreased.

Public Welfare Policies. Public welfare policies have also had an important impact on African American families and a related risk for family and community violence. For example, during the 1970s, these policies sought to control the expansion of public assistance rolls by forcing mothers to establish their own households, including single teenage mothers. These policies effectively undermined the maintenance of many households in which fathers and mothers of potentially eligible children lived together, and support from extended family members with whom some mothers previously lived in joint households.

Today, ironically, new welfare policies seek to push poor women, many of whom are black, into marriage and into the labor force, often leaving them trapped in violent relationships or forced into the labor market with few job skills, substance abuse treatment opportunities, or child care assistance. The family policies of the Temporary Assistance to Needy Families Program (TANF) seeks to restore patriarchal families, regardless of their impact on women (Mink, 2001). Forcing women into the labor market may have an especially adverse effect on black women, as their prospects for marriage are slimmer, and residential segregation, employment discrimination, and inadequate job skills lessen their chances of a successful transition from welfare to work (Edin & Harris, 1999).

Implications for A Proposed Research Framework

This analysis of research literature on African American family violence has clarified contributing factors to this problem as well as factors that can act as buffers to violence. A proactive research agenda should be developed among African American family scholars to continue some of the current research and document its effectiveness as well as gaps. A second part of this agenda is to create new areas of research related to upstream factors or those that contribute to violence from a structural perspective.

Revising/Improving Current Research

In recent decades, rates of reported intimate partner violence in the United States have declined, although they remain unacceptedly high (Gelles & Cornell, 1990). Women in general have become more economically independent and more able to escape violent relationships. Social activism has also played an important role; for example, patriarchal power has become less acceptable, and the idea that black women must remain silent to protect "black unity" is under fire (A. White, 1999). Some programs have also been developed to curtail violence against children, and many have had limited success. These initiatives primarily focus on the individual and community. Some include teaching parents more about childrearing, increasing parental self-esteem and confidence, and involving the larger community in childrearing (Hampton, 1991; Hill, 1999), which is culturally supportive to many African Americans. The National Research Council (1993) found that programs teaching nonaggressive problem-solving methods and emphasizing prosocial behaviors and peer tutoring to reduce school failure, have lessened rates of violence in children (National Research Council, 1993).

Research on these programs can be improved by exploring family and ethnic factors that may affect the outcomes of their services, either positively or negatively, and enhance the studies' cultural relevance and sensitivity (Williams, Pierce, Young, & Van Dorn, 2001). Biased beliefs of researchers or procedures that can affect the focus and outcomes of studies must be identified, for example, researchers' beliefs about individual causes of violence or methods that ignore subjects' perspectives about their behavior. This information can inform other research that seeks to replicate violence prevention studies, as well as raise questions about whether a narrow focus on this problem provides long-term individual change and/or requires any systemic changes.

Developing New Research on Upstream/Structural Factors

A more significant and lasting part of this proposed research agenda for decreasing black family violence should focus more on interrelated upstream factors, such as social class, ethnicity, and gender inequality. These inequalities have been referred to as a "matrix of domination," with each one reinforcing the other (Sherman, 1994; Wilson, 1987, 1996). For example, ethnic inequality and poverty tend to foster and perpetuate each other, and economic inequality fosters the secondary status accorded to women in both the home and workplace.

A research focus on these upstream issues requires continuous efforts to increase and document the effects of economic and social parity between black families and white families, as well as between women and men in the areas of education, job training, and employment. Admittedly, this research agenda is political in nature, as are all efforts that seek to inform structural changes or diminish the effects of upstream factors on violence. Hence, this agenda has both research and policy development/reform components. The outcomes from research on contributory upstream factors can be used to identify the types of policies and programs that are needed to effect long-term structural changes, or to document the effects of existing policies and programs on black family violence.

CONCLUSION

Family violence is a serious social problem in all ethnic groups and social classes that results in a host of adverse consequences for its perpetrators, victims, and for society. For African American families living in poverty, in particular, violence increases their diminished sense of humanity and lack of opportunity. Abused children may experience growth retardation, brain damage, emotional disorders, low self-esteem, and early death; they also suffer from hyperactivity, impulsivity, attention deficit disorder, low empathy, and low IQs (National Research Council, 1993). Coupled with these serious effects of violence, black children also suffer from ethnic oppression, discrimination, labelling, and low cultural esteem, which can increase the negative effects of violence including a potential to commit violent crimes themselves (Holden & Richie, 1991; Widom, 1992). Similarly, violence against black women and the elderly tends to impair their self and ethnic esteem, health, and ability to function effectively.

As historical economic transitions and political/social definitions of violence have shaped this behavior in African American and white families, it is natural that these factors continue to influence comtemporary issues of violence. A research and policy focus on upstream factors that contribute to violence—social class, ethnicity, and gender—has two distinct advantages. It can decrease the blaming of African Americans or black culture for this problem by dominant society, and as well, create greater understanding of the structural changes that are required to address the problem more effectively.

REFERENCES

Adams, J. A., Harper, K., Knudson, S., & Revilla, J. (1994). Examination of findings in legally confirmed child sexual abuse: It's normal to be normal. *Pediatrics, 94* (3), 310–317.

Anderson, K.L. (1997). Gender, status, and domestic violence: An integration of feminist and family violence approaches. *Journal of Marriage and the Family, 59* (3), 655–669.

Behl, L.E., Conyngham, H.A., & May, P.F. (2003). Trends in child maltreatment literature. *Child Abuse and Neglect, 27,* 215–229.

Bell, C. C. (1991). Clinical care update: Preventive strategies for dealing with violence among Blacks. In R. L. Hampton (Ed.), *Black family violence: Current research and theory* (pp. 163–174). Lexington, MA: Lexington Books.

Bennice, J.A., Resick, P.A., Mechanic, M., & Astin, M. (2003). The relative effects of intimate partner physical and sexual violence on posttraumatic stress disorder symptomatology. *Violence and Victims, 18,* 87–94.

Benokraitis, N. V. (1996). *Marriages and families: Changes, choices, and constraints* (2nd edition). Upper Saddle River, NJ: Prentice Hall.

Blassingame, J. W. (1972). *The slave community: Plantation life in the antebellum South.* New York: Oxford University Press.

Block, M. R., & Sinnott, J.D. (1979). *The battered elder syndrome: An exploratory study.* College Park, MD: University of Maryland Center on Aging.

Brown, J., Cohen, P., Johnson, J.G., & Salzinger, S. (1998). A longitudinal analysis of risk factors for child maltreatment: Findings of a 17-year prospective study of officially recorded and self-reported child abuse and neglect. *Child Abuse & Neglect, 22* (11), 1065–1078.

Butler, R.N., Lewis, M.I., & Sunderland, T. (1998). Special concerns: Race and ethnicity, older women and gender issues. *Aging and mental health: Positive psychosocial and biomedical approaches* (pp. 157–200). Boston: Allyn & Bacon.

Davis, A., & Havighurst, R.J. (1946). Social class and color differences in child-rearing. *American Sociological Review, 2,* 698–710.

DeMause, L. (1974). Our forebears made childhood a nightmare. *Psychology Today, 8,* 85–88.

Dill, B.T. (1988). Our mothers' grief: Racial ethnic women and the maintenance of families. *Journal of Family History, 13* (4), 415–431.

Dobash, R. E., & Dobash, R. (1979). *Violence against wives: A case against patriarchy.* New York: Free Press.

Edin, K., & Harris, K.M. (1999). Getting off and staying off: Racial differences in the work route off welfare. In I. Brown (Ed.), *Latinas and African American women at work: Race, gender, and economic inequality*. New York: Russell Sage Foundation.

Erickson, N.S. (1991). Battered mothers of battered children: Using our knowledge of battered women to defend them against charges of failure to act. *Current Perspectives in Psychological, Legal, and Ethical Issues, 1A,* 197–218.

Filinson, R. (1989). Introduction. In R. Filinson and S.R. Ingman (Eds.), *Elder abuse: practice and policy*. New York: Human Sciences Press.

Frazier, E.F. (1966). *The Negro family in the United States* (3rd edition). Chicago: University of Chicago Press.

Gelles, R. J., & Conte, J.R. (1990). Domestic violence and sexual abuse of children: A review of research in the eighties. *Journal of Marriage and the Family, 52*(4), 1045–1048.

Gelles, R.J., & Cornell, C.P. (1990). *Intimate violence in families* (2nd edition). Newbury Park, CA: Sage.

Gelles, R. J. (1987). *Family violence*. Newbury Park, CA: Sage.

Goetting, A. (1991). Patterns of marital homicide: A comparison of husbands and wives. In R.L. Hampton (Ed.), *Black family violence* (pp. 147–60). Lexington, MA: Lexington books.

Gutman, H.G. (1976). *The black family in slavery and freedom: 2750–192*. New York: Patheon.

Hampton, R. L. (Ed). (1991). *Black family violence: Current research and theory*. Lexington, MA: Lexington Books.

Hampton. R. L., & Gelles, R.J. (1991). A profile of violence toward black children. In R.L. Hampton, R.J. Gelles, & Harrop, J. (Eds.), *Black family violence: Current research and theory* (pp. 21–24). Lexington, MA: Lexington Books.

Hampton, R. L., Gelles, R.J., & Harrop, J. (1991). Is violence in Black families increasing? A comparison of 1975 and 1985 national survey rates. In R.L. Hampton, R.J. Gelles, & J. Harrop (Eds.), *Black family violence: Current research and theory* (pp. 3–18). Lexington, MA: Lexington Books.

Hill, R. (1972). *The strengths of black families*. New York: Emerson Hall.

Hill, S.A. (1999). *African American children: Their socialization and development in families*. Newbury Park, CA: Sage.

Hill, S.A., & Zimmerson, M.K. (1995). Valiant girls and vulnerable boys: The impact of gender and race on mothers' caregiving for chronically ill children. *Journal of Marriage and the Family, 57*(1), 43–53.

Hine, D.C. (1995). Rape and the inner lives of Black women in the middle west: Preliminary thoughts on the culture of dissemblance. In B. Guy-Sheftall (Ed.), *Words of fire: An anthology of African American feminist thought* (pp. 380–387). New York: The New Press.

Holden, G.W., & Richie, K.L. (1991). Linking extreme marital discord, childrearing, and child behavior problems: Evidence from battered women. *Child Development, 62,* 311–327.

hooks, b. (2001). *Salvation: Black people and love*. New York: Harper Collins.

Johnson, M. P. (1995). Patriarchal terrorism and common couple violence: Two forms of violence against women. *Journal of Marriage and the Family, 57,* 283–294.

Johnson, M.P., & Ferraro, K.J. (2001). Research on domestic violence in the 1990s: Making distinctions. In R.M. Milardo (Ed.), *Understanding families in the new millennium: A decade in review* (pp. 167–182). Minneapolis: National Council on Family Relations.

Kardiner, A., & Ovesey, L. (1951). *The mark of oppression: Explorations into the personality of the American Negro.* New York: World Publishers.

Kempe, C. H., Silverman, F.N., Steele, B.F., Droegemueller, W., & Silver, H.K. (1962). The battered-child syndrome. *Journal of the American Medical Association, 18* (1), 17–24.

Kurz, D. (1989). Social science perspectives on wife abuse: Current debates and future directions. *Gender & Society, 3*(4), 489–495.

Kurz, D. (1993). Physical assaults by husbands: A major social problem. In R.J. Gelles & D.R. Loseke (Eds.), *Current controversies on family violence* (pp. 88–103). Newbury Park, CA: Sage.

Lamana, M.A., & Riedmann, A. (2000). *Marriages and families: Making choices in a diverse society* (7th edition). Belmont, CA: Wadsworth.

Lau, E. E., & Kosberg, J. (1979). Abuse of the elderly by informal care providers. *Aging, 299,* 10–15.

Lewis, D.K. (1975). The black family: Socialization and sex roles. *Phylon, 36* (3), 221–238.

Mash, E.J., & Wolfe, D.A. (1991). Methodological issues in research on physical child abuse. *Criminal Justice and Behavior, 18*(1), 8–29.

McGruder-Johnson, A.K., Davidson, E.S., Gleaves, D.H., Stock, W., & Finch, J.F. (2000). Interpersonal violence and posttraumatic symptomatology: The effects of ethnicity, gender, and exposure to violent events. *Journal of Interpersonal Violence, 15,* 205–221.

McKinlay, J. B. (1994). A case for refocussing upstream: The political economy of illness. In P. Conrad and R. Kern (Eds.), *The sociology of health and illness* (pp. 509–530). New York: St. Martin's.

Mink, G. (2001). Violating women: Rights abuses in the welfare police state. *The Annals of the American Academy of Political and Social Sciences, 577,* 79–93.

Nam, Y., & Tolman, R. (2002). Partner abuse and welfare receipt among African American and Latino women living in a low-income neighborhood. *Social Work Research, 26,* 241–251.

National Research Council (1993). *Understanding and preventing violence.* Washington, DC: National Academy Press.

Nobles, W.W. (1985). Africanity: Its role in black families. *The Black Scholar, 5,* 10–17.

Richie, B. E. (1995). Battered black women: A challenge for the black community. In B. Guy-Sheftall (Ed.), *Words of fire: An anthology of African American feminist thought* (pp. 398–404). New York: The New Press.

Russell, D. (1986). *The secret trauma: Incest in the lives of girls and women.* New York: Basic Books.

Scott, J. W. (1993). African American mother-daughter relations and teenage pregnancy: Two faces of premarital teenage pregnancy. *Western Journal of Black Studies, 17,* 73–81.

Scott, R.J. (1985). The battle over the child: Child apprenticeships and the Freedman's Bureau in North Carolina. In N.R. Hiner and J.M. Hawes (Eds.), *Growing up in America: Children in an historical perspective* (pp. 193–207). Chicago: University of Chicago Press.

Sherman, A. (1994). *Wasting America's future: The Children's Defense Fund report on the costs of child poverty.* Boston: Beacon Press.

Siegel, L.J. (1998). *Criminology* (6th edition). Belmont, CA: Wadsworth.

Straus, M. A. (1994). *Beating the devil out of them: Corporal punishment in American families.* New York: Lexington Books.

Straus, M. A., Gelles, R.J., & Steinmetz, S.K. (1980). *Behind closed doors: Violence in the American family.* New York: Doubleday.

Tatara, T., & Blumerman, L. (1996). *Summaries of the statistical data on elder abuse in domestic settings: An exploratory study of state statistics for FY93 and FY94.* Washington, DC: National Center on Elder Abuse.

Tower, C.C. (1996). *Understanding child abuse and neglect* (3rd edition). Boston: Allyn and Bacon.

Turbett, P. & O'Toole, R. (1980). Physicians' recognition of child abuse. Paper presented at the Annual Meeting of the American Sociological Association. New York: American Sociological Association.

Walker, L. (2000). *The battered woman syndrome* (2nd edition). New York: Harper.

Whaley, A.L. (2000). Sociocultural differences in the developmental consequences of the use of physical discipline during childhood for African Americans. *Cultural Diversity and Ethnic Minority Psychology, 6,* 5–12.

White, A. (1999). Talking black, talking feminist: Gendered micromobilization processes in a collective protest against rape. In B. Guy-Sheftall (Ed.), *Words of fire: An anthology of African American feminist thought* (pp. 189–218). New York: The New Press.

White, D.G. (1999). *Ar'nt I a woman? Female slaves in the plantation south.* New York: W.W. Norton and Company.

White, E.C. (1985). *Chain, chain, change: For black women dealing with physical and emotional abuse.* Seattle, WA: Seal Press.

Widom, C.S. (1992). *The cycle of violence.* National Institute of Justice Research in Brief. Washington, DC: U.S. Department of Justice.

Wiese, D., & Dar, D. (1995). Current trends in child abuse reporting and fatalities: The results of the 1994 annual fifty state survey. Chicago: National Committee to Prevent Child Abuse.

Williams, J.H., Pierce, R., Young, N.S. & Van Dorn, R.A. (2001). Service utilization in high-crime communities: Consumer views on supports and barriers. *Families in Society, 82,* 409–417.

Wilson, W.J. (1987). *The truly disadvantaged: The inner-city, the underclass, and public policy.* Chicago: University of Chicago Press.

Wilson, W.J. (1996). *When work disappears: The world of the new urban poor.* New York: Knopf.

Zinn, M.B., & Eitzen, D.S. (2002). *Diversity in families* (6th edition). Boston: Allyn and Bacon.

Chapter 6

A COMMON HERITAGE OF WORK: EMPLOYMENT AND TRAINING OF AFRICAN AMERICANS

BOGART R. LEASHORE

African Americans share the common heritage of ancestors who were forcefully brought to America to work as unpaid labor for the economic, social, and political institution of slavery. As enslaved workers, irrespective of their gender and age, the ancestors of African Americans were largely agricultural workers who were required to labor from dawn to dust. Moreover, they came from an African tradition of shared labor, mutual responsibility, and interdependence. Thus, a strong work orientation has long been integral to the history of African Americans. This work ethic has been a critical strength in the common heritage of African Americans, as they have sustained themselves in a hostile environment and achieved much over the years. Their work ethic is among five cultural strengths that Hill (1972) identified.

Embedded in the strong work orientation of African American families are aspirations for improving the quality of their lives. They have a longstanding goal for their children to have a better life and to become self-reliant. This goal has been advanced by the rich structural and functional variability and diversity that exist among these families. Over time, they have had a consistent history of cooperative egalitarian arrangements and efforts (Everett, Chipungu, & Leashore, 1997; Billingsley, 1992; Landry, 1987; Lewis & Looney, 1983; Stack, 1974).

Despite institutionalized racism, sexism, discrimination, exploitation, and oppression, African Americans have long held to enhancing the quality of their lives through education and employment. Indeed, they have achieved against great odds. According to the 1990 U.S. Census, African Americans represent 12.3 percent of the resident population of the U.S. (Bennett, 1992). By the year 2005, the proportion of African American workers is expected to increase, while that of whites is expected to decline (Tidwell, 1993).

The education, income, health, and living conditions of African Americans have generally improved since the passage of important civil rights legislation in the 1950s and 1960s. However, these improvements slowed and then regressed in some instances during the 1980s. Despite a significant increase in the number of affluent and middle-income African Americans over the last decade, the net wealth of African American households is only one-tenth that of whites. This and other disparities have been attributed to the Republican dominated national politics of the 1980s, which negated the previous civil rights gains and socioeconomic advancements of African Americans.

Other authors have identified factors that increased the gap between the rich and the poor, including more opportunities for educated middle-income African Americans and fewer opportunities for the urban poor, thus polarizing these two subgroups. The changing economy and demographic factors, as well as racial discrimination, are other contributing factors that severely limit the quality of life for African Americans (O'Hare, Pollard, Mann, & Kent, 1991).

This chapter addresses the common heritage of work as a strength for African American families. It analyzes the research literature on the past and current employment and training circumstances of these families, how they might be improved by drawing upon the history of work among African Americans, and the role that future research on social policies and programs might play in providing improved opportunities for work and training. Special attention is given to the strengths perspective and the empowerment process for enhancing the well-being of African Americans, their families, and other Americans as well.

African Americans and the Labor Force: An Analysis of the Research Literature

General Labor Force Statistics on Blacks

Research shows that while African Americans constitute 10.8 percent of the total labor force in the U.S., they represent 19.9 percent of the unemployed. And, while African American women have a long history of working, the labor force participation rates for men are generally higher than for women. Further, the unemployment rate for African Americans in 1991 was twice that of whites (Bennett, 1992). This disparity, in small part, is attributed to the relatively low labor force participation rate of persons sixteen–nineteen years old, which includes thirty-eight percent for African Americans in this age group for 1994 and fifty-six percent for whites (Honer, 1996).

A larger percent of persons with work disabilities are African American, for example, in 1993, 15.8 percent of the work disabled were African Americans compared to 9.3 percent of whites, with a higher percent in all age categories for African Americans. Of individuals with work disabilities, twenty-six percent of African Americans and twenty-nine percent of whites were receiving Social Security income, with larger percentages of African Americans receiving food stamps, qualifying for Medicaid, and residing in public or subsidized housing (Honer, 1996, p. 83). Also, it should be noted that in 1994, larger percentages of African Americans than whites were members of labor unions: twenty-six percent versus nineteen percent respectively for men, and twenty-one percent versus fourteen percent for women (Honer, 1996, p. 231).

Unique Dynamics of Black Unemployment

The employment rates of African Americans have deteriorated over the past decade due to the following factors according to studies: difficulties in finding jobs; a greater likelihood of being laid-off; a decline in stable, higher-wage blue collar jobs in the industrial cities; continued racial discrimination and negative stereotyping by white employers; the dispersal of jobs from central cities to the suburbs; and limited education opportunities and increased school dropout rates.

African Americans remain unemployed for longer periods of time than whites; they sometimes work two or more jobs simultaneously to survive; and many are underemployed and work fewer hours than they prefer. Others are chronically unemployed workers who have become discouraged and have given up the search for work (O'Hare et al., 1991).

Inner-city, urban communities offer ". . . a vast range of tedious or socially demeaning jobs that require unskilled, willing and adequately inexpensive labor. . ." (Galbraith, 1992, p. 38). The flourishing economy and the relocation of industry and jobs to more desirable areas preclude the poor and near poor from benefiting from new employment opportunities. Consequently, greater resentment and unrest might be expected among poor residents in those communities across different ethnic groups (Broman, 2001; Galbraith, 1992).

Effects of Structural or Systemic Factors

Unemployment and poverty are related to structural factors, including the loss of well-paying manufacturing jobs, declining neighborhoods, and discrimination in the workplace. These are factors that go beyond African Americans' personal responsibility. Moreover, labor force participation alone will not enable many working poor families to escape poverty; additional requirements include a higher minimum wage and/or some form of earned income tax credit (EITC), negative income tax, or guaranteed income. Opportunities for training and education are also important to help African Americans upgrade their skills for better and higher paying jobs (Caputo, 1991). Affirmative action can and has abated racial and sexual discrimination. It is a part of a "redistributive chain" that should be strengthened; as noted by West (1993), "Given the history of this country, it is a virtual certainty that without affirmative action racial and sexual discrimination would return with a vengeance" (p. 64).

Consequences of Technological Advances

A shift from the production of goods to services has and will continue to be profound. Service-producing industries are expected to add twenty-three million jobs by the year 2005. However, African Americans continue to be greatly dependent on the manufacturing industry in which they are much more likely to be displaced than whites. Such displacement means that they are less likely than whites to be re-employed after displacement and more likely to experience longer periods of unemployment than whites.

It has been projected that most new jobs will require more education and higher levels of language, math, and reasoning skills. Up to the year 2005, workers at all levels of education and skills will be needed, how-ever, those with higher levels of education or training will have more options and better paying job opportunities. Technical and related sup-port jobs are expected to grow fastest (37%); followed by professional specialists (32%), service workers (29%), and executives, administra-tors, and managers (27%). Similar increases are expected in service in-dustry occupations such as home health aides, paralegals, and medical records technicians. It is very clear that African Americans will need to be much better prepared than in the past to seize these technological opportunities in the changing economy (Tidwell, 1993).

African American Work and Career Aspirations

In spite of these technological changes and structural factors, the work and career aspirations of many young African Americans have remained high and somewhat optimistic. In 1992, for example, data from national studies documented the expected occupations of twelfth graders at age 30. A majority of African Americans (55%) expected to be in professional, business or managerial occupations compared to fifty percent of whites; eight percent of African Americans compared to six percent of whites expected to be in the military or a police or se-curity officer; while seven percent of African Americans and six per-cent of whites expected to be business owners. This research also indi-cated that larger percentages of whites compared to blacks expected to be farmers (1 percent versus .6 percent), housewives (1.2 percent versus .4 percent), laborers (.7 percent versus .3 percent), and teachers (8.4 percent versus 3.7 percent) (Honer,1996, p. 112).

In the same year, the most recent types of work for employed twelfth graders, both African Americans and whites, were food service work-ers, grocery clerks or cashiers, office or clerical staff, and salespeople. In 1994, however, the most frequent occupations of employed African American adults involved a much broader range:

1. service workers: police, firefighters, guards, private household workers, health aides, food service workers, cleaning and building service staff;
2. technicians, sales, and administrative supports: technical and related supports, health technologists, engineers, salespersons, administrative supports, clerical and computer operators;
3. operators and laborers: machine operators, assemblers, inspectors, movers, equipment operators, helpers and laborers;
4. precision production, craft and repair: mechanics, repairers, and construction workers;
5. managerial and professional: executives, managerial scientists, physicians, dentists, teachers, lawyers, artists, entertainers, and athletes; and
6. farming, forestry, and fishing. (Honer, 1996, pp. 211–212)

It is important to identify factors from research that have helped blacks move into occupational fields from which they were previously excluded, especially, to broaden the aspirations of the younger generation. It is clear that African Americans draw upon a common heritage of work and related strengths to foster a better quality of life including: mutual support, a strong achievement orientation, a sense of spirituality, role adaptability, and strong kinship ties (Hill, 1972). These strengths, combined with strong national policies and programs in support of workers and families (Bischoff & Reisch, 2000; Jannson, Dodd, & Smith, 2002), can do much to enhance the quality of life for African Americans, as well as other marginalized groups.

Work, The Strengths Perspective, and Empowerment

Social Work Practice and The Black Work Orientation

Ironically, employment and unemployment are not usually a particular focus in social work practice, despite the impact these issues have on the stability and well-being of individuals, families, and communities (Briar, 1983; Sales, 1995). At best, secondary consideration is given to work as part of the mix of problems that clients present. Research findings indicate that work opportunity is an especially significant factor for engaging African American males, in particular, in clinical social work practice (Gary, Hopps, Pinderhughes, & Shankar, 1995). Employment opportunities can reduce the humiliation and hopelessness that often accompany help seeking by poor people and people of color. The exposure of children to work-oriented behaviors such as understanding

and organizing time, preparing for work, meeting transportation sched-
ules, discussing work issues at home, and taking pride in one's work can
provide positive reinforcement for children's school achievement
(Gary, Hopps, Pinderhughes, & Shankar, 1995).

The Strengths Perspective

The strengths perspective's effectiveness has been documented by
research on services to various groups and social problems including
mental illness, the elderly, women, at-risk youth, and addictions (Saleebey, 1992; Sullivan & Rapp, 1994; Weick, Rapp, Sullivan, & Kisthardt,
1989; Miller & Berg, 1995; Parsons & Cox, 1994). This perspective min-
imizes practitioners' and researchers' obsessions with pathology and
draws attention to competencies, capacities, beliefs, hopes and possibilities from within the individual or ethnic group (Saleebey, 1996).
In the context of work and achievement, African Americans place
great emphasis on education, regardless of barriers that they encounter. Historically, supporting the educational aspirations of youth has
been shared within the family and in the general community (Freeman,
1990). Extended family and even fictive kin provide encouragement
and tangible support for educational achievement.

From a strengths perspective, services for helping African Americans
to develop and identify occupational goals should include information
about the range of possibilities; the requirements necessary to achieve
them; clients' individual and ethnic strengths, in particular, cultural
models and coaches in specific fields; and available resources. Consideration should be given to black youths' interests, motivations, abilities,
and capacities. As appropriate, their work experience, formal education, training, and experiences with racism and discrimination should
also be explored and addressed.

It is also important to recognize, acknowledge, and reinforce work efforts and achievements among African Americans for whom racism
and discrimination have historically blocked the door to employment
and training opportunities. Their success can be attributed to their abilities, motivation, hard work, diligence, resilience, and cultural support
networks. With specific reference to African American males, research
has shown that the majority perceive themselves as providing very well
for their families, an important strength in spite of employment discrimination and other barriers (Taylor, Leashore, & Tolliver, 1988).

An Empowerment Approach

Empowerment involves a process of gaining control or influence over one's life circumstances (Solomon, 1976). A number of studies have documented this approach's effects when applied to various ethnic and age groups (Browne, 1995; Freeman, 2001; Gutierrez, 1990; McDermott, 1989; Price, 1988). Consequently, it can be effectively used to address issues of employment and training among African Americans, as well as other groups. The approach counters the negative value or image of African Americans often seen in the media and reinforced over a history of racism in the U.S. It counters powerlessness and hopelessness with the ability to competently address problems, beginning with a positive view of one's self and one's ethnic group (Solomon, 1976). As a social work practice goal and process, empowerment can mitigate racial oppression, discrimination, and poverty by helping African Americans to learn how to make and implement basic life decisions (Boyd-Franklin, 1989). Hence, it can promote effective coping at the individual, family, community, and organizational levels (Daly, Jennings, Beckett, & Leashore, 1995).

As in the case of postmodern feminist conceptualizations, empowerment is a process of self-liberation and that of others; it is a potential, a capacity, a growth process that includes connections with others, a sense of community, and collective identity and good, as well as social power (Browne, 1995; Gary, Hopps, Pinderhughes & Shankar, 1995; Pinderhughes, 1983; Solomon, 1976;). It involves the development of self-confidence and a belief in oneself and others, along with a belief in possibilities. Insight, risks, supportive relationships, resilience, competence and collaboration are critical aspects of an empowerment approach (Saleebey, 1996).

In both the strengths perspective and the empowerment process, it is important that services be relevant to the needs of African Americans. Broadened frames of reference and a reformulation of assessment and intervention, including practitioners' attention to personal issues, awareness, cultural sensitivity and competence, can promote more effective and relevant services (Logan, 1990). Mentoring African American children and youths can be important for promoting education, training, and career development. Interpersonal relationships can provide social support; research shows these relationships are effective for working with youth, but also can be used to support young adults, as well as various professionals including social workers (Collins, Kamya, & Tourse, 1997).

Addressing Structural Factors

A focus on empowerment and strengths is important for addressing racism, sexism, discrimination, and sexual harassment in the workplace, and in the broader society. While support and advocacy can and should be provided on an individual basis, boycotts and class action lawsuits also may be used. For example, federal lawsuits against systematic and structural employment discrimination by large companies have more than doubled. In part, this change occurred due to 1991 fed eral legislation that, by increasing the potential payoff to workers and their lawyers and making discrimination easier to prove has brought more high profile cases to the courts. Those cases involve Texaco, State Farm, Shoney's, Denny's, and Lucky Stores.

Although the federal Equal Employment Opportunity Commission has sharply reduced the number of bias cases it files to 160 per year, down from 643 in 1990 and 1,174 in 1974, there were sixty-eight discrimination suits/class actions in 1996 and seventy-one in 1995, up from thirty in 1992. New cases are more often about pay and promotion discrimination and harassment, rather than hiring discrimination. Increasingly, these cases concern sexual rather than racial discrimination, such as the confinement of women to dead-end jobs. The new law permits claims for workplace changes and back pay, and also in cases of intentional discrimination, for distress, humiliation and punitive damages.

Further, this law allows discrimination cases to be heard by juries, whereas previously, only judges heard these cases. Of the discrimination cases heard by juries in 1994, workers won forty-three percent, but they only won twenty-two percent of those heard by judges (Myerson, 1997). Empowering, supporting and advocating for workers who may be fearful about taking legal action against employment discrimination, and assisting them in securing effective legal counsel are strategies that social workers should undertake more often to effect structural changes.

Using Community Rebuilding Approaches

Black communities, in the more conventional sense, can create preconditions for work by transmitting expectations and definitions of success including preparation for and entrance into careers. Rebuilding communities and mobilizing residents and institutions therein can promote achievement, and foster business development and residents' employment. Improved schools and educational reforms, effective training programs, and opportunities for higher education can have powerful effects on employment outcomes.

For example, informal cultural networks are valuable sources of information about jobs, and community organizations and agencies can help in the job development and job-seeking processes. Communities can seek better access to and linkages with public transportation to the areas where jobs are located, by advocating for expanded routes. Empowerment zones, community development corporations, and other community-building initiatives should be used for the creation of employment and economic opportunities in communities where African Americans reside. Efforts also should be made to negate cultural stereotypes of these communities and the people who live in them (Coulton, 1996).

A Culturally Relevant Research Framework: Employment, Public Policy, and Private Initiatives

The Research Framework

A well-planned research framework is required to guide a much-needed interrelated process of policy development, policy analysis, and policy reforms. This research framework can help researchers and practitioners to address public policy and private initiatives related to employment and training programs for African Americans. Despite the retreat from public policies that promote the employment and general well-being of African Americans and all Americans, Wilson (1996) states that bold, comprehensive, and thoughtful public policies are needed. He calls for public policies that integrate and mobilize resources from both the public and private sectors to alleviate social inequality.

Education and Employment Policy

This research framework should focus on policies that link employment and education, and family support systems. For example, research is needed for establishing and analyzing the effects of policies on national performance standards for public schools, as well as teacher development, funding, curriculum resources, and improvement of dilapidated schools. Research based on this framework can also reveal gaps in public policies and identify particular areas for which private initiatives are needed. For instance, the private sector, including corporations, local businesses, civic clubs, churches, and community centers, could fund and support computer-competency training in inner-city public schools.

The Goals 2000: Educate America Act, which was passed in 1994, encourages states to apply for grants to improve their schools in the domains of instruction, curriculum, technology, professional development, and parental and community involvement (Wilson, 1996). This policy should receive a larger appropriation from the U.S. Congress to accomplish its goals in this broad range of domains. Research could effectively document the need to reform this policy through an analysis of its impact upon each of these domains and identification of critical gaps in its scope and implementation.

In regard to employment policy, integration of city-suburban work resources is critical to the development of healthy metropolitan regions and to the well-being of the nation as a whole. Affordable housing, public transportation, car-pool and van-pool networks to suburban employment sites are needed resources. Further, policies that help create more public-sector jobs should be established to enhance employment opportunities for low-skilled workers, focused on infrastructure maintenance areas such as repairing roads, highways, and bridges; addressing the shortage of day-care aides, and training playground assistants to upgrade their status and pay. In fact, Wilson (1996) recommends the creation of low-wage public-sector jobs with universal health insurance, child care programs, and earned income tax credits.

In the current conservative political climate, it is necessary for broad-based coalitions to use social action to advocate for these goals (Leashore, 1994). Research on social and political action to improve work opportunities for marginalized groups such as African Americans has been a low priority for policy analysts and other researchers. However, the proposed research framework provides a strong rationale for studies that explore best practices in developing and retaining these low-wage public-sector jobs for African Americans and others (Brodsky & Ovwigho, 2002). This framework also reinforces the importance of research on analyzing the effects of current systemic barriers, including nonsupportive policies on such efforts.

Related Family Support Policy

Research has shown that a number of family supports are needed as complements to the above enhanced employment opportunities. However, additional policy analysis and reform research is needed on the specific effects of family supports, which include universal preschools, infant care programs and high-quality nursery schools, and national health insurance. School-to-work transition programs, if adequately funded and researched, could help address wage inequality and economic marginality among high school graduates from different ethnic groups and social classes. The School-to-Work Opportunities Act of 1994 provides a national framework for the school-to-work transition by supporting demonstrations in which businesses work with educators in reforming school systems and integrating work and school, yet this legislation was funded for less than $500 million. Again, policy research could be used to document significant gaps in funding and needed reforms; while intervention research could help to identify best practices related to the school-to-work transition and the implications for successful adult work.

Formal resources such as unemployment benefits and services should be addressed, especially the length and coverage of benefits. Informal cultural sources of help for African Americans, such as family, friends, and indigenous leaders, are a frequent critical resource. Sales (1995) found that for all job loss groups, use of informal sources remains high and relatively consistent, involving tangible help from family and friends. Use of these informal supports was higher during the second year of unemployment, with other sources of income most likely used by workers between six and twelve months after their job loss. After two years of unemployment, however, workers were less likely to receive economic help from their informal support network.

Long-term unemployed or discouraged workers may need special supports and services to maintain their identification with work. Displaced workers should be linked to these services so as to retain and strengthen their employment interest and potential. These services may include job search assistance and retraining, and support groups

(Harknett, 2001; Sales, 1995). Research is needed to clarify ethnic and social class differences and similarities in this informal helping process, especially related to long-term unemployed African Americans, and to describe how those factors interact with formal employment and income services.

There is a need for quality, affordable child care; high-quality, readily accessible, affordable infant and toddler day care, and care for special needs children. Flextime and permanent part-time jobs with good benefits are needed, as well as: employee assistance programs that provide counseling for family problems; greater support for Head Start; family-sensitive policies for family leave and national health insurance coverage; income supplements for the working poor; and the strengthening of adult education, job training, and job placement programs (Chilman, 1993). Job or employment programs should address enhancing the capacity of recipients to achieve long-term self-sufficiency.

Educational components for employment programs might include literacy training, adult basic education, general equivalency diploma preparation, and secondary and postsecondary education. These services are often available through local public schools and community colleges without cost. Job skills training should be available in critical areas such as word processing; health services need expanding, including nurse's assistants, licensed practical nurses, and health and home care attendants; as well as child care and construction jobs. Job readiness services can focus on resume preparation, job interviewing skills, information about workplace expectations, and job development and placement services (Hagen & Lurie, 1995). The proposed research framework can guide studies designed to explore the cultural relevance of the identified family supports, as well as studies that document policy implementation barriers and strengths.

Related Public Welfare Policy

While welfare as we know it no longer exists with the passage of the Personal Responsibility and Work Opportunities Act of 1996, there are several issues related to this policy that should not be ignored. National concern has been expressed about the lack of nondemeaning, minimum wage jobs, employment benefits, and adequate child care. Workfare without decent and minimum wage jobs is not fair or equitable. It is antidemocratic, antiwomen, and it reinforces social injustices.

With specific reference to education and training, this legislation makes it very difficult for welfare recipients to get postsecondary education. They must perform work activities for at least twenty hours a week in order to maintain their benefits under the new law. Vocational education training is allowed for up to twelve months, however, the policy does not permit students to earn an associate's degree. The legislation does not mention higher education specifically, thus it is not certain whether enrollment in college is permitted. This provision as written could preclude many African Americans who value education from receiving college degrees. It will have a special impact on black women and those in other ethnic groups who disproportionately receive AFDC benefits (Brodsky & Ovwigho, 2002; Cleaveland, 2002; Reynolds, 1997). A state-by-state policy analysis is gravely needed to identify policy inconsistencies and barriers that are hindering the effectiveness of this policy in work and education areas.

CONCLUSION

African American families and communities have been described as both vulnerable and enduring amidst constant social, political, and economic changes. There are thousands of businesses owned by African Americans; thousands of churches; more than 100 predominately African American colleges and universities; fraternal and sorority organizations; and political, social, and professional organizations (Billingsley, 1992). Many of these black businesses and organizations have developed social and human service programs involving after school, family support, food and shelter, transportation, educational scholarship, and mentoring programs (Leashore, 1995). Some have employment services components, however, many more can and should develop such services, thus, continuing the self-help and mutual aid tradition among African Americans.

Private business initiatives should be developed to locate businesses in African American communities and neighborhoods and to hire low-skilled residents. African American businesses in particular should be provided access to loans and other supports. Private foundations should pursue and support initiatives to create jobs and to assist long-term

unemployed workers to find and keep jobs. For example, the Rocke-
feller Foundation in partnership with the Chase Manhattan Bank and
the U.S. Department of Housing and Urban Development, has a project to help residents of public housing become employed. Residents
are trained for entry-level jobs, provided job-search assistance, and provided support services after finding jobs such as child care workers (*The
New York Times,* 1997).

Regardless of the issues, problems, and challenges, the strengths perspective and the empowerment process are approaches that can effectively promote employment and training opportunities for African
Americans. Further, although research on employment and training
has increased in frequency and scope, additional research is clearly
needed to explore the world view of African Americans and its impact
on work and employment. Their world view involves their perceptions
of themselves in relation to other people, institutions and nature; it also
involves their view of the world and their role and place in it, including
the meaning and value of work. Unique and important experiences
shape the world views of African Americans, and to varying degrees,
how they prioritize traditional attributes such as strong kinship ties, religious orientation, achievement orientation, work ethic, and egalitarian
role-sharing (English, 1997; Hill, 1972). These traditional attributes are
consistent with and can be utilized in combination with the strengths
perspective and the empowerment process to establish and reform public policies related to employment and training.

REFERENCES

Bennett, E.C. (1992). U.S. Bureau of the Census: Current population reports, population characteristics. In *The Black population in the United States* (pp. 420–464).
Washington, DC: U.S. Government Printing Office.

Billingsley, A. (1992). *Climbing Jacob's ladder: The enduring legacy of African American
families.* New York: Simon and Schuster.

Bischoff, U.M., & Reisch, M.S. (2000). Welfare reform and community-based organizations: Implications for policy, practice, and education. *Families in Society, 81,*
95–105.

Boyd-Franklin, N. (1989). *Black families in therapy: A multisystems approach.* New York:
The Free Press.

Briar, K. (1983). Unemployment: Toward a social work agenda. *Social Work, 28,*
211–216.

Brodsky, A.E., & Ovwigho, P.C. (2002). Swimming against the tide: Connecting
low-income women to living wage jobs. *Journal of Poverty, 6,* 63–87.

Broman, C.L. (2001). Work stress in the family life of African Americans. *Journal of Black Studies, 31,* 835–846.

Browne, C. (1995). Empowerment in social work practice with older women. *Social Work, 40*(3), 358–364.

Caputo, R.K. (1991). Patterns of work and poverty: Exploratory profiles of working-poor households. *Families in Society, 72*(8), 451–460.

Chilman, C.S. (1993). Parental employment and child care trends: Some critical issues and suggested policies. *Social Work, 38,* 451–460.

Cleaveland, C.L. (2002). "Why don't those people just get a job? Fragile work attachment in a cohort of welfare recipients." Doctoral Dissertation. Massachusetts: Bryn Mawr College.

Collins, P.M., Kamya, H.A. & Tourse, R.W. (1997). Questions of racial diversity and mentorship: An empirical exploration. *Social Work, 42,* 145–151.

Coulton, C.J. (1996). Poverty, work, and community: A research agenda for an era of diminishing federal responsibility. *Social Work, 41*(5), 509–519.

Daly, A., Jennings, J., Beckett, J.O., & Leashore, B.R. (1995). Effective coping of African Americans. *Social Work, 40,* 240–248.

English, R.A. (1997). Diversity of world views among African American families. In J.E. Everett, S.S. Chipungu, & B.R. Leashore (Eds.), *Child welfare: An Africentric perspective* (19–35). New Brunswick, NJ: Rutgers University Press.

Everett, J.E., Chipungu, S.S., & Leashore, B.R. (1997). *Child welfare: An Africentric perspective.* New Brunswick, NJ: Rutgers University Press.

Freeman. E.M. (1990). The Black family's life cycle: Operationalizing a strengths perspective. In S.M.L. Logan, E.M. Freeman & R.G. McRoy (Eds.), *Social work practice with Black families: A culturally specific perspective* (pp. 55–72). New York: Longman.

Freeman, E.M. (2001). *Substance abuse intervention, prevention, rehabilitation, and systems change strategies: Helping individuals, families, and groups to empower themselves.* New York: Columbia University Press.

Galbraith, J.K. (1992). *The culture of contentment.* New York: Houghton Mifflin Company.

Gary, L., Hopps, J., Pinderhughes, E., & Shankar, R. (1995). *The power to care: Clinical practice effectiveness with overwhelmed clients.* New York: The Free Press.

Gutierrez, L. (1990). Working with women of color. *Social Work, 35,* 149–154.

Hagen. J.L., & Lurie, I. (1995). Implementing JOBS: From the rose garden to reality. *Social Work, 40,* 523–532.

Harknett, K. (2001). Working and leaving welfare: Does race or ethnicity matter? *Social Service Review, 75,* 359–385.

Hill, R. (1972). *Strengths of the Black family.* New York: Emerson Hall Publishers.

Honer, L.L. (1996) (Ed.). *Black Americans: A statistical sourcebook.* Palo Alta, CA: Information Publications.

Jannson, B.S., Dodd, S.J., & Smith, S. (2002). *The Social Policy Journal, 1,* 5–18.

Landry, B. (1987). *The new Black middle class.* Berkeley, CA: University of California Press.

Leashore, B.R. (1994). Social policies, Black males, and Black families. In R. Staples (Ed.) *The Black family: Essays and studies* (5th ed.). New York: The Free Press.

Leashore, B.R. (1995). African Americans overview. In R.L. Edwards (Eds.), *Encyclopedia of social work* (19th Edition). Washington, DC: National Association of Social Workers Press.

Lewis, J.M., & Looney, J.G. (1983). *The long struggle: Well-functioning working-class Black families*. New York: Brunner/Mazel, Publishers.

Logan, S.M.L. (1990). Black families: Race, ethnicity, culture, social class, and gender issues. In S.M.L. Logan, E.M. Freeman, & R.G. McRoy, (Eds.), *Social work practice with Black families: A culturally specific perspective*. New York: Longman.

McDermott, C.J. (1989). Empowering elderly nursing home residents: The resident's rights campaign. *Social Work, 34,* 155–157.

Miller, S.D., & Berg, I.K. (1995). *The miracle method: A radically new approach to problem drinking*. New York: W.W. Norton.

Myerson, A.R. (1997, February 3). As federal bias cases drop, workers take up the fight. *The New York Times* (pp.1 and 14).

O'Hare, W.P., Pollard, K.M., Mann, T.L., & Kent, M.M. (1991). African Americans in the 1990s. *Population Bulletin, 46*(1). Washington, DC: Population Reference Bureau, Inc.

Parsons, R.J., & Cox, E.O. (1994). *Empowerment-oriented social work practice with the elderly*. Pacific Grove, CA: Brooks/Cole.

Pinderhughes, E.B. (1983). Empowerment of our clients and for ourselves. *Social Casework, 64,* 331–338.

Price, K. (1988). Empowering preadolescent and adolescent leukemia patients. *Social Work, 33,* 275–276.

Reynolds, W.A. (1997). For student on welfare, degrees pay dividends. *The Chronicle of Higher Education, 38*(28), 60–68.

Saleebey, D. (1992). *The strengths perspective in social work practice*. White Plains, NY: Longman.

Saleebey, D. (1996). The strengths perspective in social work practice: Extensions and cautions. *Social Work, 41,* 296–305.

Sales, E. (1995). Surviving unemployment: Economic resources and job loss duration in blue-collar households. *Social Work, 40,* 483–494.

Solomon, B.B. (1976). *Black empowerment: Social work in oppressed communities*. New York: Columbia University Press.

Stack, C.B. (1974). *All our kin: Strategies for survival in a Black community*. New York: Harper and Row.

Sullivan, W.P., & Rapp, C.A. (1994). Breaking away: The potential and promise of a strengths-based approach to social work practice. In R.G. Meinert, J.T. Pardeck, & W.P. Sullivan, (Eds.), *Issues in social work: A critical analysis* (pp. 83–104)). Westport, CT: Auburn House.

Taylor, R.J, Leashore, B.R., & Tolliver, S. (1988). An assessment of the provider role as perceived by black males. *Family Relations, 37,* 426–431.

Tidwell, B.J. (Ed.) (1993). African Americans and the 21st century labor market: Improving the fit. *The state of Black America 1993* (35–57). New York: National Urban League, Inc.

The New York Times (1997). Editorial, February 3, 1997.

Weick, A., Rapp, C., Sullivan, W.P., & Kisthardt, W. (1989). A strengths perspective for social work practice. *Social Work, 34,* 350–354.

West, C. (1993). *Race matter.s* Boston: Beacon Press.

Wilson, W.J. (1996). *When work disappears: The world of the new urban poor.* New York: Alfopf.

Chapter 7

RESEARCH ON SUBSTANCE ABUSE WITHIN THE BLACK COMMUNITY

Edith M. Freeman

Effective research on black drug abuse rates and treatment outcomes can help policy makers, service providers, and black families and leaders to address the overwhelming effects of drugs on such families (Freeman, 1999; U.S. Department of Health & Human Services, 1990). However, much of the research conducted on these topics uses a colorblind perspective, often failing to produce useful data on best practices with African Americans for two reasons: (1) The research objectives and methodology are seldom focused on cultural factors that are important in black clients' addiction and recovery, and (2) The research does not explore how well equally colorblind mainstream programs address black clients' cultural needs as part of their recovery (Amuleru-Marshall, 1991). Methodological limitations such as these often produce culturally biased and insignificant results. Moreover, treatment failure rates in this research are blamed frequently on black clients, labeling them as unmotivated and too sensitive culturally.

These practice and research limitations must be considered within the context of how seriously drug abuse affects black communities today. Rowe and Grills (1993) believe, in fact, that: "The impact of drugs and the resultant chemical slavery have been devastating to the African American community" (p. 21). Various social indicators support their conclusion, for example, in terms of high drug-related rates of cirrhosis, pancreatitis, HIV/AIDS, heart disease, and hypertension among blacks. In the area of crime, drugs have been implicated as strong influences on black family and community violence, prostitution, burglaries, and other illegal activities. Other important drug-related indicators in those communities include chronic rates of unemployment, school dropouts, and homelessness (Clifford & Jones, 1988; Curtis-Boles & Jenkins-Monroe, 2000; Gordon, 1993; Greenfield, 1998; Rowe & Grills, 1993). While these indicators are obviously related to individual, family, and community factors, the effects of structural or systemic factors on black addiction and recovery also need to be addressed by research (Banks, 1997; Gray, 1995). More information is needed, too, on cultural strengths and resilience factors that prevent some blacks from becoming addicted, and aid other blacks in their recovery from drugs, in spite of this combination of factors (Freeman, 1999).

This chapter analyzes research on black drug abuse and treatment outcomes in order to clarify if and how cultural strengths are identified in these studies, along with the level of this research's cultural sensitivity in related areas. Methodological limitations and specific findings of these studies are also summarized, highlighting how the findings may affect treatment and criminal justice policies regarding African Americans. The chapter ends with a proposed new framework for research on black drug abuse treatment that is designed to improve the objectives, methods, cultural sensitivity, and outcomes of that research.

Review of Research Literature on Black Drug Abuse

Overview

This review includes an analysis of research on black children and youth, and on black adults. Cross-cultural research, as well as research on black populations alone, is included because both types of research may heavily influence important policy decisions. Although the major focus of this analysis is on treatment/prevention outcome research, some epidemiological research has been reviewed to determine cultural drug abuse patterns and to clarify other unique aspects of this problem in black communities.

Research on Black Children and Youth

The Focus of This Research. The literature contains studies in three main areas related to drug abuse and black children and youth. These areas include the effects on children and youth who live with addicted family members, addiction rates among children and youth, and treatment and prevention outcomes with this population.

Family Addiction Research Results. Research on family addiction reveals that many black children and youth, as well as those from other cultural groups, are affected in terms of school failure, parental abuse and neglect, increased access to drugs, and homelessness (Freeman, 1993; Kaminer, 1991; Smyth, 1995; Treadway, 1989). Some research reveals differences in prevalence rates for black youth who are exposed to family drug abuse compared to white youth. For example, in a national sample of 43,000 adults, more white respondents reported they had lived with an alcoholic during their first eighteen years of life (18.5%), than did black respondents (15.6%) (Schoenborn, 1991). Other data indicate that an estimated nine to twelve million Americans are directly affected by alcohol and other drug abuse by a family member, including minor children in families across all racial-ethnic groups and locations (NIDA, 1992, 1993a; OSAP, 1991; Stewart, 2002).

Epidemiological Research Findings. Some epidemiological research indicates that drug use rates among African American youth differ from those of other youth. Within the twelve to seventeen year age range, for instance, black youth have lower marijuana use rates than white youth. Although blacks have comparable illicit drug use rates to those of whites in this age group, more black and Hispanic males tend to perceive a lack of risk in the occasional use of marijuana and in cocaine experimentation, compared to whites (NIDA, 1987; 1992). Gender comparisons across racial-ethnic groups reveal a different picture. Black females in this age range have lower rates of overall drug use than white females (Johnston, O'Malley, & Bachman, 1999; SAMHSA, 1999).

Treatment Outcome Research. In terms of treatment outcome research, Freeman (1991) found that recovery rates for black and Hispanic youth in her study (N = 83) were affected by their need to develop positive individual and ethnic identities, and by the program's pattern of minimizing the influence of racial stress on their addiction and recovery. This mainstream rehabilitation program served black, Hispanic, and white youth. Its age-appropriate, but colorblind treatment approach focused on the role of family and peer conflicts in their clients' addiction and recovery.

However, the program failed to help black and Hispanic clients learn nondrug-related alternative ways to cope with racial stress and conflicts (Freeman, 1991). Some other research has documented the effectiveness of peer mentors from the same ethnic background as participants in helping them to cope with and address these factors (Chang, 1993). In addition, other authors conclude that contemporary fiction (Brisbane, 1985); family and cultural narratives (Freeman, 1992); and Africentric values, principles, and interactive exercises (Gordon, 1993; Moore, 2001; Oliver, 1989) are effective in teaching black youth how to cope with racial stress and conflicts and prevent drug abuse.

Prevention Outcome Findings. While most prevention literature in the past consisted of program descriptions, in recent years, increasing numbers of prevention outcome studies have been reported in the literature. Malekoff's (1994) sample of white, Hispanic, and black youth developed a drug abuse prevention program in collaboration with the local high school and a drug-free club operated by study participants for their peers. Outcomes included increased leadership and drug resistance skills among the participants. In addition, Stephens, Braithwaite, & Taylor (1998) studied the use of hip-hop music as a prevention strategy with African American adolescents. This culture-specific procedure was effective in stimulating cooperative learning among the participants related to HIV harm reduction and drug abuse prevention. Other youth drug prevention programs in black communities are noteworthy because they have documented adolescents' nonuse or abuse of drugs for periods ranging from a few months to two years after program completion (Harper, 1991; Freeman, 1992; Hansen, 1988; Malloy, 1989).

Research on Black Adults

Findings from Epidemiological Studies. While in some instances, the drug abuse rates for black children and youth are lower than those of white youth, examination of research findings on black adults reveals different patterns. For example, blacks aged thirty-five and over are more likely than whites or Hispanics of the same age to have used cocaine at least once during their lifetimes, during the past year, or during the past month (NIDA, 1987). Also some studies show that a little over seven percent of African American adults abuse *illicit* drugs compared to 6.6 percent of whites (NIDA, 1992). Other research findings, however, are in conflict with those prevalence rates. For example, a national survey on drug abuse documents that fewer African Americans than Hispanics and whites use drugs *in general* (NIDA, 1993b).

The literature indicates that African Americans have higher alcohol binge rates than whites, but in contrast, they have greater overall alcohol abstinence rates than whites (SAMHSA, 1999). Statistically, blacks are less likely than whites to have consumed alcohol in their lifetime, in the past year, and in the last month (SAMHSA, 1999). Black women, on the other hand, have significantly higher abstinence *and* heavy drinking rates than white women (Herd, 1986; NIDA, 1993b). This finding does conflict, however, with studies that indicate equal proportions of African American and white women are heavy drinkers (Anderson, 1995; SAMHSA, 1999).

A number of other epidemiological studies focus on cross-cultural samples that include black adults. Some of those studies are focused on prevalence rates, while others attempt to identify psychosocial correlates to drug abuse within those samples, such as impulsivity, threats of violence, spousal battering, child abuse and neglect, chronic unemployment, homelessness, and other factors. Other studies are focused on treatment effectiveness with culturally diverse clients, including black adults (Willenbring, Ridgely, Stinchfield, & Rose, 1991; Wallace, 1991; Zelvin, 1993). Yet the findings of both types of studies often fail to focus on relevant cultural factors in addition to social factors (Plutchik & Plutchik, 1988; Wallace, 1991), even when black participants in these studies are in the majority and have obvious culturally-related medical or psychosocial needs (Dunlap, Johnson, & Rath, 1996; Zule, Flannery, Wechsberg, & Lam, 2002; Gilbert, El Bassel, Schilling, & Friedman, 1997; Hutchison, 1999).

Treatment Outcome Research Results. Regarding this type of research, some studies conclude that holistic approaches focused on the mind and body connection are effective with African Americans (Kammer, 2002). Baker & Bell (1999) and Vontress & Epp (1997) found that addressing racial identity and culturally unique physiological reactions to medication and other drugs improves recovery outcomes. Gender-specific strategies have been helpful to some African American males and females in recovery (Beckerman & Fortana, 2001; Walton, Blow, & Booth, 2001; Washington & Moxley, 2001). More specifically, active problem-solving, religious involvement, and family support facilitated the recovery of black women in Curtis-Boles and Jenkins-Monroe's group intervention study (2000). Similarly, Fagan & Stevenson (1995) were able to use a co-facilitated self-help group parenting intervention to improve low-income fathers' skills in coping with violence and substance abuse. Related positive outcomes included enhanced parenting and teaching skills in these areas regarding their children and peers.

SUMMARY: LIMITATIONS OF RESEARCH ON BLACK CHILDREN, YOUTH, ADULTS

Level of Cultural Sensitivity

Some researchers today acknowledge the importance of and continue to strive toward making their research more culturally sensitive (Baker & Bell, 1999; Stephens, Braithwaite & Taylor, 1998; Chang, 1993; Freeman, 1991, 1992; Malekoff, 1994; Vontress & Epp, 1997). Much of the research analyzed in the previous section, however, tends to be culturally insensitive (Dunlap et al., 1996; Gilbert et al., 1997; Hutchinson, 1999; Johnston et al., 1999; Plutchik & Plutchik, 1988; Schoenborn, 1991; Wallace, 1991; Willenbring et al., 1991; Zelvin, 1993). Freeman (1999) defines culturally insensitive research as that which ignores the unique cultural and developmental context, traditions, values, experiences, beliefs, and meanings of a cultural group related to a certain phenomena, such as substance abuse. This research also ignores context in terms of political, policy, power, structural, and other systemic factors that affect cultural groups regarding the phenomena under study.

Such research views people of color, women, the elderly, gays and lesbians, the disabled, and other oppressed groups as the targets of research rather than as local experts who should be actively involved in the process and outcomes. From this perspective, the researcher is expected to bring the only expertise and decision-making power that matter to the knowledge development process. A familiar proverb attests to this limitation of culturally insensitive research: "Text without context is pretext" (Anonymous).

Culturally insensitive research on blacks in the area of substance abuse often fails to explore this multidimensional context of the problem in the following specific ways:

1. The cultural world views of black participants are not acknowledged or addressed, especially their views about normal developmental transitions, illness, problems, substance abuse, self-medication, recovery and relapse, racial stress and how to cope with this issue if it is relevant, the meaning of family and family relationships, and other sources of cultural supports-barriers that can influence resistance to drugs and recovery.

2. Researchers' goals are frequently too narrow, i.e., to gather data about a particular phenomena such as recovery outcomes, transitional housing, or cognitive behavioral treatment, without utilizing the research process as a capacity building opportunity for black participants. Examples of culturally sensitive research goals related to capacity building include participants' improved assessments of cultural supports and barriers in their families/communities and in the larger environment, and the effects on their ethnic identity and recovery. This research also fails, often, to explore to what extent rehabilitation programs use treatment approaches that foster culturally meaningful capacity-building opportunities for black clients.

3. Black clients are seldom involved in helping to design, implement, interpret, and disseminate the research findings. Few researchers use pre-research contacts with potential participants in order to identify cultural issues, questions, and methods that could help to make the process less culturally biased and more culturally relevant to black participants' resistance to and recovery from drugs.

4. Many of these researchers may have an individualistic value base that causes them to ignore or misinterpret black values such as collectivism and interdependence, hence they often do not collect data on relationships that are culturally relevant to black participants' recovery (e.g., a grandmother, minister, healer, or "play uncle"), or involve those cultural coaches as study participants. Many of these key informants may have local knowledge and cultural coping skills that are contributing factors to the primary participants' recovery and other outcomes.

5. Environmental factors that may have a differential impact upon black people's abilities to resist or recover from substance abuse are seldom the focus of research on use and abuse patterns or treatment outcomes. Examples include conflicting child welfare and substance abuse treatment policies related to the timing and criteria for reunification between addicted mothers and their children, and racial discrimination in education and employment. This discrimination may be a major influence on recovery and resistance to self-medication among black adults and youth.

6. Cultural strengths and resilience unique to black youth and adults, the effects on their recovery and resistance, and on their coping with developmental transitions have been ignored by a majority of researchers. This gap may reinforce researchers' emphasis on individual and cultural group pathology in their findings, recommendations, and design of future studies, as well as impede their respect for black participants' as experts with valuable local knowledge.

7. Common factors that affect black substance abusers and those from other cultural groups have not been explored or identified by researchers, perhaps because studies on this topic require a culturally aware, rather than a color-blind, perspective. This aspect of culturally insensitive research may be a barrier to discovering whether certain treatment components are essential for substance abusers from all cultural groups, based on those common factors. Common treatment components could be explored by researchers, in combination with various culturally-specific components for different groups. (Fitzpatrick & Gerald, 1993; Freeman, 2001; Gordon & Zrull, 1991; Yeich & Levine, 1992)

Other Methodological Issues

In addition to these issues of cultural insensitivity, this analysis reveals a number of other important methodological limitations in the identified research. Some of these limitations affect the quality of substance abuse research in general, while others are particularly relevant to black communities because of social justice and equity concerns. Primm (1992) validates the importance of sound substance abuse research on African American and Latino communities, given the higher risks imposed on them by the current inequitable social system, involving "a triad of poverty, disease, and unemployment" (p. 616). The following methodological limitations are apparent from this research literature:

1. Researchers' value biases related to research on black substance abusers or at risk subgroups are seldom acknowledged, for example, whether they have a colorblind or social class bias, do not believe they have a social responsibility to study the supply side as well as the demand side of the problem, or lack interest in social equity issues such as culturally-biased sentencing patterns for drug-related offenses by blacks, Hispanics, and women. Those biases often affect the design of their studies, the methods used (surveys versus life histories or narratives), interpretation of data, recommendations, and dissemination of findings.

2. Researchers need to clearly define and study complex multiple outcomes, rather than focusing only on whether the participant maintains recovery, because abstinence from drugs is only ten percent of lifetime recovery. Recovery has been shown to include long-term interrelated cycles of abstinence and relapse, therefore, researchers should explore how participants use relapse to

inform the abstinence side of their cycles. Other outcomes that affect recovery and their effects need to be clarified, such as improved ethnic and self-esteem, more productive work and school activities, enhanced communication, and the effective use of cultural coaches.

3. Much of this research focuses on individual outcomes at the micro-level, so the focus should be broadened to include other micro-outcomes related to family, peer, and work relationships; mezzo outcomes involving key organizations and aspects of the community that are relevant to participants' recovery; and macro-outcomes that require important policy reforms and changes in large social systems.

4. The components of substance abuse treatment need to be described more clearly and behaviorally (e.g., more clearly than case management, methadone maintenance, or group counseling approaches), so that effective and ineffective aspects of particular treatments can be delineated for study participants whose characteristics also need to be described more clearly (e.g., participants were from a low-income diverse community), especially those with specific addictions (e.g., methamphetamines or crack addictions).

5. While some studies have attempted to collect follow-up data on substance abusers in recovery or high-risk participants in prevention programs, most of this research fails to conduct more long-term follow-up to determine if outcomes are maintained over time and factors that influence the process. Further knowledge is needed about long-term post aftercare changes in abstinence-relapse cycles, cultural and social support factors as well as barriers, the nature of substance abuse resistance over time, how future developmental transitions are handled, and the recovery process in black participants who abuse drugs versus those who sell *and* abuse drugs. (Carroll, Rounsaville & Garwin, 1991; Nowinski, Baker & Carroll, 1995; Pratt & Gill, 1990; Woodhouse, 1990)

Effects of The Research Findings and Methodological Issues

These methodological and cultural limitations of research on black substance abuse and resistance have influenced important attitudes and decisions. Examples include program funding decisions, criminal justice policies, recommended treatment and prevention approaches, general resource allocations for black communities; mutual help within those communities; and media stereotypes that have politicized the problem and people's attitudes.

Effects on Media Stereotypes and Policy Decisions

Unfortunately, media coverage of the war on drugs has taken on the quality of a war against people and communities of color, and the poor.

Media sources include newspapers, magazines, television (including dramatic shows and coverage of research reports on this topic), movies, and popular music. These sources have influenced attitudes of the general public and policy makers in four important ways. First, media stereotypes of drug abusers and dealers reinforce ideas that people in poverty and ethnic groups of color commit most drug abuse, related violence, and other street crimes. Culturally-biased research reports, especially those about blacks and Hispanics, may be one source of these media stereotypes, while the media often ignore other research outcomes confirming that "most substance abusers and addicted people are white, most people who use substances are not poor, and most of the poor do not use drugs" (Freeman, 2001, p. 65).

In spite of these contrary findings, media stereotypes about people of color and poor people related to substance abuse may also influence sentencing patterns within the criminal justice system. Uniform federal mandatory sentencing guidelines were passed in 1992 to resolve social class, race, and other biases within the justice system (Greenfield, 1998). However, subsequent data have revealed that people in poverty, people of color, and women still have higher incarceration rates than affluent, white, male populations with the same drug possession charges (Beckerman & Fortana, 2001). One may assume that particular systemic or structural barriers are impeding uniform sentencing patterns across cultural and social class groups, including personal attitudes and biases that are, no doubt, reinforced by media.

A related media bias has led to a failure to report on white-collar drug-related crimes with a similar intensity. This lack of adequate media coverage helps to hide the extent and integration of such crimes into legitimate professions and industry, including law, transportation, banking and investment companies, real estate, and the collection of fine art and other assets as drug money laundering devices. Few policies and laws have either been enacted or implemented to address the many forms of drug-related white-collar crimes, in comparison to laws for street crimes in this area (Taylor, 1994). An explanation for these vastly different approaches to law enforcement is that drug-related white-collar crimes are largely invisible, thanks to the media. Moreover, these crimes are committed by a socially accepted, privileged, and powerful group that has the cultural respect of the media.

Finally, the media's concentration on the demand versus supply side of the drug problem perpetuates the myth that there are no structural aspects to this problem. Most research also focuses on demand reduction (treatment/prevention) strategies and outcomes, hence, the findings tend to reinforce the media's political decision to ignore the supply side and related ramifications. Media concentration on the demand reduction aspects is consistent with blaming individuals for this problem, such as people of color and the poor, and lamenting the costs to the country as a whole. In reality, however, this country's laws and policies provide more resources for supply-side programs, resulting in lackluster results that are generally ignored by the media. Saunders (1995) notes that "federal spending for the war on drugs has remained at about seventy percent for supply-side programs and (only) thirty percent for demand-side programs" (p. 2338).

As local experts, black communities may have insights about such resource allocations, the social policies and media biases that support those inequities, and their unique cultural needs. However, because researchers and policy makers seldom solicit those insights from black participants, policies and media reports continue to focus on pathology and individual/cultural deficits. Chapin (1995) indicates that "Inclusion means public policy is more likely to reflect consumers' realities because they are on the policy making team" (p. 509), while exclusion maintains peoples' powerlessness and the social and political conditions that are risk factors for substance abuse.

Impact Upon Black Communities' Mutual-Help Efforts

Members of black communities read these same culturally-biased media reports and experience the negative effects of biased criminal justice and treatment policies. These communities are not only affected by the inadequacy of resources allocated to address risk factors that are common to substance abuse, violence, unemployment, lack of economic development opportunities, inadequate housing, and health problems. However, many of these communities are also affected by a loss of hope, general self-sufficiency, and quality of life.

Other black communities have used media and policy biases to mobilize their members to resist the seductive power of the implied negative messages. These community mobilization or mutual-help efforts are based on the reframing of such messages as opportunities to redefine substance abuse as a community problem and solution. Examples of black communities' solutions have included the following mutual-help efforts, which need to be documented/supported by culturally sensitive research:

1. Development of grass roots community-centered, culture-specific, substance abuse treatment and prevention programs for black communities.
2. Use of more comprehensive service approaches in those programs with a focus on health care and health promotion, employment and economic development, education, housing, legal issues, community service, African history and traditions, and cultural coping supports (e.g., meditation, exercise, healing rituals).
3. Establishment of specialized black substance abuse prevention materials for key children's settings and needs, such as black Sunday School or religious school curricula and conflict resolution materials for black boys and girls clubs.
4. Integration of 12-step programs into the normal life of black communities, including churches, community centers, health clinics, political clubs, and housing developments.
5. Creation of drug-free transitional housing in black communities for recovering people in aftercare, particularly for women with children, with more realistic definitions of transitional periods (ranging from 1–4 years).

Proposed Framework for Black Substance Abuse Research

Life Span Assumptions and Conceptual Framework

The life span perspective provides a strong set of assumptions and a conceptual framework for guiding researchers in conducting more culturally-sensitive studies on black substance abuse. It normalizes and draws attention to the context in which black participants resist and recover from drugs, including developmental, cultural, and political aspects of this context.

Developmental Aspects of This Context. In terms of the developmental aspects, this perspective focuses on normal (nonpathological) life changes and processes. It assumes that life is a series of transitions, events, and processes that occur at particular points, subject to unpredictable sequences, and affected by unexpected disruptions and disorders (Berger, McBreen, & Rifkin, 1996). Blacks and other individuals can exhibit growth, resilience, or mere survival, as well as unique responses to and ways of coping with those changes. The life span perspective assumes normal developmental transitions present opportunities for such growth, and that response variations are based on "Cultural and historical contexts, variations in sexual orientations, and the influence of poverty and oppression" (Germain, 1994, p. 259). Researchers need to explore how black participants understand and respond to normal developmental transitions as a context for their ability to resist or recover from substance abuse.

Cultural Aspects. Building on these developmental aspects, assumptions about the cultural context emphasize attention to black people's narratives about important life span events and how culture shapes their meanings and beliefs about those events. Those stories may also reveal culturally-biased environmental barriers that black people believe inhibit their opportunities to grow from life span transitions. Hence, those stories can be sources of cultural information for researchers about black participants' substance abuse patterns over the life course, reactions to chronic losses, resilience, and supportive traditions.

Political Aspects. This life span perspective also helps researchers to focus on issues of social equity and justice as part of the political context, a reality that confronts black participants on a daily basis. The perspective can help researchers raise questions about policies and practices that inhibit recovery and resistance, that reinforce self-medication as a method for coping with the underlying racial stress, along with those that support recovery and resistance. Using this perspective means that researchers should be skilled in eliciting such information, because black participants may blame themselves solely for their substance abuse problems, without acknowledging contributing environmental factors. Or they might believe the assumptions of traditional colorblind treatment approaches, that to consider the role of those contributing factors means excusing the individual's responsibility for the abuse (Freeman, 2001). This perspective also requires that research focus on whether programs under study address social equity and justice issues related to participants' life span transitions as part of prevention and treatment, or whether they are colorblind.

An Example of Life-Span Substance Abuse Research

This discussion about the context, aims, and benefits of life span research provide a useful background for the following research example.

This example addresses some of the cultural sensitivity and methodological limitations of research described in a previous section. It also includes attention to the developmental, cultural, and political context of the black participants in the study, related to the normative life span perspective. The research methodology and outcomes are included in this discussion.

The Research Methodolgy. Table 7.1 reflects the methodology for this research example focused on black adults in recovery. The research objectives are framed from a culturally centered life span perspective, including key events and the effects. The research design and sampling strategy are consistent with a focus on the participants' stories about recovery within the context of other life span transitions (qualitative time series design), involving participants who met the criteria of being a black adult in treatment (convenience sample). These participants were part of a larger national sample of twelve treatment and five prevention programs. Eight of those programs were coed and four were for women only (Freeman, 2001). Table 7.1 indicates the identified sub sample includes seventy-five participants in four of those coed treatment programs; a majority of them were poly-addicted and had multiple treatment admissions. The identified research procedures focused on local knowledge from the expert participants, emphasizing the importance of their voices, realities, meaning, life span experiences, and their cultural transitions and strengths.

The Research Outcomes. These outcomes are reported in four main areas: (1) The participants' views of life span events/issues, (2) How they defined coping and resilience, (3) The effects of culture on those attributes/strengths, and (4) Supports and barriers to their coping. Interestingly, many participants viewed recovery as a life-changing period or transition, as part of their ongoing life course. They believed that as a life transition, recovery brought to the surface past unsuccessful or incomplete developmental transitions (past "screw-ups"), such as not establishing a positive black identity. Their natural focus on history (past transitions) and culture (ethnic and family substance abuse patterns) is consistent with definitions of life span transitions and the life course from the literature. This finding goes beyond those definitions, however, because it reframes recovery as an important part of the life course of these participants. The meaning they identified from that reframe is that addiction and other life events such as deaths, parenthood,

Table 7.1 Methodology: A Life-Span Research Case Study

Areas of Methodology	How Areas Were Addressed in Research Case Study
Research Objectives:	1)Identify key life span transitions and their effects on the participants' addiction and recovery. 2)Define and identify effects of coping and resilience on recovery. 3)Clarify effects of supports and barriers on coping-resilience during transitions and recovery. 4)Explore the role of culture on participants' coping and resilience during addiction and recovery.
Research Design:	Qualitative, time series, organizational design
Sampling Strategy:	Convenience sample
Sub Samples:	N=75 (30 females and 45 males), receiving services in 4 black or predominantly black coed treatment programs. Most were poly-addicted; 87% had been in rehab 2 or more times; all had different combinations of multiple employment, legal, family, housing, and health problems
Research Procedures:	1)Narrative inquiry: stories about life transitions/coping and related local knowledge 2)Focus groups: Sessions for planning research Member checking sessions (pre-testing, data analysis, dissemination strategies) 3)Ethnographic interviews: Participants/social supports 4)Direct observation of rehab groups/12 step meetings

relationship break-ups, and hence recovery, happened for a reason. Many believe they are or will be better African Americans and individuals as a consequence. Often, participants also reframed their survival from addiction by drawing upon various cultural and personal strengths, as evidence of thriving, of a miracle based on the difficulties they had encountered.

Participants identified a range of sources for their coping and resilience examples. Two main sources were the new meanings and interpretations they were able to develop about their narratives or stories and the self-knowledge they gained from those reinterpretations. Some were able to reframe many of their old "war stories" about how they became addicted to stories about how they survived and the cultural strengths that contributed to their survival, including key mentors (a grandmother) and attributes (cultural humor). Their enhanced self-knowledge often led to a redefinition of themselves as recovering individuals who are worthy of cultural and personal respect, and so the process also enhanced their self-value. Other sources of coping involved knowledge gained about relapse triggers and tools and their application to daily life; understanding, believing in, and making good choices (they had learned how to make mistakes and were good at that); problem-solving skills such as consulting mentors; and a sense of power (a natural high) from successfully using these and other skills.

Some participants were able to identify how culture has affected their coping and resilience, primarily those who were in later aftercare phases of treatment. Having personal and racial shame validated by peers and staff improved their coping and reinforced trust of their own reactions. Another support involved assuming cultural responsibility by doing community service as a form of giving back to communities they had taken from during their addiction. Giving back activities, such as black voter registration, community trash clean-ups, and participation in the Million Man March in Washington, D.C., often helped to restore some of their cultural pride. Those activities frequently made it possible for black participants to repair family, peer, and community relationships that they had harmed during addiction, and to recreate sober cultural supports and networks so essential for their recovery.

Finally, a number of participants were able to identify supports and barriers to these examples of improved coping. At a personal level, some of their supports included cultural pride, a belief in God, or spirituality; while barriers involved "stinking thinking (negativity or believing they can take drugs again without being addicted) and loss of hope. At the interpersonal level, some participants identified cultural resources as supports, including a black or multicultural 12-step group and family support. Barriers included intergenerational drug use by family members and peers and stressful relationship cut-offs, as well as the challenge of staying away from those relationships which, though risky for recovery, were still desirable in some ways. Not surprisingly, some participants identified systems level supports and barriers related to their recovery. For example, safe drug-free transitional housing and having a medical card were high priority supports. On the other hand, resource gaps such as a lack of transitional housing, cultural or gender insensitivity by the treatment program or social agencies, and power games (blaming) were identified as disempowering for their recovery.

Life Span Research Principles

A number of specific research principles can be inferred from this example, for improving the cultural sensitivity of black substance abuse studies. These principles are intended as guidelines rather than inflexible rules, based on the developmental, cultural, and political context previously discussed regarding the life span perspective. In substance abuse studies with African American participants, researchers should:

1. Develop a repertoire of prompts to elicit definitions and examples of coping, resilience, and other strengths related to life span transitions and recovery, in recognition that some participants' perspectives about these factors may be affected by their ethnic identity stage, low racial and self-esteem, or stigma about addiction from negative media coverage and treatment staff attitudes.
2. Explore examples of coping and resiliency and related supports and barriers with these participants at the interpersonal and large systems levels, in addition to the personal level, to avoid a culturally biased data collection and analysis process.
3. Allow participants to recount significant experiences in their own words (narratives) and discuss the meaning of those experiences for recovery as a source of rich cultural data that may not emerge from a sole use of direct questions about culture.
4. Use a culturally sensitive approach to identify and elicit information about life span developmental tasks that these participants consider to be essential for their successful recovery from an African American perspective.

5. Explore and analyze whether treatment programs provide skill-based life span interventions that address the participants' life transition needs and their reactions to power cut-offs, inequitable policies, and other social justice issues.
6. Finally, select research paradigms and methods that emphasize a participatory, ethnographic, and culturally-sensitive process to encourage black participants to reexamine, heal, and bring closure to the life transitions they are concerned about.

CONCLUSION

The life span research principles in the previous discussion underscore the importance of structuring the research process so that it provides opportunities for African Americans in recovery to empower themselves. In part, enhanced empowerment opportunities are a natural byproduct when researchers embrace a life span developmental perspective. That perspective helps to create a normative and non-blaming environment in which black research participants are acknowledged as local experts on their experiences and recovery. The use of a cultural awareness approach is another part of what helps to create a nonblaming environment, in contrast to a colorblind approach. Only by involving black participants throughout the process of research planning, design, data collection, analysis, and dissemination, is it possible to effectively limit cultural bias by researchers. At the same time, this approach can help to establish researchers' trustworthiness in very tangible and observable ways with African Americans in recovery.

REFERENCES

Amuleru-Marshall, O. (1991). African-Americans. In J. Kinney (Ed.), *Clinical manual of substance abuse*. St. Louis, MO: Mosby Year Books.

Anderson, S.C. (1995). Alcohol abuse. In R.L. Edwards (Ed.), *Encyclopedia of social work (19th Edition)* (pp. 203–215). Washington, DC: National Association of Social Workers.

Baker, F.M. & Bell, C. (1999). Issues in psychiatric treatment of African Americans. *Psychiatric Services, 50,* 362–368.

Banks, R. (1997). Race, representation, and the drug policy agenda. In C. Herring (Ed.), *African Americans and the public agenda: The paradoxes of public policy* (pp. 209–223). Thousand Oaks, CA: Sage.

Beckerman, A. & Fortana, L. (2001). Issues of race and gender in court-ordered substance abuse treatment. *Journal of Offender Rehabilitation, 33*(4), 45–61.

Berger, R.L., McBreen, J.T., and Rifkin, M.J. (1996). *Human behavior: A perspective for the helping professions.* White Plains, NY: Longman.

Brisbane, F.L. (1985). Using contemporary fiction with black children and adolescents in alcohol treatment. *Alcoholism Treatment Quarterly, 2,* 179–197.

Carroll, K.M., Rounsaville, B.J., and Garwin, E.J., (1991). A comparative trial of psychotherapies for ambulatory cocaine abusers: Relapse prevention and interpersonal psychotherapy. *American Journal of Drug and Alcohol Abuse, 17,* 221–247.

Chang, V.N. (1993). Prevent and empower: A student-to-student strategy with alcohol abuse. *Social Work in Education, 15,* 207–213.

Chapin, R.K. (1995). Social policy development: The strengths perspective. *Social Work, 40,* 483–495.

Clifford, P.R. & Jones, W. (1988). Alcohol abuse prevention issues and the Black community. *Evaluation and Health Professions, 11,* 272–277.

Curtis-Boles, H. & Jenkins Monroe, V. (2000). Substance abuse in African American women. *Journal of Black Psychology, 26,* 450–469.

Dunlap, E., Johnson, B.D., & Rath, J.W. (1996). Aggression and violence in households of crack sellers/abusers. *Applied Behavioral Science Review, 4,* 191–217.

Fagan, J., & Stevenson, H. (1995). Men as teachers: A self-help program on parenting for African American men. *Social Work with Groups, 17,* 29–42.

Fitzpatrick, J.L. and Gerard, K. (1993). Community attitudes toward drug use: The need to assess community norms. *International Journal of the Addictions, 28,* 947–957.

Freeman, E.M. (1991). Social competence as a framework for addressing ethnicity and teenage alcohol problems. In A.R. Stiffman & L.E. Davis (Eds.), *Ethnic issues in adolescent mental health* (pp. 247–266). Newbury Park, CA: Sage.

Freeman, E.M. (1992). The use of storytelling techniques with African American males: Implications for substance abuse treatment. *Journal of Intergroup Relations, 29,* 53–72.

Freeman, E.M. (1993). Developing alternative family structures for runaway, drug-addicted adolescents. In E.M. Freeman (Ed.), *Substance abuse treatment: A family systems perspective* (pp. 48–70). Newbury Park, CA: Sage.

Freeman, E.M. (1999, January). Culturally sensitive research on African Americans and culturally-specific treatment programs. Paper presented at the Society for Social Work & Research Conference. Austin, Texas.

Freeman, E.M. (2001). *Substance abuse intervention, prevention, rehabilitation, and systems change strategies: Helping individuals, families, and groups to empower themselves.* NY: Columbia University Press.

Gilbert, L., El Bassel, N. Schilling, R.F., & Friedman, E. (1997). Childhood abuse as a risk for partner abuse among women in methadone maintenance. *American Journal of Drug and Alcohol Abuse, 23,* 581–595.

Germain, C. (1994). Emerging conceptualizations of family development over the life course. *Families in Society: Journal of Contemporary Human Services, 75,* 259–267.

Gordon, A. and Zrull, M. (1991). Social networks and recovery: One year after in-patient treatment. *Journal of Substance Abuse Treatment, 8,* 143–152.

Gordon, J.U. (1993). A culturally specific approach to ethnic minority young adults:

In E.M. Freeman (Ed.), *Substance abuse treatment: A family systems perspective* (71–99). Newbury Park, CA: Sage.

Gray, M.C. (1995). Drug abuse. In R.L. English (Ed.), *Encyclopedia of social work (19th Edition)* (pp. 795–803). Washington, DC: National Association of Social Workers.

Greenfield, L. A. (Ed.). (1998). *Alcohol and crime: An analysis of national data on the prevalence of alcohol involvement in crime.* Prepared for the Assistant Attorney General's National Symposium on Alcohol and Crime. Washington, DC: U. S. Department of Justice.

Hansen, W. (1988). Effective school-based approaches to drug abuse prevention. *Education Leadership, 12,* 9–14.

Harper, F.D. (1991). Substance abuse and the black American family. *Urban Research Review, 13,* 1–5.

Herd, D. (1986). A review of drinking patterns and alcohol problems among U.S. blacks. *Report of the secretary's task force on black and minority health* (pp. 77–132). Vol. 7 of Chemical dependency and diabetes. Washington, DC: U.S. Department of Health and Human Services.

Hutchison, I.W. (1999). Alcohol, fear, and woman abuse. *Sex Roles, 40,* 893–920.

Johnston, L.D., O'Malley, P.M., & Bachman, J.G. (1999). *Drug trends in 1999 are mixed.* University of Michigan News and Information Services. Ann Arbor, MI: {On Line}. Available: www.monitoring the future.org: Accessed 4/27/2000.

Kaminer, Y. (1991). Adolescent substance abuse. In R.J. Frances and S.I. Miller (Eds.), *Clinical textbook of addictive disorders* (pp. 320–346). NY: Guilford.

Kammer, R.E. (2002). Predictors of black and Hispanic women's involvement in Alcoholics Anonymous and Narcotics Anonymous. *Dissertation Abstracts International: The Humanities and Social Sciences, 63*(4), 1558-A.

Malekoff, A. (1994). Action research: An approach to preventing substance abuse and promoting social competency. *Health and Social Work, 19,* 45–53.

Malloy, D. (1989). Peer intervention: An exploratory study. *Journal of Drug Issues, 19,* 319–336.

Moore, S.E. (2001). Substance abuse treatment with adolescent African American males: Reality Therapy with an Afrocentric approach. *Journal of Social Work Practice in the Addictions, 1*(2), 21–32.

National Institute on Drug Abuse (1987). *Drug abuse among ethnic minorities* (DHHS Publication No. ADM 87–1474). Washington, DC: U.S. Government Printing Office.

National Institute on Drug Abuse (1992). *Annual emergency room data: Data from the Drug Abuse Warning Network.* Rockville, MD: U. S. Department of Health and Human Services.

National Institute on Drug Abuse (1993a). *National household survey on drug abuse: Population estimates 1992.* Washington, DC: U.S. Department of Health and Human Services.

National Institute on Drug Abuse (1993b). *National survey results on drug use from the monitoring the future study,* 1975–1992 (NIH Publication No. 93–3597). Rockville, MD: U.S. Department of Health and Human Services.

Nowinski, J., Baker, S., and Carroll, K. (1995). Twelve-step facilitation therapy manual: A research guide for therapists treating individuals with alcohol abuse and dependence. Rockville, MD: U.S. Department of Health and Human Services, Public Health Service, National Institute of Health, National Institute on Alcohol Addiction and Abuse.

Office of Substance Abuse Prevention (1991). *Prevention plus III.* (DHHS Publication No. ADM 91–1817). Washington, DC: U. S. Government Printing Office.

Oliver, W. (1989). Black males and social problems: Prevention through Africentric socialization. *Journal of Black Studies, 20,* 15–39.

Plutchik, A., & Plutchik, R. (1988). Psychosocial correlates of alcoholism. *Integrative Psychiatry, 6,* 205–210.

Pratt, C.W., and Gill, K. (1990). Sharing research knowledge to empower people who are chronically mentally ill. *Psychosocial Rehabilitation Journal, 13,* 75–79.

Primm, B.J. (1992). Future outlook: Treatment improvement. Unpublished paper. Washington, DC: National Institute of Drug Abuse.

Rowe, D. & Grills, C. (1993). African-centered drug treatment: An alternative conceptual paradigm for drug counseling with African American clients. *Journal of Psychoactive Drugs, 25,* 21–31.

Saunders, D.N. (1995). Substance abuse: Federal, state, and local policies. In R.L. Edwards (Ed.), *Encyclopedia of Social Work, 19th Edition* (2338–2347). Washington, DC: National Association of Social Workers.

Schoenborn, C.A. (1991). Exposure to alcoholism in the family: United States, 1988. *Advance Data, 205,* 1–13.

Smyth, N.J. (1995). Substance abuse: Direct practice. In R.L. Edwards (Ed.), *Encyclopedia of social work (19th Edition)* (pp. 2328–2338). Washington, DC: National Association of Social Workers.

Stephens, T., Braithwaite, R.L., & Taylor, S.E. (1998). Model for using hip-hop music for small group HIV/AIDS prevention counseling with African American adolescents and young adults. *Patient Education and Counseling, 35,* 127–137.

Stewart, C. (2002). Family factors of low-income African American youth associated with substance abuse: An exploratory analysis. *Journal of Ethnicity in Substance Abuse, 1*(1), 97–111.

Substance Abuse and Mental Health Services Administration (1999). *National household survey on drug abuse: Main findings 1999.* Washington, DC: Department of Health and Human Services.

Taylor, J. (1994). Rules on electronic transfers of money are being tightened by U.S. Treasury (Economy). *The Wall Street Journal, XCIV,* (26 September), A2.

Treadway, D.C. (1989). *Before its too late: Working with substance abusers in the family.* NY: Norton.

U.S. Department of Health and Human Services (1990, September). Alcohol and other drug use is a special concern for African American families and communities. In *The fact is. . . . Washington, DC: Author.*

Vontress, C.E., & Epp, L.R. (1997). Historical hostility in the African American client: Implications for counseling. *Journal of Multicultural Counseling and Development, 25,* 170–184.

Wallace, B.C. (1991). *Crack cocaine: A practical treatment approach for the chemically dependent.* NY: Brunner/Mazel.

Walton, M.A., Blow, F.C., & Booth, M. (2001). Diversity in relapse prevention needs: Gender and race comparisons among substance abuse treatment patients. *The American Journal of Drug and Alcohol Abuse, 27*(2), 225–240.

Washington, O.G.M. & Moxley, D.P. (2001). The use of prayer in group work with African American women recovering from chemical dependency. *Families in Society, 82*(1), 49–59.

Willenbring, M.L., Ridgely, M.S., Stinchfield, R., & Rose, M. (1991). *Application of case management in alcohol and drug dependence: Matching techniques and populations* (DHHS Publication No. ADM 01–1766). Washington, DC: U.S. Government Printing Office.

Woodhouse, L. (1990). An exploratory study of the use of life history methods to determine treatment needs for female substance abusers. *Response, 13*, 12–15.

Yeich, S. and Levine, R. (1992). Participatory research's contribution to a conceptualization of empowerment. *Journal of Applied Social Psychology, 22*, 1894–1908.

Zelvin, E. (1993). Treating the partners of substance abusers. In S.L. Straussner (Ed.), *Clinical work with substance-abusing clients* (p. 196–213). NY: Guilford.

Zule, W.A., Flannery, B.A., Wechsberg, W.M. & Lam, W.K. (2002). Treatment issues of African Americans in recovery. *The American Journal of Drug and Alcohol Abuse, 28*(3), 525–544.

Chapter 8

AFRICAN AMERICAN YOUTHS: PROMOTING EDUCATIONAL ACHIEVEMENT AND CULTURALLY-SENSITIVE RESEARCH THROUGH THE STRENGTHS PERSPECTIVE

PAULA ALLEN-MEARES

This chapter explores the literature and research on the educational achievement and outcomes of African American students in the wake of recent educational trends. Furthermore, it examines emerging and continuing societal, environmental, and school factors that have been documented as impediments to students' educational progress. Much has already been written about the need to reform schooling in America and the failure of many of our youths to achieve (*Nation at Risk,* 1983). Much of this discussion has focused on increasing standards and assessing competencies at specific stages of schooling, while too little attention has been paid to factors that contribute to poor academic performance and the tracking of students along race, socioeconomic and gender lines (Allen-Meares & Fraser [forthcoming]; Allen-Meares, Washington, & Welsh, 1996), or to the quality of research in this area.

This chapter provides an overview of the current status of African American youths' educational performance in selected areas, the role of poverty and educational practices in preventing their full intellectual development according to research, and the various theoretical frameworks and perspectives useful for understanding the unique strengths of these youths, their families and communities. Some general guidelines or approaches for improving research in this area are also presented. As Murrell (1994) argues, we desperately need to promote an understanding of the unique cultural practices of the African American community in order to develop effective teaching strategies:

> Educators are not likely to develop a pedagogical knowledge base of critical aspects of class and culture for minority group learners unless a theory is developed that addresses how these students make sense of the curriculum in the context of their unique racial, ethnic, cultural, and political identities. . . . This necessitates that teachers acquire a deep understanding of the discourse routines and dynamics of the educational settings these students find themselves in. (p. 556)

Environmental Impact on Students' Performance

Interaction of Social, Educational, Political, and Economic Factors

It is well known that schooling in America has advanced the economic and political well-being of selected groups, too often at the expense of those belonging to a racial and/or ethnic group underrepresented in the power hierarchy. In the past, public rhetoric and–to some degree–legislation have declared that the educational system should promote equal opportunity. Bowles and Gintis (1976), however, argue that, rhetoric aside, American education has always served the needs of capitalism by perpetuating the inequality of the status quo:

> Education in the United States plays a dual role in the social process whereby surplus value, i.e., profit, is created and expropriated. On the one hand, by imparting technical and social skills and appropriate motivations, education increases the productive capacity of workers. On the other hand, education helps defuse and depoliticize the potentially explosive class relations of the production process, and thus serves to perpetuate the social, political, and economic conditions through which a portion of the product of labor is expropriated in the form of profits . . . Schools foster legitimate inequality through the ostensibly meritocratic manner by which they reward and promote students. They create and reinforce patterns of social class, racial, and sexual identification. (p. 11)

Despite our knowledge of the various factors contributing to unequal academic achievement, some scholars insist that all children have the same opportunity to learn and achieve, and that schools have the ability to offer this opportunity effectively (Bloom, 1976; Edmonds, 1983). Some of these scholars implicitly blame poor African American children and their families for their unfavorable educational outcomes in comparison to their white counterparts. We have even seen a resurgence of the genetic explanation for poor academic performance with the publication of The Bell Curve (Hermstein & Murray, 1994). These authors suggest that intelligence is more a function of genetics than environment, and that success in life is tied to "good genes" that yield a higher IQ. Under their survival-of-the-fittest schema, poverty, divorce, poor parenting, institutional racism, and school failure are all genetically determined, so that only those of low intelligence experience these social problems.

These authors blatantly ignore the influence of environmental conditions on academic, economic and social success, particularly for African American youth and other youth of color. Poor academic performance is all too often the result of such social and economic factors as poverty, racism, sexism, inadequate health care, and educational policies, practices, and curricula that either push these pupils out or relegate them to second-class citizenship and opportunity. Research has shown that development and achievement cannot be viewed as fixed or predetermined by genetics; instead multiple determinants—including environmental conditions—impact developmental outcomes.

Racism: Separate is not Equal in America

For African Americans, racism is one of the foremost environmental factors impacting childhood development and individual achievement, profoundly influencing each child as she/he comes to terms with both institutional and individual racism. African American children not only face limited opportunities for success; they themselves learn to doubt their abilities as they internalize racist ideology. Racism has influenced research on educational achievement as well: as Perry (1993) convincingly argues, past attempts to develop an explanatory model for African American school achievement have focused disproportionately on the fact of failure rather than the reasons for failure. In order to uncover some of the reasons for poor academic performance among African American students, we need to examine the persistent denial of educational opportunity to African Americans, from the time of slavery to the present.

African Americans have struggled for centuries to achieve equal educational opportunity in the U.S. In the nineteenth century, educating slaves was a crime. After slavery was abolished, African Americans no longer faced the same legal barriers to education, but new Jim Crow barriers were created to insure that the education they received was not the same as that of their Caucasian counterparts. *Plessy v. Ferguson* (1896)[1] enunciated this doctrine of separate but equal which, when applied to education, sanctioned the development of two entirely separate and inequitable systems of education.

Plessy v. Ferguson was not overturned until 1954 when, in *Brown v. the Board of Education*,[2] the Supreme Court ruled that state-mandated public school segregation on the basis of race was inherently unequal and therefore unconstitutional. The differential effects of segregation on minority children, in particular the impact on their self-worth, motivation, and learning opportunities, were cited as the basis for outlawing this practice. The Brown decision was the beginning of three decades of U.S. policy designed to overhaul the segregated—and therefore unequal—educational system. The policies enacted were often controversial, as the public demonstrations over school busing and desegregation attest.

However, during the 1970s and early 1980s the general public appeared to value racial integration and equal educational opportunity for vulnerable groups of pupils, and was relatively open to experiments such as busing, magnet schools, and the development of other compensatory programs. Nancy St. John (1975), in an analysis of conditions that determined successful school desegregation identified the following as variables that led to successful integration: black self-determination; no discrimination by administrative and school staff; equal access of blacks and whites to high quality educational programs; a commitment to pluralism; within-school integration, and individualized instruction.

In later years, however, America has frighteningly slipped backward, and antibusing sentiments and the "separate but equal" doctrine have become more pronounced in public rhetoric and in law/legislation. Through a series of adroit political manipulations, antibusing proponents have met with some success, including the landmark decision

---

1. *Plessy v. Ferguson* itself was concerned with maintaining separate railway carriages in Louisiana, but the case gave rapid rise to a host of segregated systems and institutions.

2. *Brown v. Board of Education of Topeka,* 347 U.S. 483 (1954).

of *Freeman v. Pitts* (1992),[3] which ruled that school districts are under no requirement to remedy a racial imbalance caused by demographic factors. This decision declares that it is not unconstitutional to have a majority of either African Americans or white pupils in a particular school if the majority is a function of neighborhood patterns, although such patterns often exist because of unacknowledged institutionalized racism in the housing area.

Gary Orfield (1978), a leading expert on school desegregation, systematically analyzed records of court decisions and congressional and state agencies, and concluded that little has actually been accomplished by desegregating our schools. He found that the recent movement towards resegregation and the retreat from both the magnet school concept and voluntary desegregation has undermined our progress toward integration. Orfield views busing as one strategy to integrate our nation's schools, but the U.S. has seemingly abandoned it as a strategy to eliminate racial isolation.

The Effects of Poverty

A history of limited educational opportunity is not the only burden shouldered by today's African American children; all too often they also struggle under poverty. In 1990, it was estimated that 12.7 million children under the age of eighteen years lived below the poverty level (Bureau of Census, 1990). Children of color were three times as likely as white children to be poor, and their parents were most often members of the working poor and/or welfare dependent. Chan and Rueda (1979) point out that poverty has a detrimental influence on parent-child relationships and learning. Chronic unemployment or underemployment can negatively influence parents' mental health and thus the quality of their interactions with their children; the home and community environment can lack educational opportunities and resources; and nutritional deprivation can cause fatigue, inattentiveness, and illness. Minority children, particularly those of African American heritage are more likely to live in poverty as a result of racial discrimination within the opportunity structure of America.

---

3. *Freeman v. Pitts* Supreme Court Decision (1992). In Bierlen (1993) *Controversial issues in educational policy.* Newbury CT: Sage Publications.

Unfortunately, poverty and inadequate education are often mutually reinforcing, as Ogbu (1986) has noted:

> . . . not only does American society provide blacks with inferior education, which contributes to inferior performance, but blacks also receive fewer economic and other rewards in the form of employment status, level, and type of employment, and wages. This experience also contributes to lower school performance. (p. 42)

The review of the literature and research that follows provides an up-to-date assessment of the educational achievement of African American students, conceptual perspectives used to develop educational programs and initiatives, the strengths perspective, and what schools can do to facilitate the academic development of these pupils.

An Analysis of the Research Literature

Some Positive Trends in African American Achievement

American educational policy has failed to reach its goal of equal educational opportunity for all; African American students, disproportionately poor and often environmentally deprived, continue to lag behind in overall academic achievement. There are some recent indications that African Americans have made some educational gains, however, in spite of this well-established achievement gap between white and racial/ethnic minority students. Table 8.1 and corresponding Figures 8.1–8.3 show national data collected by the federal government comparing students' reading achievement levels and the SAT scores of African American students with their white and Latino counterparts. As indicated in Table 8.1, reading achievement among African American children has steadily increased over the past two decades at a rate faster than that of white students. This holds true for nine, thirteen, and seventeen-year-olds and has served to reduce the reading achievement gap between black and white students, although the gap remains significant. For reasons that are not clear, in late years the rate of increase in reading achievement has leveled off for African American students and even decreased for seventeen-year-old students. The same is true for the math achievement of African American students.

Furthermore, the dropout rate among African American students has shown a steady decline. In 1970, the rate was thirty percent for African

Table 8.1 Average Student Proficiency in Reading, By Age and Selected Characteristics of Students: 1971 to 1992

Selected characteristics Of students	9-Year-Olds						13-Year-Olds						17-Year-Olds					
	1971	1980	1984	1988	1990	1992	1971	1980	1984	1988	1990	1992	1971	1980	1984	1988	1990	1992
Total	208	215	211	212	209	211	255	259	257	258	257	250	285	286	289	290	290	290
Sex																		
-Male	201	210	208	208	204	206	250	254	253	252	251	254	279	282	284	286	284	284
-Female	214	220	214	216	215	215	261	263	262	263	263	265	291	289	294	294	297	296
Race/ethnicity																		
-White	214	221	218	218	217	218	261	264	263	261	262	266	291	293	295	295	297	297
-Black	170	189	186	189	182	185	222	233	236	243	242	238	239	243	264	274	267	261
-Hispanic	*	190	187	194	189	192	*	237	240	240	238	239	*	261	268	271	273	271
Parental Education																		
-Not h.s. grad.	189	193	195	193	193	195	238	239	240	247	241	239	261	262	269	267	270	271
-Graduated hs	208	213	209	211	209	207	256	254	253	253	251	252	283	278	281	282	283	281
-Post h.s.	224	226	223	220	218	220	270	271	268	265	267	270	302	299	301	300	300	299
Control of School																		
-Public	<<	214	209	210	208	209	<<	257	255	256	255	257	<<	285	287	289	287	288
-Private	<<	227	223	223	228	225	<<	271	271	268	270	276	<<	298	303	300	311	310

(*): Test scores of Hispanics were not tabulated separately during the identified years.

(<<): Data not available during the identified years.

Table 8.1 (continued)

Selected characteristics of students	9-Year-Olds						13-Year-Olds						17-Year-Olds					
	1971	1980	1984	1988	1990	1992	1971	1980	1984	1988	1990	1992	1971	1980	1984	1988	1990	1992
Community type:																		
-Advantaged urban	230	233	231	222	227	234	273	277	275	266	270	281	306	301	302	301	300	303
-Disadvantaged urban	179	188	192	192	186	184	234	242	239	239	241	231	260	258	266	275	273	267
-Extreme rural	200	212	201	214	209	207	237	255	255	262	251	257	277	279	283	287	290	285
-Other	208	215	211	211	210	212	255	258	257	257	258	261	285	287	290	288	291	293
Regions:																		
-Northeast	213	221	216	215	217	218	261	260	260	259	259	265	291	286	292	295	296	297
-Southeast	194	210	204	207	197	199	245	253	256	258	256	254	271	281	285	286	285	278
-Central	215	217	215	218	213	216	260	266	259	256	257	264	291	287	290	291	294	294
-West	205	213	208	208	210	209	254	256	254	258	256	258	284	287	288	289	287	290

Note: These test scores are from the National Assessment of Educational Progress (NAEP). The NAEP scores have been evaluated at certain performance levels. A score of 300 implies an ability to find, understand, summarize, and explain relatively complicated literary and informational material. A score of 250 implies an ability to search for specific information, interrelate ideas, and make generalizations about literature, science, and social studies materials. A score of 200 implies an ability to understand, combine ideas, and make inferences based on short uncomplicated passages about specific or sequentially related information. A score of 150 implies an ability to follow brief written directions and carry out simple, discrete reading tasks. Scale ranges from 0 to 500.

Source: U.S. Department of Education, National Center for Education Statistics, National Assessment of Educational Progress, The Reading Report Card, 1971-88 and NAEP 1992 Trends in Academic Progress, by Education Testing Service.

Americans and fifteen percent for whites, but by the mid 1990s the rates had dropped to fifteen percent and ten percent respectively. The gap between white and African American SAT scores has closed slightly over the past twenty years, although it remains significant. While African American scores have risen slightly, white achievement has essentially remained unchanged.

Conceptual Frameworks or Strategies to Promote Academic Achievement

Overview. While there have been some gains in African American academic achievement, clearly additional strategies are needed to help these students reach their potential. The question before us *is:* Where can we be most effective in enhancing the well-being of these students? Knowing that institutions like the school are slow to change and to adopt new ways of operating, African Americans must look to other conditions and entities over which they can exert more control and influence. This does not mean that we should abandon efforts to address institutional racism, poverty, the inferiority of schools serving primarily minority communities, and other conditions that perpetuate the status quo. Instead, the author is suggesting that we seek to influence proximal factors/conditions that will in turn affect the short- and long-term outcomes for our children. No one answer exists for the failure of African American children to succeed, and the relative weight of contributing factors varies according to both the community and the individual. Recent social work research is increasingly using conceptual frameworks that tie the academic performance of African American students and other at-risk groups to the closeness of relationships between home, school, and community (Freeman & Pennekamp, 2002). These conceptual models from the research and practice literature provide insight into the impact that individuals can make on a child's educational outcome.

Ecology of Schooling Framework. In late years, there has been renewed interest in the ecology of schooling and the importance of relationships among school, home/families, and neighborhoods (Crowson & Boyd, 1993). Under this theoretical framework, communities and neighborhoods are viewed as critically important to a child's well-being, and the interactions/ transactions/relationships between schools,

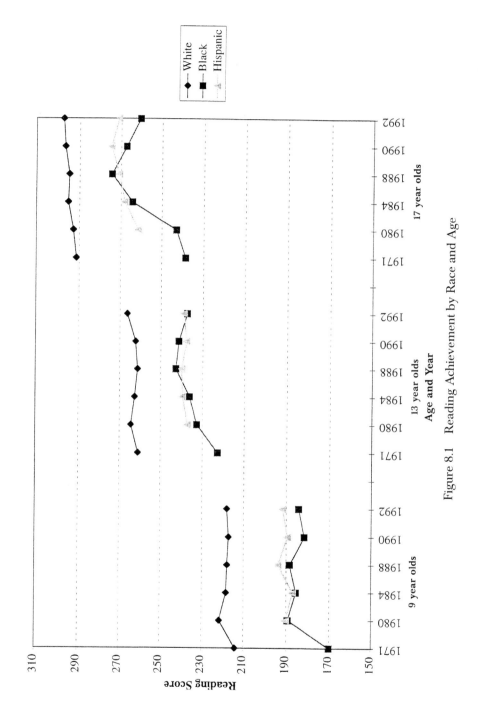

Figure 8.1   Reading Achievement by Race and Age

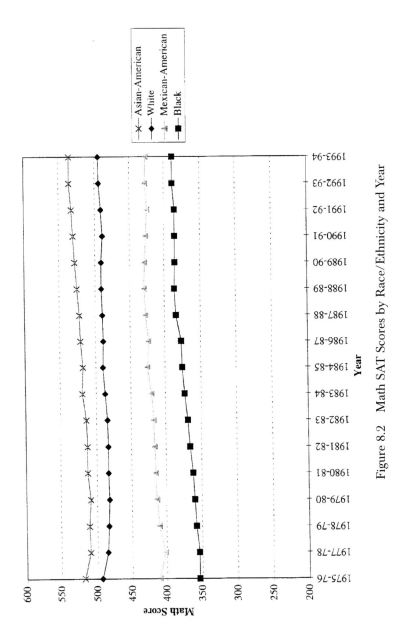

Figure 8.2   Math SAT Scores by Race/Ethnicity and Year

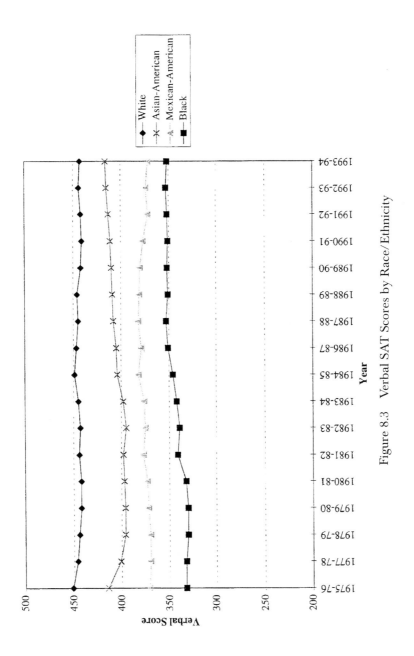

Figure 8.3   Verbal SAT Scores by Race/Ethnicity

neighborhoods, economic development, and the availability of health services play a major part in the child's development. The ecological perspective suggests that important entities in the student's immediate environment have a profound impact on learning and development (Freeman & Pennekamp, 2002).

An illustrative example of this perspective is the new school-linked service approach. This approach requires schools, human service agencies, parents, health services, and other relevant service providers to form partnerships to provide integrated services to children and their families. Collaboration and getting beyond agencies' organizational boundaries are the terms used to describe this approach (Freeman & Pennckamp, 2002).

Investment Perspective/Framework. Another point of view that has gained considerable recognition is the "investment" perspective in which education is seen as an investment in human capital that pays off in renewed economic and social strength. However, evidence is growing that investing in education alone for at-risk students does not yield significant results unless a concomitant investment is made in housing, health, family support programs, and community development services (Hawley, 1990).

An illustrative example of the investment perspective is when parents invest their time to participate in their child's education and in the decision-making process in school and related matters that bear on the educational program. On the mezzo and macro levels, this perspective advocates that the public invest or reinvest significant resources in schooling.

Child Development Perspective/Framework. James Comer has been the major developer of the child development emphasis in which schools are seen as caring institutions. Under this perspective, successful developmental outcomes for black children are closely tied to the extent to which home, family, and school share in children's social, moral and emotional development. Critical developmental pathways in the lives of children are rooted in home and family backgrounds, but these need to be merged effectively with developmental reinforcers found in the school. For example, Ianni (1989) speaks of the importance of schools and parents communicating "reinforcing messages to children," emphasizing the need for the partners to work together to promote the child's well-being and thus academic achievement.

Comer & Haynes (1992) have developed a specific model that includes coordination and cooperation among all adults concerned with the child's educational best interest. Regular meetings with parents and opportunities for their involvement in the governance of the school are critical components of the approach. Other aspects include a no-fault approach to decisions and training for the educational staff to promote understanding and a caring learning environment. Researchers have found that this program produced statistically significant improvements in students' reading and mathematics, behavior adjustments to school, self-concept, and positive classroom climate.

General Conceptual Frameworks Applied to African Americans

Cultural Relevance of These General Frameworks. The three-macro perspectives/frameworks discussed in the previous section on schools and the relationship between family and neighborhood/community can increase our understanding of some of the reasons for academic nonachievement. But how do they apply specifically to African American students? What cultural practices and norms among African American communities impact student achievement? How does the family–the primary agent for passing on values–differ in African American communities? What theories or perspectives can assist us to understand the functioning of the African American family? It is very clear that many of the proposed theories to date have failed to offer fruitful directions for intervention and for prevention of school failure among black children and youth.

The Strengths Perspective/Framework. This perspective or framework seems critically important to successful intervention and interaction of educators with African American parents/students/families. For educators to adopt this perspective is in contrast to the long-standing practice of targeting problems and pathologies onto this group, and then unilaterally trying to fix the problems. There is a growing body of literature and research that identifies specific strengths that must be acknowledged and built upon in service interventions to assist black children and to enhance their educational outcomes. High levels of familialism, including fictive kin networks, have been seen as characteristic of the African American family (Oyserman, Gant, & Ager, 1995). Familialism and discrimination, according to these authors, may function to make parent-adolescent relations in these families closer and more intimate. Further, African American identity is strongly rooted in three components–a sense of community, solidarity against racism, and the need for individual effort–all of which serve to increase school persistence and performance (Hill, 1995; Neisser, 1986; & Schultz, 1993).

Ford (1993) and Johnson (1992) found that the actual structure of African American families had a positive effect on children. New empirical evidence suggests that, contrary to popular perception, dysfunctional family structures are not primarily to blame for poor educational performance by African Americans. Hatchett and James (1993) found little support for the dysfunctional family stereotype; instead their research showed that these families have great intra- and extra-household extendedness, that this extendedness is a response to situational constraints in daily living, and that there is closeness or family solidarity. Family structure itself was not a reliable indicator of academic success; instead the family's quality of interaction, expectations, resources, and focus on academic behavior were much more significant indicators of African American student success.

Perhaps educators use family structure, race, and community conditions as excuses for their sometimes lack of institutional sensitivity to these students. A correlational study that examined relationships between socioeconomic advantage, achievement, motivation, and academic performance in 130 African American and Hispanic fourth–sixth graders found that urban teachers must demonstrate and communicate their belief in student ability to both the student and the parents. When intellectual potential is realized by both parents and children, motivation increases and student achievement scores rise.

The African American family and community have enormous strengths and capacities that too often go unrecognized. Without any analysis or examination, differences in African American families from the cultural "norm" have often been labeled disease, rather than seen as equally valid cultural practices. Littlejohn and Darling (1993) and Logan (1996) have promoted a strengths perspective on families rather than the deficit or pathological model. Littlejohn and Darling (1993) define family strengths as those relationships, patterns, interpersonal competencies, and social and psychological characteristics that create a sense of family identity (p. 461). While most of the literature on families is focused on Euro-American families, there is a growing body of literature that examines the African American family from a positive or strengths perspective.

Littlejohn and Darling (1993) also describe the strengths of African Americans as follows: a deep commitment to religion and spirituality, the willingness of the family to absorb others into the household of kin-structured networks, the substantial economic and moral support family members offer one another, and the ability of families to expand and to contract in response to both internal and external pressures. Others authors such as King & Hall (1982) note that African American parents provide their children with an important resource: information for negotiating social, economic, and educational systems both in the society as a whole and in the African American community. African American parents also teach their children to take pride in themselves and their accomplishments.

How do African American parents prepare their children for the continual stereotyping and discrimination that they will face? Marshall (1995) identifies essentially three basic types of ethnic socialization— (1) cultural experience; (2) minority experience; and (3) mainstream experience. African American parents usually focus on their minority experiences—specifically sharing with their children the struggle they have themselves experienced—in order to prepare their children to survive in a racist society (McAdoo, 2001).

Ethnic socialization is concerned with the intergenerational transmission of certain messages and behaviors from parents to their children, that relate to group identity, and the relationship between a group and the larger society (Marshall, 1995). It would appear that African American parents emphasize humanistic values over more ethnic specific values. Although Marshall's (1995) conclusions are called into question by the small sample size (58) and the inclusion only of middle-class African American children attending a predominantly white suburban elementary school, the findings are still very suggestive; the parents in the study did emphasize humanistic values. Some may find these findings problematic because they believed that cultural pride or ethnic specific values should be the priority for these parents. Perhaps the most immediate concern for these parents is providing an orientation to the daily struggle of being black in a white society and facilitating the bicultural adaptability of their children as they learn to live in two worlds.

African American parents socialize children to obtain the best from both worlds–the dominant culture and the African heritage–through survival techniques. According to some, parents will exhaust their resources to provide entry for their children into the economic and political structures (King & Hall, 1982). In other words, African American families, through the conceptual lens of a structural functionalist view, have adapted successfully to many difficult conditions over the decades. Managing to live in two worlds that frequently overlap or conflict can be an indicator of an ethnic group's adaptability and strength, rather than pathology.

African American Parental Involvement Framework. Since African American parents have a large impact on their children's emotional and social development, in order to formulate strategies to promote student achievement, the interactions between parents and the school need to be examined more closely. By and large, at least in the early years, the relationship between African American parents and the schools can be described as cooperative. A study that examined the effects of parental involvement in schooling on eighth grade achievement for a large representative sample of middle school students found little support for the conjecture that low socioeconomic parents were less involved in their children's schooling than those of higher economic status (Ho & Willms, 1996). Since parents of low socioeconomic status are disproportionately African American, these findings help to belie the myth of their disengagement from their children's education.

This study examined four components of parental involvement in education: (1) parent-child discussions about school activities, (2) parental monitoring of school activities, (3) parent-school personnel contact, and (4) parent volunteer activities and attendance at parent-teacher conferences. It was found that involvement at home, particularly in discussing school activities and helping children plan their programs, strongly spurred achievement. African American parents tended to have a slightly higher level of involvement than did whites on all dimensions, except school participation. Thus, contrary to popular belief, the lower tendency of African American parents to attend parent-teacher conferences regularly cannot be seen as evidence of a lack of concern or involvement, or as the strongest factor in their children's academic success.

African American families are often very supportive of the school. In a study that examined the influence of parental attitudes and behavior on scholastic and social adjustment of 729 low-income inner-city black children, ninety percent of these parents reported being satisfied with the quality of the school. The same percentage indicated that they held high educational expectations for their children. Contrary to media depictions, these low-income, urban parents held the same positive educational expectations for their children as other parents (Reynolds & Gill, 1994). From personal experience and through observation, the author of this chapter has similarly found black parents to be very supportive of the educational system. In my several years of experience as a school social worker, I have seen numerous instances in which the parent insisted that the child obey the educational staff and acknowledge its authority.

Given the strong impact African American families have on their children's attitudes toward schooling, a recent study is troubling because it shows that both the quality and quantity of parental contacts with the school decline as children age (Puma, Jones, Rock & Fernandez, 1993). During the first grade, fifty-two percent of the interactions between families and schools are positive (relating to the good academic performance of the child). But by the seventh grade, the proportion of positive contacts drops to thirty-six percent, and the proportion of negative contacts rises to thirty-three percent. The proportion of parents serving as volunteers drops as well. This evidence shows that over time the relationship between parents in general and the school becomes increasingly hostile; it is therefore not surprising if some African American students cease to value or respect the school.

To reverse this trend, Rioux and Berla (1993) emphasize the need to think beyond the ordinary ways in which parent-family involvement in education is considered and approached. Rutherford and Billig (1995) argue that schools have a tendency to keep certain parents at arms length as a way of buffering teachers and administrators from complaints and diverse ideas about educational practices. It is this pattern of buffering that undermines the development of cooperative working relationships between school personnel and African American families/parents. Rutherford and Billig also argue that building and fostering relationships with families/parents helps to improve the knowledge of both educators and families, builds upon everyone's strengths and leads to increased success for students.

SUMMARY: RECOMMENDED SCHOOL
IMPROVEMENTS FROM RESEARCH

Despite the growing amount of research on parent involvement and strengths in high-poverty urban schools and a number of practices to choose from, it is too early to say what works in the long-term and why. Iglesias (1992) points out that the present parent programs are a conglomerate of different approaches that differ in their goals, format, and durations. It is thus very difficult to compare research results and to draw firm conclusions.

Research has established some common factors that can positively impact African American parent-school relationships. Comer and Haynes (1992) describe five guiding principles for involving African American and low-income parents in schools:

- A no-fault approach (focusing not on who is to blame, but on what can be done);
- Coordination and cooperation among all adults concerned with the child's best educational interests;
- Decisions by consensus;
- Regular meetings; and
- Active involvement

Many federal and local programs aim to improve the academic achievement of urban and disadvantaged students by mandating a parent involvement component and providing funding for it. Research shows that Parent Centers in the schools have been especially successful; essentially, these parent centers are based on four principles. If these principles are adhered to, parents become empowered and their commitment to achieving educational objectives is enhanced:

- Parents plan their center;
- Personal contact among all team members promotes success;
- Everyone learns from everyone else, so that the parent center is seen as essential to the school's operation; and
- The center must be accessible and hospitable. (Yates, 1993)

There are concrete actions that schools and families can take according to the research literature to make their schools productive and humanistic environments in which students maximize their potential. Schools should establish family-school partnerships, make learning relevant to the student's cultural and racial backgrounds, and emphasize early childhood education. Studies show that establishing school practices that encourage parental participation is more likely to promote individual educational achievement than family characteristics such as parental education, family size, marital status, socioeconomic level, or student grade level (Dauber & Epstein, 1993; Gilbert, 2003).

A PROPOSED FRAMEWORK FOR CULTURALLY SENSITIVE RESEARCH

Summary: Current Research Limitations

Much of the relevant literature and research compare the behaviors, achievement and educational status of African American pupils to those of the majority population. This literature and research often ignores cultural and racial issues that impact on achievement and learning and cause emotional stress, treat all African Americans as if they are alike, ignore institutional racism that exists within the larger society as well as within the school as an institution, and ignore the diversity of learning styles and the sterility of the school's curriculum for African American youth. These research limitations are extremely problematic. In fact, all too often the literature and research reinforce negative perspectives about this group of learners and treat the educational process as if it exists in a vacuum. In this chapter, the author has presented some studies that move the discussion beyond those that have previously dominated the discourse on this topic.

Proposed Research Framework and Improvements

In the author's opinion, research on this topic could be greatly improved if the conceptual frameworks used were more comprehensive and included contextual and environmental variables that impact upon the educational outcomes for African American pupils. Too often researchers' perspectives on the topic under study are tainted with racist misperceptions, and faulty assumptions about these students and their families. Researchers need to include the voices of their subjects, their specific life circumstances, and in this case, the unique African American culture. The inclusion of qualitative data, in which African American families and pupils share their experiences and reactions to interventions is desperately needed. Such narrative data can enrich our understanding and perhaps lead to the development of effective educational and social interventions (Crew & Anderson, 2003; Dart & Davies, 2003; London, Zimmerman, & Erbstein, 2003).

The focus of this qualitative research should not only include the experiences, wisdom, and needs of African American families, but also the impact of particular educational policies on these youths and their families and the related policy improvements that are needed at the individual school, school district, and/or federal level (Freeman, Franklin, Fong, Shaffer, & Timberlake, 1998). Finally, ethnic modeling is needed in qualitative research. For this to take place, African American researchers and those from other ethnic groups need to redefine their relationship with the black participants of their study and their community. Such research should become a partnership process in which all stakeholders are acknowledged to have expert knowledge and experiences that can enrich the research planning and discovery endeavor (Chawla, 2001; James & McGillicuddy, 2001; Sabo, 2001; Stanfield, 1994).

CONCLUSION

In recent years, a number of encouraging signs of increased African American academic achievement have been observed. Achievement statistics have risen in some cases; the body of theoretical and empirical literature identifying the strengths of this ethnic group has grown; and clarity about the changes that can be implemented by the school system to the benefit of students has increased. However encouraging these signs are, they are hardly all of the ingredients required for success.

With escalating poverty rates, America is retreating from the ideals of racial integration and equality of educational opportunity, and reducing welfare and other supports for certain groups. Despite their family, community, and internal strengths—African American children born to poverty may thus be hindered in their pursuit of educational achievement, and indeed some of them will fail. According to Mickelson (1990) "Without fundamental change in the larger opportunity structure, the underachievement of minority and working class students is likely to persist, even in the face of the best designed and most lavishly funded educational reforms (p. 60)". It is true that underachievement among African American students is influenced by many societal, economic, social factors, neither made nor controlled by the students themselves. These factors must be remedied so that each child has a chance to succeed according to his or her own merits.

Social work academicians and practitioners have critical roles to play in the elimination of factors that place African American youth at risk. We, too, have sometimes failed to build upon the strengths of these students, families, and communities, and to provide interventions that are culturally sensitive and founded on empowering models/theoretical frameworks. We have sometimes failed to engage actively in the formulation of social policies that benefit this group and others, and to promote social justice for all. We have sometimes failed to hold the educational system accountable for its failure to educate all youths, and to fulfill our historical mission of social reformers. But we cannot look ceaselessly at past missteps; while our eyes are on the past a new generation of students will encounter the same problems. Armed with new knowledge, we can make a difference in many students' lives, helping all students–regardless of race–to reach their academic potential.

REFERENCES

Allen-Meares, P., & Fraser, M.W. (Forthcoming). *Intervention with children and adolescents.* Needham Heights, MA: Allyn & Bacon.

Allen-Meares, P., Washington, R., & Welsh, B. (1996). *Social work services in schools* (2nd ed.). Needham Heights, MA: Allyn & Bacon.

Bloom, B. (1976). *Human characteristics and school learning.* New York: McGraw Hill.

Bowles, S. & Gintis, H. (1976). *Schooling in capitalist America: Educational reform and the contradictions of economic life.* New York: Basic Books.

Brown vs. Board of Education of Topeka, 347 U.S. 483 (1954).

Chan, K., & Rueda, R. (1979). Poverty and culture in education: Separate but equal. *Exceptional Children, 45*(6), 422–431.

Chawla, L. (2001). Evaluating children's participation: Seeking areas of consensus. *Participatory learning and action notes: Children's participation: Evaluation effectiveness.* London: International Institute for Environment and Development.

Comer, J., & Haynes, N. (1992). Educating students outside the mainstream. *The Education Digest, 58*(28), 28–30.

Crew, R.E. Jr., & Anderson, M.R. (2003). Accountability and performance in charter schools in Florida: A theory-based evaluation. *American Journal of Evaluation, 24,* 189–212.

Crowson, R.L., & Boyd, W. (1993). Coordinated services for children: Designing arks for storms and seas unknown. *American Journal of Education, 101*(2), 140–179.

Dart, J., & Davies, R. (2003). A dialogical, story-based evaluation tool: The most significant change technique. *The American Journal of Evaluation, 24,* 137–156.

Dauber, S., & Epstein, J. (1993). Parent attitudes and practices of parent involvement in inner-city elementary and middle schools (Paper). Center for Research on Elementary & Middle Schools. Baltimore, MD: The Johns Hopkins University.

Edmonds, R. R. (1983). Implications of programs of school improvement. The *Education Digest, 48,* 19–21.

Ford, D. (1993). Black students' achievement orientation as a function of perceived family achievement, orientation and demographic variables. *Journal of Negro Education, 62*(1), 47–66.

Freeman v. Pitts Supreme Court Decision (1992), see Bierlen (1993). In *Controversial issues in educational policy.* Newbury, CT: Sage Publishing.

Freeman, E.M., Franklin, C.G., Fong, R., Shaffer, G.L., & Timberlake, E.M. (1998). *Multisystem skills and interventions in school social work practice.* Washington, DC: National Association of Social Workers.

Freeman, E.M., & Pennekamp, M. (2002). Administration of integrated services programs serving children, youths, families, and communities. *Social work practice: Toward a child, family, school, community perspective* (2nd ed) (pp. 256–278). Springfield, IL: Thomas.

Gilbert, D.J. (2003). Multicultural assessment. In C. Jordan & C. Franklin (Eds.), *Clinical assessment for social workers: Quantitative and qualitative methods* (2nd Edition) (pp. 313–350). Chicago: Lyceum Books, Inc.

Hatchett, S., & James, J. (1993). African American extended kin systems. In H. McAdoo (Ed.). *Family ethnicity strength in diversity* (pp. 90–108). Newbury, CA: Sage Publications.

Hawley, W. D. (1990). The theory and practice of alternative certification: Implications for the improvement of teaching. *Peabody Journal of Education, 67,* 3–34.

Hermstein, R. J., & Murray, C. (1994). *The Bell Curve: Intelligence and class structure in American life.* New York: Free Press.

Hill, N. (1995). The relationship between family environment and parenting style: A preliminary study of African American families. *Journal of Black Psychology, 21*(4), 408–423.

Ho, E., & Willms, J. (1996, April). Effects of parental involvement on eighth-grade achievement. *Society of Education, 69*(2), 126–141.

Iglesias, A. (1992). *Parent programs: Past, present, and future practices.* Unpublished paper. Philadelphia: Temple University for Research in Human Development & Education.

Ianni, F. A. J. (1989). Providing a structure for adolescent development. *Phi Delta Kappan, 70,* 673–682.

James, T., & McGillicuddy, K. (2001). Building youth movements for community change. *Nonprofit Quarterly, 8,* 1–3.

Johnson, S. (1992). Extra-school factor on achievement attainment and aspiration among junior and senior high school-age African American Youth. *Journal of Negro Education, 61*(1), 99–119.

King, G. C., & Hall, E. H. (1982). Working with the strengths of black families. *Child Welfare, 61,* 536–44.

Littlejohn-Blake, S. M., & Darling, C. A. (1993). Understanding the strengths of African American families. *Journal of Black Studies, 23*(4), 460–471.

Logan, S. L. (Ed.). (1996). *The black family: Strengths, self-help, and positive change.* Boulder, CO: Westview Press.

London, J.K., Zimmerman, K., & Erbstein, N. (2003). Youth-led research and evaluation: Tools for youth, organizational, and community development. *New Directions for Evaluation, 98,* 33–46.

Marshall, S. (1995). Ethnic socialization of African American children: Implications for parenting, identity development and academic achievement. *Journal of Youth & Adolescents, 24*(4), 377–396.

McAdoo, H.P. (Ed.) (2001). *Black children: Social, educational, and parental environments.* Thousand Oaks, CA: Sage.

Mickelson, R .A. (1990). The attitude-achievement paradox among Black adolescents. *Sociology of Education, 63,* 44–61.

Murrell, R. (1994). In search of responsive teaching for African American males: An investigation of students' experience of middle school mathematics curriculum. *Journal of Negro Education, 63,*(4), 556–569.

National Commission on Excellence in Education. (1983). A nation at risk: Imperative for education reform. U.S. Department of Education. Washington, DC: US Government Printing Office.

Neisser, V. (Ed.). (1986). *The school achievement of minority children: New perspectives.* Hillsdale, NJ: Laurence Erlbaum & Associates.

Ogbu, J. (1986). The consequence of the American caste system. In Neisser, V. (Ed.). *The school achievement of minority children: New perspectives.* Hillsdale, NJ: Laurence Erlbaum & Associates.

Orfield, G. (1978). *Must we bus? Segregated schools and policy.* Washington, DC: Brookings Institute.

Oyserman, D., Gant, L., & Ager, J. (1995). A socially contextualized model of African American identity: Possible selves and school persistence. *Journal of personality, 69*(6), 1216–1232.

Perry, T. (1993). *Toward a theory of African American school achievement.* (ERIC Document No. ED366 418).

Puma, M. J., Jones, C. C., Rock, D., & Fernandez, R. (1993). Prospects: The congressional mandated study of educational growth and opportunity. Interim Report. Bethesda, MD: Abt Associates.

Reynolds, A. J., & Gill, S. (1994). The role of parental perspectives in the school adjustment of inner city black children. *Journal of Youth & Adolescents, 23*(6), 671–694.

Rioux, J., & Berla, N. (1993). *Innovations in parent and family involvement.* Princeton Junction, NJ: Eye on Education.

Rutherford, B., & Billig, S. (1995). Eight lessons of parent, family, and community involvement in the middle grades. Phi *Delta Kappan, 77*(l), 64–68.

Sabo, K. (2001). The benefits of participatory evaluation for children and youth. *Participatory action and learning notes.* London: International Institute for Environment and Development.

Schultz, G. F. (1993). Socio-economic advantage and achievement motivation: Important mediators of academic performance in minority children in urban schools. *Urban Review, 25*(3), 221–232.

Stanfield, J. H. (1994). Ethnic modeling in qualitative research. In N. K. Denzin & Y. S. Lincoln (Eds.), *Handbook of Qualitative Research* (pp. 175–188). Thousand Oaks, CA: Sage Publishing.

St. John, N. (1975). *School desegregation outcomes.* New York, NY: John Wiley.

U.S. Department of Commerce Bureau of the Census (1990). *Statistical Abstract of the United States.* Washington, DC: Author.

U.S. Department of Commerce Bureau of the Census (1990). *Current population report.* Washington, DC: Author.

Yates, L. (1993). *Building a successful parent center in an urban school. Digest Number 9.* Clearing House on Urban Education (ERIC).

Chapter 9

BLACK WOMEN AND FAMILIES:
A RESEARCH ANALYSIS

SADYE L. LOGAN

I am a black woman
tall as a cypress
strong beyond all definition
still defying place and time
and circumstance
assailed
impervious
indestructible
look
on me and be
renewed

–Mari Evans

Evans's poem is a testament to the courage and inner strength of black women over time and space. In nearly four centuries since their ancestors were brought to the United States, black women have not only survived but have thrived (Lanker, 1989). They used their inner strength to find safety and security within themselves. The larger society, and perhaps the world, could not believe black women's persistence, fortitude, and dauntless courage in living from day-to-day and staying alive (Cash, 2001). Their tenacious holding on has become fertile ground for numerous myths and works of fiction about black women and their families. They are often, if not always, described in pejorative terms in both popular and scholarly literature (hooks, 1999). "They were shown as 'Aunt Jemimas' with arms and jaws pouched in laughter or leering buxom wenches with round heels, open thighs and insatiable sexual appetites" (Angelou, 1989, p. 8). A parallel view is that of the "overbearing matriarch with a steel demeanor, super strength, eye cutting glances and castrating behavior" (Angelou, 1989, p. 8). Given the myriad distortions and persistent half-truths about black women, it is imperative to ask questions such as: Who is the black woman? Where has she been? Where is she going? How will she get there? What happens after she arrives? These questions can guide explorations into the existing body of literature on black women.

The journey for black women has been, and in many ways continues to be, an arduous task, but it is goal-directed (Alexander, 2001). In this regard, despite her scars and suffering, the black woman has moved continuously toward self-definition and self-hood. This chapter describes the evolution of that journey over time by analyzing the research literature on black women and the central themes that emerged during slavery and the post-slavery period. It includes an African centered feminist perspective for research on African American women, using the historical and cultural context synthesized from the literature analysis. This proposed perspective is in response to the scientific paradigm, which dominates the literature and tends to denigrate African American women as a group.

Literature Review: An Historical Perspective on Black Women

Overview

The goal of this analysis of the research literature is to provide an historical perspective on the unique experiences of black women. A number of social, political, and economic conditions contributed to the oppression of black women over time, which effectively silenced their voices. This silence means that, until the latter part of the twentieth century, the literature often excluded or stereotyped information about black women's life experiences and strengths. For these reasons, this review and analysis includes information from the more culture specific, nonmainstream literature as well as from the professional literature.

To further place this review in context, it is important to summarize what is known about African American women as a subgroup within the general black population. Today there are over thirty million African Americans in the United States. Females constitute over one-half of this number (58%). A majority of these women are single heads of households with children, due to divorce and separation. Many live in cities and large metropolitan areas (Billingsley, 1992; Logan, 2001; Leashore, 1995).

Current data indicate, however, that African Americans as a group have developed a trend toward movement back to the South. According to early census reports, at one time ninety percent of all African Americans lived in the rural South. In the 1940s, over one million African Americans migrated from the South to northern and midwestern states for better jobs and, in some instances, for educational opportunities (Painter, 1977; Leashore, 1995). Currently, African Americans make up more than forty percent of the civilian labor force that are employed in technical, sales, and administrative support fields, and as service entrepreneurs (Billingsley, 1992; Logan, 2001). This profile of African Americans, and of black women in particular, is a foundation for a discussion of the following themes: estrangement and survival; rebuilding and growth; and identity expansion, empowerment and self-determination. These themes capture and reflect the experience of African American women historically within the American society.

Themes of Estrangement and Survival

Coping with Loss. It is common knowledge that African Americans are descendents of West Africa tribes primarily, who came to the United States of America as slaves. Due to rape and sometimes consensual sexual relationships, as well as interracial marriages, many African Americans also have partial European and Native American ancestry. As slaves and freed blacks, they suffered numerous losses and inhuman degradation. The forced journey from their homeland resulted in total estrangement from Africa and a familiar way of life. They suffered countless deaths, loss of family and community, loss of their native language, and above all, loss of their rights to be free human beings. Life was not about living, but about existing and surviving.

The early literature about slavery in the United States rarely, if ever, addressed the experiences of female slaves. Generally, enslaved African American women were discussed in terms of their economic value to their slave owners as breeders of children, who were then sold on auction blocks (Berry & Blassingame, 1982; Franklin, 1969; Franklin & Moss, 1988). Freed African American women were not discussed at all. Although historians were aware of volumes of primary data collected during the 1920s and 1930s about slaves who had been freed, they questioned the validity of those data. It was not until after the civil rights struggles of the 1960s that scholars began to allow the voices of enslaved and freed African American women in nineteen-century America to be heard (hooks, 1981; Sterling, 1997; Collins, 1990).

Those voices showed a rich diversity among African American women, yet a single-minded purpose, to support the survival of less fortunate African Americans in their communities (Dickerson, 2001). The voices revealed joys, sorrows, pain, hope, courage, steadfastness, and even some within group prejudices (Cooper, 1892; Forten, 1953; Harley, 1978 & Harper, 1981). Perhaps most striking in those revelations is how their voices force us to revise old assumptions and stereotypes about the lives and experiences of African American women.

Prioritizing Gender and Ethnic Issues. Despite the inner strengths and accomplishments of nineteenth century African American women and even beyond, these women were all subjected to the indignities and routine injustices of Jim Crow laws. It did not matter if they were the wives and daughters of black politicians, ministers, or educators who had been exposed to the finer things of life, or were intellectuals and scholars educated at prestigious schools such as Fisk and Oberlin. They were still slapped or verbally abused by white men, and were not admitted to or were thrown out of ladies rooms in train stations or other segregated public places.

During this period, their concerns for "the welfare of the race" may have caused many of these women to consciously choose to fight for race issues over gender issues (hooks, 1981; Harper, 1981; Sterling, 1997). Although some women like Frances Harper, writer and lecturer, prioritized race over gender issues, they were nevertheless strong activists for women's rights. Harper, for example, not only lectured on the subject of domestic violence, she directed husbands to refrain from beating and abusing their wives. She was one of the first black women to support the America Women's Suffrage Association (Sterling, 1997).

Although free black women in the North had slightly different experiences than black female slaves in the South, both had to work. Free black women not only worked, but they also organized benevolent societies against slavery for mutual aid and self-education (Sterling, 1997; Hutchinson, 1989; Lowenberg & Bogin, 1976). As early as 1821, Washerwomen and Domestics of Philadelphia and Daughters of Africa Societies were pooling their resources to pay sick and death benefits to needy members. In 1831, several Colored Ladies' Literary Societies were organized in major cities in the northeast. In 1832, black women organized the nation's first Female-Anti-Slavery Society in Salem, Massachusetts (Sterling, 1997). Sojourner Truth, Frances Ellen Watkins, and Sarah Remond were employed as antislavery speakers who traveled all over the United States enthralling their audiences with charm, eloquence, and a creative use of language.

Sterling (1997, p. xiii), among other authors, commented that "to be a black women in nineteenth-century America was to live in the double jeopardy of belonging to the 'inferior sex' of the 'inferior race'." Despite this double jeopardy, two million slaves and 200,000 free African American women of that era survived and often thrived. In short, their tenacious spirit, endurance, and great courage supported the survival of African American people as a whole.

Themes of Rebuilding and Growth

Participating in Social and Political Activism. Despite unimaginable cruelties and injustices, African American women endured. During and after the Civil War they worked to build better lives for their families and children. The 1867 Reconstruction Acts, designed to rebuild the South after the Civil War, were a catalyst for black women activists. African American women fought back and refused to submit to the cowardly, though often deadly, tactics of the Ku Klux Klan. These Reconstruction Period women registered complaints against their white male protagonists, defied the authority of ex-slave owners, and suffered severe and brutal retaliations. "Splitting a nigger woman," along with

severe beatings, was a common practice by white men in the Reconstruction south (Haley, 1976; Sterling, 1997; hooks, 1999).

During this period black women worked as schoolteachers who were
often very effective. Additionally, they ran boarding houses, restau-
rants, and grocery stores; sold fresh fruits and vegetables; and were
domestic workers and washerwomen. Washerwomen worked as independent contractors, sometimes in their own homes. They soon began to organize themselves into Washing Societies and to strike for pay
increases. According to Sterling (1997), striking societies included
workers in Jackson, Mississippi in 1866; Galveston, Texas in 1877; and
Atlanta, Georgia in 1881. The Atlanta strike was probably the largest
and best organized of those strikes. Cooks, nurses and other servants
joined approximately 3,000 washerwomen in their demands for pay
increases. White Atlanta retaliated. Strike leaders were arrested for dis-
orderly conduct and threatened with placement on chain gangs. Landlords increased the women's rent and the city council proposed an
annual license fee of twenty-five dollars for each washerwoman. The
license fee caused some strikers to withdraw and others to respond with
defiant letters to the mayor of Atlanta, as in the following example (Sterling, 1997, p. 338):

Mr. Jim English, Mayor *Washing Society*
Dear Sir: *Atlanta, Georgia, August1, {1881}*

*We, the members of our society, are determined to stick to our pledge and make extra charges
for working and we have agreed, and are willing to pay $25 or $50 for licenses as protection, so we can control the washing for the city. We can afford to pay these licenses, and
will do it before we will be defeated and then we will have full control of the city working
at our own prices, as the city has control of our husband's work at their prices. Don't forget
this. We hope to hear from your council Tuesday morning. We mean business this week or
no washing.*

Yours respectfully,
From 5 societies, 486 members

Using Passive Resistance Strategies. Bold and audacious, these
brave and courageous women stood their ground, but lacking the economic power to hold out indefinitely, they were forced to return to
work at the old rate of pay. Although they lacked the power to bargain
for a better rate of pay, they found other ways to assert their dissatis-
faction with their very low wages. In what Sterling (1997) describes as

sit-out strikes, the washerwomen who had worked all weekend could be "too ailing" to arrive on time on Monday, and by mid-week they might develop "a mis'ry" in their backs, which kept them at home unable to work. Of the many tasks they had to complete, they might do them poorly or not at all. The down side, however, is that these acts of courage tended to reinforce white people's stereotypes about blacks as tardy and sloppy, and a "what-can-you expect from them" reaction.

Black women were extraordinary contributors to the rebuilding process during the decades following the Civil War. However, when the broad question was raised of equality in all spheres of life for black women, black male leaders of the time often took the position of their white counterparts. Consequently, black women were denied membership and equality in male-dominated literary societies, in the councils of churches, in the press, and they were even denied equality in their private lives (hooks, 1981; Daniels, 1970; Duster, 1970).

Themes of Identity Expansion, Empowerment and Self Determination

Confronting Economic and Employment Barriers. Despite the U.S. Constitution's guarantee of black men's right to vote and civil rights laws designed to end discrimination in public places, black people continued to experience numerous hardships. While black men were paid much lower incomes than whites, black women were paid even less. Furthermore, in large cities such as Philadelphia, Washington, DC, and New York following the Civil War, black males' mortality rates were so high that more than twenty-five percent of black women with children were widowed by their early forties.

Under the influence of northern missionaries, schoolteachers, and the Freedmen's Bureau, black families were told that the man was the head of the household and must provide for his family, and that women should stay at home. The gap between this fantasy and the reality of poor black families' lives at that time was not bridgeable. The reality of living on one income was extremely challenging, if not impossible. However, since whites in general rejected the suggestion that black women were similar or equal to white women, they insisted that black women and their children work alongside their husbands and fathers in the fields as sharecroppers.

The decades after the Civil War found most black women confined to the kitchen or other service positions, in the classrooms, or as field hands on farms. Educated women with skills such as sewing or typing were frequently forced to clean houses, wash clothes, or work as chambermaids because of racial prejudice. Often, in responding to an advertisement for a desirable position, black women were told to call again later, that they were not suited for the position, or simply that if they were hired all the white women would walk off the job. Themes of prejudice and stress related to living in a hostile brutal world greatly impacted these women and still echo among African American women today. Only a few generations removed from slavery, many discrimination laws existed in all spheres of life, which continuously assaulted these earlier women.

Women of the Anti-Slavery Society strove to live up to the standards of their white counterparts. Those fortunate enough to attend educational institutions such as Oberlin College in Ohio, Women's Medical College of Pennsylvania and Meharry Medical College in Tennessee pushed themselves to excel. A majority of them felt an overwhelming responsibility for uplifting other black people as a group. For example, one applicant wrote the following statement when applying to the American Missionary Association for a teaching post:

> I am myself a colored woman, born to that ignorant, degraded long enslaved race. They are socially and politically my people; and I have an earnest and abiding conviction that the All-Mighty Father requires me to devote every power with which he has endowed me to the work of ameliorating their conditions. (Sterling, 1997, p. 263)

Sterling (1997) concluded that young women teachers such as the one above were all northern born, from middle-income families, single and childless. They were generally in their twenties with above average educations from the Oberlin Institute for the Black Youth or from a normal school near their homes. These and other black women who were a part of the antislavery movement were considered "representative colored women." This term did not mean typical; it meant these women had absorbed the values, mannerisms, and lifestyles of Southern or New England whites, and that they were accepted as "representatives" of their people by whites. The women were often labeled as coloreds instead of Negroes. They, as well as whites, referred to the women's lighter complexions as slightly tinged with African blood, or as having a slight admixture of Negro blood. Many of these women adopted white identities and lived as white people.

Seizing New Opportunities. As educational opportunities became more available, some of these "representative" women pursued careers in areas other than teaching. They entered medical or nursing schools, and many like the brilliant Ida B. Wells published their own newspapers, while others wrote for newspapers and magazines, or became editors. Despite the lack of support these women received from the "representative" men of the time, by the later part of the nineteenth century the former were recognized for their extraordinary successes in business, acting, and lecturing, and as singers (Harley & Terborg-Penn, 1978; Duster, 1970).

Although within a different context, black women of the South held a vision of success for themselves and their families, not unlike northern black women. Their work included being wives, mothers, homemakers, domestics, and working alongside their husbands as field hands. Generally husbands saw their responsibility as providing food and rent, while women took care of all other expenses. Believing the husband to be in charge of the family, many women worked nights to allow their husbands to go to school and or to minister to a church congregation, which provided little or no income. Black women wanted their children to be cared for, and they wanted to own a piece of land and a home.

Surviving Gender and Self-Determination Barriers. An adage, the more things change the more they remain the same, captures the experience of contemporary black women. They see being a woman and black as their two primary disadvantages, not unlike women in nineteenth century America. Black women and men struggled equally in the nineteenth century to end slavery and construct a more just society. However, the "representative" men of the time upheld patriarchal values and encouraged black women to assume a more subservient role. Gradually, evidence of the intellectual and political contributions of nineteenth century black women in America faded. The silencing of black women's voices became more evident in the twentieth century. While they continued to participate equally with black men to maintain a home and family life by entering the work force, many did not advocate for an end to gender oppression.

The civil rights movement began in the 1950s. It was not unlike the

Reconstruction period with its goal to free all blacks. These two movements were also alike in that neither raised questions the unfairness of patriarchy. Perhaps one striking difference in the 1960s civil rights movement was that some black male activists publicly affirmed their stance on sexist roles for black women. Black women were told that they should take care of household needs and breed warriors for the revolution (Cade, 1970). Some women activists attempted to resist such dominance, while others simply acquiesced (Alexander, 2001).

The oppression and denigration of black women is also reflected in the stereotypical image of the "strong" black women. This "strength" label implies that although black women are victims of oppression, their strength and ability to survive adversities allows them to circumvent the dehumanizing impact of oppression. bell hooks (1999) points out, however, that being strong when dealing with oppression is not the same as transformation and growth. Within this context, it is imperative to recognize that sexism operates in tandem with racism to perpetuate the dual oppression of black women. bell hooks (1999) goes on to say that black women, perhaps like no other group in America, have had their identity socialized out of existence.

AN AFRICAN CENTERED FEMINIST PERSPECTIVE
FOR RESEARCH ON AFRICAN AMERICA WOMEN

Limitations of Current Philosophical and Research Perspectives

Educator Carter G. Woodsen (1933, p. 84) spoke of the need for self-definition and the importance of thinking for oneself:

> If you control a man's thinking, you do not have to worry about his action. When you determine what a man shall think you do not have to concern yourself about what he will do. If you make a man feel that he is inferior, you do not have to compel him to accept inferior status, for he will seek it himself.

Although Wooden (1933) refers to the male gender in the above quote, the implications are equally true for all humans regardless of gender. However, with regard to African American women, the need for self-definition has been a recurring theme. Nearly two decades ago, bell hooks (1981) pointed out that black women were rarely recognized as a group separate and distinct within themselves. She goes on to say:

When Black people are talked about, sexism mitigates against the acknowledgement of the interests of Black women (because the focus tends to be on Black men). When women are talked about, racism mitigates against a recognition of Black females interests (because the focus tends to be on white women). . . . (hooks, 1981, p. 7)

Although literature on black women has changed in some respects, what exists currently is still insufficient. Comprehensive studies by African American women are needed on the social status of black women, articulating their experiences across the life cycle, their beliefs; and the impact of racism and sexism on their lives, their hopes, and dreams. A pervasive Eurocentric, masculine perspective has further contributed to the lack of research on black women, which requires:

1. Separation or distancing from the "object" of study.
2. The absence of emotions from the research process.
3. The elimination of ethics and values in the research process.
4. The reporting of only findings that confirm previously hypothesized relationships.
5. Adversarial debates as the preferred method of determining the truth of a position. (Collins, 1990)

A Proposed Alternative Research Framework

An African-Centered Feminist Epistemology. In order for research on black women to move beyond current limiting methodologies, such as the traditional framework, an African-centered feminist perspective is being proposed. This perspective is not new and has been discussed by Patricia H. Collins (1990) and other black feminist authors. An Africanist perspective or world view incorporates the traditional cultural beliefs and values of West Africa societies. This world view is holistic. It is based on the interconnectedness of all things; a oneness of mind, body, and spirit; group or collective identity; a consanguineous family structure; consequential morality; nondualistic thinking; a present time orientation; and a spirituality that supports and affirms the holistic view of human beings and gives meaning and purpose to life (Turner, 1991, Asante, 1988, 1989).

Despite historical differences among blacks, their societies all over the world reflect this world view and share common oppression experiences with racial domination. Similarly, women share a history of gender oppression that transcends, and yet has been influenced by, ethnicity, race, social class, sexual orientation, and religion. This universal oppressive history of women forms the basis of a feminist epistemology. Furthermore, Africentric and feminist perspectives can be integrated to reflect epistemological elements that are unique and culturally meaningful to black women.

Interconnected Cultural-Gender Elements. These elements include black women's concrete everyday experiences, such as the use of cultural dialogue, individual and unique experiences, appropriateness of emotions, a capacity for empathy, and personal accountability (Collins, 1990). As interconnected elements, they reflect black women's ways of knowing, doing, and being in the world. Hence, this group of elements can guide the selection of research topics for investigation and the methodologies to be used, because such elements acknowledge the centrality of black women in their families, organizations, and communities. Essentially their centrality provides a unique position for sharing stories about their lived experiences within a caring relational context. This context allows for individual uniqueness, and appropriate expression of emotions, as well as a capacity for empathy or the understanding of another person's feelings. In terms of personal accountability, new knowledge shared by individuals who are respected for their ethnical and moral behavior is more credible than knowledge offered by someone who is less respected (Collins, 1990).

Useful Next Steps Regarding This Research Framework. This expanded research framework can promote a body of self-defined knowledge about black women, which is expected to evolve from the scholarship of other committed black female researchers. The framework provides a culture- and gender-specific process for developing as well as critiquing a more relevant epistemology. Only with this strong combination of a culturally meaningful epistemology and sound research methods will knowledge about black women transcend the results of current pathology-focused studies.

CONCLUSION

African American women are the foundation and the healing force within black families and communities. Their experiences in surviving the worst forms of human degradation and continued oppression have provided them with a unique view of the world. Surviving such experiences has allowed them to remain connected to their compassion for others. As a result they are able to see the beauty, the hope, and the possibilities, as well as the injustices of the world, from a wholistic rather than narrow perspective. Collectively, they have journeyed through time and space from estrangement and survival to empowerment and self-determination (Ruiz, 2001). As they have moved into the twenty-first century, black women have continued to expand their definitions of self and selfhood (Martin & Martin, 2002). A cadre of culturally-centered researchers is needed to explore and document the unique journey of these women, and to influence policy makers whose decisions can continue to significantly influence the life opportunities of black women.

REFERENCES

Alexander, A. (2001). *Fifty black women who changed America*. New York: Citadel Press, Kensington Publishing Corp.

Angelou, M. (1989). They came to stay. In B. Summers (Ed)., *Brian Lanker, I dream a world: Portraits of black women who changed America* (pg. 8–9). New York: Stewart, Tabori & Change.

Asante, M.K. (1988). *Afrocentricity*. Trenton, NJ: Africa World Press.

Asante, M.K. (1989). *Kemet, Afrocentricity and knowledge*. Trenton, NJ: Africa World Press.

Berry, M.F. & Blassingame J.C. (1982). *Long memory: The black experience in America*. New York: Oxford University Press.

Billingsley, A. (1992). *Climbing Jacob's ladder. The enduring legacy of African American families*. New York: Simon & Schuster.

Cade, T. (1970) (Ed.). *The black woman*. New York: Signet.

Cash, F.B. (2001). *African American women and social action*. Connecticut: Greenwood Press.

Collins, P. (1990). *The black feminist thought: Knowledge, consciousness, and the politics of empowerment*. Boston: UnWin Hyman.

Cooper, A.J. (1892). *A voice from the south: By 2 black women of the south*. Xenia, OH: Aldine Printing House.

Daniels, S. (1970). *Women builders*. Washington, DC: Association Press.

Dickerson, J.G. (2001) Margaret Murray Washington: Organizing rural African American women: In I. B. Carlton-LaNey (Ed.), *African American leadership: An empowerment tradition in social welfare history* (pp. 55–74). Washington, DC: NASW Press.

Duster, A. (1970) (Ed). *Crusade for justice. The autobiography of Ida B. Wells*. Chicago: University of Chicago Press.

Forten, C. (1953). *The journal of Charlotte L. Forten.* New York: Vintage Press.

Franklin, J.H. (1969). *From slavery to freedom: A history of Negro Americans (3rd ed.).* New York: Vintage Books.

Franklin J.H. & Moss, A.A. (1988). *From slavery to freedom: A history of Negro Americans.* New York: Knopf.

Haley, A. (1976). *Roots: The saga of an American family.* Garden City, New York: Doubleday & Company, Inc.

Harley, S. (1978). Anna Julia Cooper: A voice for black women. In S. Harley & R. Terborg-Penn (Eds.), *The Afro-American struggles and images* (pg. 87–96). Port Washington, NY: Kenn Kar Press.

Harley, S & Terborg-Penn, R. (1978) (Eds.), *The Afro-American struggles and images.* Port Washington, NY: Kenn Kar Press.

Harper, F.E.W. (1981). *Sketches of southern life.* Philadelphia, PA: Ferguson Bros & Co.

hooks, b. (1999). Selling hot pussy: Representation of black female sexuality in the cultural marketplace. In K. Conboy, N. Medina & S. Stanbury (Eds.), *Writing on the body's female embodiment and feminist theory* (pp. 113–128). New York: Columbia University Press.

hooks, b. (1981). *Ain't I a woman: Black woman and feminism.* Boston, MA: South End Press.

Hutchinson, L. (1989). *Anna J. Cooper.* Trenton, NJ: African World Press.

Lanker, B. (1989). *I Dream a world: Portrait of black women who changed America.* New York: Stewart, Tabor & Change.

Leashore, B.R. (1995). African Americans overview. In R. L. Edwards. (Ed), *Encyclopedia of social work: 19th ed.* (pp 101–115). Washington, DC: NASW Press.

Logan, S. (2001) (Ed.). *The black family: Strengths, self-help and positive change* (2nd ed.). Colorado: Westview Press.

Lowenberg, B.J. & Bogin R. (1976) (Eds.). *Black women in nineteenth-century American life.* University Park, PA: Pennsylvania State University Press.

Martin, E. P., & Martin J.M. (2002). *Spirituality and the black helping tradition in social work.* Washington, DC: NASW Press.

Painter, N. (1977). *Exodusters: black migration to Kansas after reconstruction.* New York: Knopf.

Ruiz, D.S. (2001). Traditional helping roles of older African American women: The concept of self-help. In I.B. Carlton-Le Nay (Ed.), *African American leadership: Empowerment tradition in social welfare history* (pp. 215–228). Washington, DC: NASW Press.

Sterling, D. (1997) (Ed.). *We are sisters: Black women in the nineteenth century.* New York. W.W. Norton.

Turner, R.J. (1991). Affirming consciousness: The Afrocentric perspective. In J. Everett, S.S. Chipungu, & B.R. Leashore (Eds), *Child welfare: An Afrocentric perspective.* New Brunswick, NJ: Rutgers University Press.

Woodsen, C. (1933). *The miseducation of the Negro.* Washington, DC: Association Press.

Chapter 10

EPISTEMOLOGICAL, THEORETICAL, CONCEPTUAL AND METHODOLOGICAL ISSUES IN CONDUCTING RESEARCH ON AFRICAN AMERICAN MEN

Janice Matthews Rasheed

It is clear that many research projects that pertain to the lives of Black people are political; therefore, any study of their lives is political.
—Robert L. Williams (1980)

In traditional social science research, epistemological and theoretical questions about methodology are usually divorced from substantive subfield concerns (such as research on African American males) and are typically discussed in a vacuum, as philosophy of social science considerations (Stanfield, III, 1993). These important epistemological, theoretical, conceptual and methodological questions about research, specific to the study of African American men, are raised in this chapter.

In particular, this chapter addresses the issue of how the conceptualization of research problems and interpretations of data collected in research on African American men has typically been preceded by a priori ideological and cultural biases that profoundly determine the production of this so-called "objective knowledge." Thus, the gathering and interpretation of research data on African American men has historically served the function of lending a professional gloss to what, in reality, is nothing more than cultural and social stereotypes about black men. This chapter examines these ideological intrusions that plague research about African American men.

Although social scientific research has traditionally emphasized males, it has not studied **men as men;** research has largely been genderless (Thompson & Pleck, 1995). Research has studied the experiences of men–but not necessarily as **males.** Over the last twenty years empirical research on men's problems has lagged far behind theory in the social science literature (O'Neil et al. 1995). Consequently, little is known about men's gender roles from a scientific perspective. Even less is known, empirically speaking, about men of different ages and from different ethno-cultural backgrounds, class levels, and sexual orientations. Hence, theory development on men, especially men of color, is still in its early stages of development; as research activities on men of color which are critical to theory development, are conspicuously missing from the literature.

In light of this pivotal gap in the literature, research is sorely needed that does not pathologize the behaviors of African American men and that can generate a fuller understanding of the strengths of black men. To this end, this chapter presents emergent theoretical and conceptual frameworks for research that have the potential to generate a more holistic and contextually-based examination of the dilemmas and cultural strengths of African American men. This chapter strives to facilitate research on African American men, in view of the fact that research is the foundation of and gives guidance to important theory, practice, programming, and policy activities.

HISTORICAL CONTEXT OF AFRICAN AMERICANS, RACE, AND RESEARCH

Scientific Racism in Research

In the seminal works of Stephen Jay Gould (1981), he focused on the reanalysis of classical data sets in craniometry and intelligence testing. Gould (1981) was able to locate a priori prejudice, leading scientists to invalid conclusions from adequate data. Gould (1981) was also able to locate prejudices being played out in more subtle roles in what he calls "absurd experimental designs . . . gross errors in measurement and measurement procedures . . . and the distorting of the gathering of the data itself" (pp. 26–27). Unfortunately, the formal challenging of these early pseudo-scientific studies or rather exercises in scientific racism did not occur early enough in the scientific community in order to subvert future lines of research inquiry that have continued into the culmination of more contemporary scientific racist research efforts.

More recently, Herrnstein and Murray (1994) in their book, *The Bell Curve,* continue this pseudo-scientific, racist tradition in their scandalous disregard for scientific objectivity. In their book they unabashedly assert that scientific evidence demonstrates the existence of genetically-based differences in intelligence among social classes and races (Herrnstein & Murray, 1994). However, in *The Bell Curve,* these authors repeatedly fail to distinguish between the elementary research concepts of correlation and causation; and thus, draw many inappropriate biased conclusions.

The Consequences For Social Problem Formulations

These reports are key examples of how, historically, research on African Americans fails to treat racism as a significant variable, either in the research design, procedures and/or the interpretation of data. Research on African American men similarly suffers the consequences of this critical conceptual failure. One of the most notorious illustrations of this conceptual failure is the Moynihan Report (1965), which was based on the hypotheses that African American men were emasculated by slavery and thus emerged as irresponsible breadwinners. Moynihan (1965) attributed the social problems found in African American families to black men's economic dependence on black women as heads of household. By focusing on black men's inadequacies in meeting traditional gender role functions, Moynihan (1965) sidestepped the societal issues of racism, oppression, and injustice. Fortunately, a more enlightened generation of research scholars have acknowledged the importance of reconciling cultural and male identities with economic and social obstacles in their research on African American men and other men of color (Lazur & Majors, 1995).

In summary, research on African Americans has historically suffered from five essentially racist strategies identified in journal articles by Howitt and Owusu-Bempah (1994), namely: (1) stereotyping, (2) marginalizing racism, (3) avoiding the obvious, (4) neo-imperialism, and (5) blaming the victim. Consequently, research specific to the study of African American men has suffered a similar plight.

SUBSTANTIVE AREAS OF RESEARCH

Recent Trends in Research

Research on African American males is located loosely across disciplines, with no one discipline housing a significant number of studies (Gadsden & Smith, 1994). This trend is a healthy one in that interdisciplinary research efforts have the potential to facilitate diverse foci and value orientations–as professional and discipline socialization no doubt serve to influence research efforts in this regard.

The past twenty years have witnessed a tremendous increase in the quantity, quality, and diversity of research on African American men. However, this recent resurgence of research in the social and behavioral science literature comes after decades of neglect. Taylor, Chatters, Tucker, & Lewis (1990) in their decade review on developments in research on black families conclude that the role of black men in families is one of the most conspicuously neglected areas of family research.

Principal Foci and Findings of the Research Literature

The foci and principal findings of the research literature on African American men has been conceptualized here into three different waves of research and/or three different generations of researchers. Hence, this section presents these three generations of research findings along with critiques of their cultural relevance and sensitivity, methodological adroitness, and the implications and impact for African American men and their communities.

The First Wave/Generation of Research on Black Men. Racial differences in temperament, childrearing practices, and moral and social development topped the research agendas on African American males from the mid-1920s until the 1950s (Evans & Whitfield, 1988). However, a significant research focus exclusively on black men as males, as opposed to merely including them as research subjects, did not occur in the social and behavioral science literature until the very late 1970s and/or early 1980s, during the third wave/generation of research.

Research on African American men in this first wave of research seems to be conducted more out of intellectual curiosity than from any real concern for African American men. The researchers tended to be white middle-class males who imposed biased culture- and class-bound research questions and hypotheses into their methodologies. Research in this era was typically conducted from an assumption of cultural deficiency regarding black males, devoid of an ecological context and an emic (group-specific) view or perspective. By and large, much of the research in this era consisted of studies that were no more than thinly-veiled social, cultural, and racial prejudices posing as genuine pursuits of truth and knowledge. To this end the cumulative impact of these works served to reinforce and legitimize the inequitable and oppressive environments of African American men, thus rationalizing the maintenance of the status quo in the larger society.

The one notable exception to the above critique is the legendary works of E. Franklin Frazier (1932a, 1932b, 1939). Frazier concluded that acculturation to the values and lifestyles of mainstream society was a key to the advancement of black Americans. His thesis and its rationale catalyzed studies in the next wave of research, wherein researchers began to explore a new link to pathology and dysfunction for African American families, i.e., the primacy accorded the prevailing cultural norms of the dominant core culture (Tidwell, 1990).

The Second Wave/Generation of Research on Black Men. The social concerns of the 1960s and the 1970s led to research on a broader range of psychosocial, behavioral, and social status issues that affect African American men (Evans & Whitfield, 1988; Alejandro-Wright, 1982). Three basic themes dominated research on blacks in this era, namely: intellectual capacity and achievement, self-concept, and family life (Alejandro-Wright, 1982). Hence, research on African American males closely parallels these themes during this period. This research focus did not necessarily attempt to uncover explicit male or gender issues unique to black men, with the exception being research conducted on their roles as fathers and husbands.

This era of research is especially interesting as well as promising because it represents a changing of the guards, so to speak; in that a new set of gifted, vastly better informed researchers arrived on the research scene. As a result, research on African Americans in this period demonstrated greater conceptual and methodological rigor. Closer attention was paid to underlying epistemological and conceptual biases that can profoundly impact problem formulation, allowing researchers to frame their efforts within a more bicultural, emic (i.e., group-specific) view or perspective. Hence, this research began to uncover strengths in African American males that had been distorted and misrepresented in prior studies by Moynihan (1965), Kardiner and Ovesey, (1951) Etzkowitz and Schaflander (1969), and others.

This second generation of researchers concluded that the issue of black men being peripheral within their families is vastly overstated; rather these researchers interpreted the familial behaviors of black men as flexible, adaptive, egalitarian (not emasculated), highly functional and effective (Billingsley, 1968, 1992; Rainwater, 1966, 1970; Willie, 1970; Staples, 1971; Scanzoni, 1971; Hill, 1972, 1999; Nobles, 1978; Stack, 1974; McAdoo, 1978).

In spite of the vigor of these well-conceptualized lines of research, one cannot help but consider how the efforts of these gifted researchers could have been spent engaging in proactive rather than reactive research. Banks (1980) refers to the latter research as deconstructive or falsification research, that is, research that demonstrates the fallacy of inferences and/or methodological distortions of traditional research. Essentially, this research is a process of undoing the destructive inferences about African American men emanating from traditional research. Deconstructive research involves theoretical dismantling as well as empirical rebuttal.

It is highly unfortunate that these reactive or deconstructive lines of research became so necessary to counter the deleterious impact of earlier misguided research efforts. These earlier works profoundly and quickly reinforced negative images of black men in the mass media; and thus also shaped pathology-focused public policy and important social programming.

In spite of this detour involving deconstruction research, ground-breaking research specifically exploring the experiences of African American men emerged during this period in the works of Elliot Liebow (1967), and Grier and Cobbs (1968). These scholarly pieces represent an important widening of the previous family research in that they explored respectively the coping and adaptational experiences of low income, unemployed black men and the impact of racism on personality development and masculinity. These works were among the first to examine the internal world of black men, thus validating its importance, and equally significant, conceptually weaving into their analysis and interpretation the profound influence of environmental variables on psychosocial functioning, such as racism and oppression.

The Third Wave/Generation of Research on Black Men. The 1980s and 1990s witnessed a widening of prior research interests specifically targeting the unique dilemmas of African American males, especially young, urban, unmarried fathers. With the alarming decline in social status indices for young African American males and a shift toward the highest rates of social maladjustment among all subgroups, African American men were aptly labeled an endangered species in this period (Gibbs, 1988). Descriptive and exploratory research was conducted on many areas, such as: mortality, morbidity, health, education, unemployment, crime and imprisonment, family life and paternal role functioning, mental health and substance abuse. Additional lines of research on black men were investigated for the first time, namely: male gender role-strain, psychosocial adaptation and coping, and personality development.

This third wave/generation of researchers directly benefited from the efforts of prior researchers in that they were not held hostage by misguided and misinformed research and were free to address proactively the contemporary concerns of African American men. Additionally, this generation of researchers has continued to improve upon the conceptual, theoretical, and methodological skills gained by the previous generation of researchers. Numerous edited volumes replete with rich, well-executed research studies on African American men, as well as exciting conceptual and theoretical chapters emerged during this era (Taylor and Wilkinson, 1977; Gary, 1981; Gibbs, 1988; Jones, 1989; Majors & Billson, 1992; Majors & Gordon, 1994).

A selected summary is listed below of major research findings on African American men during this period:

- the average life expectancy for black men is 64.6 years (versus 72.9 years for white men)
- the black male HIV infection mortality rate is 72.9% (versus 52% for white males), and the HIV mortality rate for African American males has more than doubled in the past ten years
- homicide, especially gang-related violence in poor urban areas, is the leading cause of death for black males, 15–34 years old, and the second leading cause of death for black men, 25–44 years old, (eight times higher than the homicide rate for white males)
- alcohol abuse, substance abuse, and depression have been recognized as the most significant mental health problems facing black men
- suicide is the third leading cause of death for young black men
- it is estimated that 44% of black men are functionally illiterate
- there is a 40–70% high school dropout rate for black males, the highest dropout or push out rate of all racial/gender group classifications in the U.S.
- the number of black men obtaining college degrees has not changed in the past twenty years
- 50% of prisoners in the United States and in federal prisons are African American; most are black men although black men comprise only 6% of the total U.S. population, (they are incarcerated six times the rate for white males)
- although 95% of all African American men are not in prison, by the time a black male reaches the age of 19, one in six will have been arrested
- 29% of all African American men live in poverty (versus 9.8% of white men), although the percentage of minor black males living in poverty is 45%
- 23% of black men ages 20–24 and 12% of black men ages 25–44 are unemployed, twice the unemployment rate for white men
- working-, middle-, and upper-class black men are more likely than white males to experience somatic stress reactions or ailments that include headaches, low back pain, diabetes, heart trouble and high blood pressure
- provider role-strain was found to adversely affect life happiness among a sample of married black fathers
- black men are highly involved in their parental and childrearing roles. (Taylor, 1995; Austin, 1996; Gibbs, 1988; Parham & McDavis, 1987; Majors & Gordon, 1994; Bowman, 1985; J. McAdoo, 1993; Stier & Tienda, 1993)

Many of these findings point to the fact that African American men are worse off today than they were twenty years ago (Gibbs, 1988; Taylor, 1987). In fact, African American men are the only racial/gender classification group that has experienced such a downward spiraling of social condition(s), as evidenced by these social status indicators from the research literature.

Future Directions Needed for Research on African American Men

Even though the breadth of research on African American males is encouraging, and appears to be widening, one major criticism of research in this area continues to be its lack of depth, especially theoretical or explanatory depth. Contemporary research on African American males continues to devote primary attention to descriptive research on current social problems. More in-depth theoretical understanding of the nature of these well-documented social problems is acutely needed. It is time for researchers to move beyond the prior descriptive and exploratory focus and begin to examine programmatic solutions to these social problems.

Future lines of research need to focus on creating a better understanding of the impact of racism, sexism, and discrimination on intrapsychic functioning and the role functioning behaviors of black men. That is, research needs to be based on the life span development of African American males, to increase understanding of the developmental shifts and changes that are catalyzed by black men's unique situations and stressors. Other lines of research that are needed are: studies of strength and resilience; understanding the interplay of socio-historical-politico-economic forces and their impact on elderly black men, black gay and bisexual men, and biracial (black) men; the long-term effects of adolescent fatherhood; the affective roles and functions of black men in African American families; the dilemmas and issues of low income, unmarried noncustodial fathers, as well as the barriers and incentives to their paternal involvement; and finally a host of phenomenally-based research studies exploring special issues and circumstances and how these circumstances may differentially affect African American men, for example, homelessness, substance abuse, depression, suicide, HIV/AIDS infection.

EPISTEMOLOGICAL, THEORETICAL AND CONCEPTUAL ISSUES: CRITIQUE OF EXISTING CONCEPTUAL AND THEORETICAL FRAMEWORKS USED IN RESEARCH ON AFRICAN AMERICAN MEN

Overview of Perspectives

This section presents a critique of existing conceptual and theoretical perspectives specifically used to guide research on African American males and their experiences. This overview of perspectives uses classification schemes developed from the works of Bowman (1989) and Oliver (1989).

There are many theories that attempt to understand and explain the socio-politico-economic status of African American males. Many of these frameworks have been used as the theoretical and conceptual underpinnings for research efforts, policy-making and social service interventions with African American men. In reviewing these frameworks, it is clear that there are common themes and assumptions shared between the various theoretical/conceptual formulations. Thus, it has been possible to classify specific theories into broader categories or schemes according to their shared assumptions about African American men. Using Bowman's (1989) and Oliver's (1989) classification schemes, the following theoretical perspectives emerge: the deficit/pathology perspective, the oppression perspective, the coping perspective, and the ethno-cultural perspective.

The Deficit/Pathology Perspective

This perspective focuses research on and labels black males in terms of maladaptive behaviors. It supports the hypothesis that cultural, psychological and/or genetic deficits are the primary cause(s) of the maladaptive behaviors under study (Garrett, 1961; Jensen 1973). This perspective dominated the earlier first wave/generation studies on black males (Evans & Whitfield, 1988; Gary, 1981). A variation of this deficit perspective is the culture of poverty orientation (Banfield, 1970; Moynihan, 1965). Proponents of this orientation argue that the cause of social problems can be found in the distinctive cultural values and traditions within lower class communities.

The Oppression Perspective

The second perspective also focuses research on maladaptive rather than adaptive behaviors. Unlike the deficit/pathology perspective, external societal barriers are considered as the fundamental causes of maladaptive behaviors (Clark, 1965; Glasgow, 1980; Kunjufu, 1982; Taylor & Wilkinson, 1977). The emphasis in this perspective is on the victimization of African American males by existing race and class barriers. In this perspective, institutional racism, internal colonialism, underclass entrapment, urban poverty, and the technological transformation of the economy leading to joblessness, are considered as primary causes of the marginal status of African American males.

The Coping Perspective

The focus of research from this perspective is directed toward those African American males who manage effective responses to stressful obstacles. While oppressive environments are acknowledged, the coping perspective focuses positively on understanding adaptive rather than maladaptive behaviors (Bowman, 1985; Cazenave, 1981; Billingsley, 1992; McAdoo, 1997; Logan, 2001). Further attention is given to understanding processes that enable many at-risk African American males to struggle against adversity and to excel, despite the odds.

The Ethno-Cultural Perspective

Studies grounded in this perspective similarly focus on adaptive modes of cultural expression rather than on maladaptive behaviors (Braithwaite, 2001). This perspective emphasizes the cultural foundations of proactive responses to institutional barriers. Attention is given to the subjective aspects of culture and to the psychological, attitudinal and expressive behavioral patterns unique to any given culture. Within this perspective are two orientations. One orientation supports the proposition that African American ethnic patterns are reactions to America's racial oppression (Sudarkasa, 1980, 1981); it is called the discontinuity orientation (see Chapter 1). The other orientation, the African survival framework (see Chapter 1), views the unique ethnic patterns of African American males as African adaptations rather than as cultural residues of oppression (Akbar, 1991; Asante, 1981; Baldwin, 1981; Myers, 1985; Oliver, 1989; Davis, 1999).

The Integrative Theoretical Conceptual Perspective

Bowman (1989) suggests that each of the four previous perspectives merely illuminates disparate but important aspects of the African American male experience. For example, the deficit/pathology perspective, though identifying the maladaptive behaviors of at-risk African American males, tends to reinforce a victim-blaming ideology. The oppression perspective, in giving attention to the destructive aspects of race and class barriers, tends to depict African American males as helpless victims. The coping perspective, in emphasizing adaptive responses to societal barriers, may minimize the underclass entrapment of African American males. Finally, the ethno-cultural perspective, while having the ability to identify indigenous cultural resources available to black males, may underemphasize the adaptive responses that the coping perspective could potentially serve to illuminate. Therefore, both Bowman (1989) and Oliver (1989) call for an integrative theoretical/conceptual perspective that incorporates the unique features of each of the other perspectives into a comprehensive, balanced, and culturally-sensitive conceptual framework for research.

Bowman's (1989) Role Strain and Adaptation Model. Bowman (1989) views this integrative theoretical conceptual perspective as a role strain and adaptation model. The model examines the objective difficulties and subjective reactions to obstacles faced by African American men as they engage in valued social roles. The obstacles and difficulties that they encounter are a result of barriers which exist in the social environment, personal limitations and/or conflicts at the environment-person interface.

Oliver's (1989) Structural-Cultural Model. Oliver (1989) proposes a structural-cultural model which suggests that the high rate of social problems among African American men is the result of structural societal pressures and dysfunctional cultural adaptations to those pressures. He theorizes that African American men have failed to adequately respond to white racism, and this gap has resulted in specific styles of behaviors that these men have developed in response to structurally-induced social pressures. Oliver (1989) believes that even the most problematic dysfunctional adaptation involves two factors: the failure of African American men to develop an Africentric cultural ideology; and the tendency of African Americans, especially lower-class blacks, to tolerate the tough guy and the player of women images, as acceptable alternatives to traditional or white definitions of manhood.

EPISTEMOLOGICAL, THEORETICAL AND CONCEPTUAL FRAMEWORKS NEEDED FOR FUTURE RESEARCH ON AFRICAN AMERICAN MEN

To guide research on African American men, a proactive/heuristic, bicultural, Africentric, emic, ecological, postmodernist-informed framework/perspective is proposed in this section. The oppression, coping and role strain perspectives, as summarized in the previous section, are major elements of the ecological component of this framework. Additionally, the ethno-cultural and structural-cultural perspectives are also embodied within the Africentric aspects of the framework discussed in this section. Each component/aspect of this research framework is described, along with implications for how the components are interrelated.

Proactive/Heuristic Research

It is important that third wave/generation research continue its direction of forging innovative, functionally relevant research agendas that respond to the contemporary needs and dilemmas facing African American men (Mickel, 2001; Davis, 1999). Bowman (1991) defines heuristic research as having the ultimate goal of articulating culturally adaptive styles and demonstrating benefits which come from adapting those styles. In addition, careful conceptual or methodological critiques of shoddy or misleading studies should continue to be written and published. This combined strategy is proposed in light of the ground that has been lost historically by some second-wave researchers who concentrated almost exclusively on reactive deconstruction research, rather than forging ahead with important and neglected proactive/ heuristic research agendas.

Emic *Perspective*

One of the most important contributions of cross-cultural psychologists to research methodology in the social and behavioral sciences has been the distinction between phenomenon that are considered to be universal (or etic) versus phenomenon that are considered to be group-specific (or emic) (Brislin, 1970). A danger in conducting research on so-called minority populations or cross-cultural research, wherein the subjects are of a different ethnocultural background from the researcher, is to erroneously assume the universality of a concept or construct. Whenever universality is assumed, it is called an imposed ethic (Berry, 1969) or pseudoetic (Triandis, 1972). These are cases where the researcher imposes a world view that is culture-specific by assuming the panculturality (or universality) of etic constructs.

It has always been the norm in the social sciences to assume that Eurocentric empirical realities can be generalized to explain the realities of people of color. Thus, validity checks are a necessary step in the research process, be it in the construction of questionnaires or in the examination of coding schema in qualitative data. Hence, it is important for researchers to consider whether conceptual and operational definitions of key variables are also valid emic (or insider/group-specific) constructs accepted by African American men as a subgroup.

Africentric Research

Africentrism is a perspective or a cognitive map that reflects an individual's world view. Africentrism is a juxtaposing of the African and American ways, and an integration of the values derived from the historical experience of African Americans to provide the clearest perspective on the unique group of people called African Americans (Asante, 1988). In essence, Africentrism is reflected in an individual's philosophical and spiritual acceptance, the intellectual acknowledgement and celebration of the unique hybrid and historical development of the African American ethno-cultural heritage. This means that researchers who are non-African Americans can similarly adopt an Africentric perspective in their research (Rasheed & Johnson, 1995).

One of the most significant aspects of this perspective is that is takes the ontological position that behavioral observations are, at best, approximates to visualizing the true nature of the human being; because spirituality is viewed as endemic to the human make-up (Akbar, 1991). Thus, inherent in this perspective is the notion that research can only hope to approach knowing or understanding its subjects, a vastly different perspective as espoused by logical positivists who seek ultimate truth. Additionally, this perspective encourages a holistic approach to methodology, that is, attempts to study people in a non-fragmented way.

The researcher's conceptual system becomes grounded in Afrocentrism by paying unique attention to culturally-based and functional sex-role differences. Hence, research can infuse the ontological values of Afrocentrism into the hypotheses and subsequent problem formulation, the conceptualization and operationalization of constructs, the data collection instruments, and into the interpretation of data. Future research efforts need to focus on establishing levels of validity and reliability with existing standardized instruments, specifically for African American males, as well as developing new instruments with culture-specific or emic Afrocentric criteria used in their development.

Bicultural Research

It is important to make a subtle, but critical distinction here regarding the difference between the Africentric and bicultural perspectives in research. Research conceptualized within a bicultural perspective, research that does not impose ethnocentric notions of normality and cultural superiority and does not view ethno-cultural differences as pathology, does not necessarily embrace the emic perspective of Africentrism (Rasheed & Johnson, 1995). Africentricity ensures that the subjective culture of the research population is captured and reflected throughout the research process. A bicultural perspective, on the other hand, as opposed to a cultural deficiency perspective, is a necessary but not sufficient perspective for culturally sensitive research. The use of an Africentric perspective, along with the bicultural perspective, is essential to a research process that seeks to understand and explain issues and behaviors of African American communities.

In assuming a bicultural perspective, the researcher is able to be more objective in examining the ecological context and impact of any given behavior, that may be adaptive or dysfunctional, depending on the interplay of contextual variables at different points in time. Thus there is an assumption that all cultures have cultural vulnerabilities. That is, any given sociocultural trait or pattern may serve as a strength in one regard; and then may render the person more vulnerable in another regard, hence, the double-edged-sword of cultural characteristics. The notion of cultural vulnerabilities is not to be construed as implying cultural inadequacies or cultural structural weaknesses or flaws. Rather, this notion serves as a safeguard against ethnocentric assumptions that any given cultural characteristic is somehow inherently pathological or flawed. It also prevents romanticizing cultural characteristics, based on an unwillingness to admit to the dysfunctionality of a characteristic, for fear of being viewed as racist or ethnocentric.

Ecological/Developmental Framework

The community context is intricately linked to the life status and experiences of African American men (see for example: Poitier, 2000). Often the social vitality and the physical resources of poor, urban African American communities are not examined or linked in a systematic method that explores the synchrony between the socioeconomic structure and the life expectations and opportunities for African American males. This missing component represents a conceptual failure in understanding the life cycle development, behaviors, and ecology of African American males and their environments.

The collective and interdependent nature of the African American community, however, provides a legitimate basis for the development of an ecological research approach for studies on black men. Thus, research studies attempting to comprehensively understand the experiences and dilemmas facing African American men must systematically build in methodologies that seek to understand the complex interplay of micro and macro systems factors that dynamically interact with each other and profoundly shape the life space of African American men. Hence, there is a need for future research to be more holistic in examining the dilemmas of African American men and to discontinue the study of potentially interrelated issues, such as institutionalized racism, education, employment, crime, violence, gang behavior, and family relationships, in isolation of each other.

Postmodern Perspective

Lincoln and Guba (1989) lay the blame for research's failure to meet the needs of its subjects at the feet of an unquestioned reliance on the scientific/positivistic research paradigm. Based upon relativism, these authors espouse a unity between the knower and the known. The postmodern research paradigm, with its emphasis on a subjective epistemology, has the potential to unite the researcher and the stakeholder in a research process that emphasizes empowerment and the enfranchisement of the stakeholder, as well as an action orientation.

The postmodernist framework for conceptualizing research on African American men can also be an important tool against the fallacies of homogeneity and a monolithic racial identity. The positivists' search for a grand theory has marginalized and discouraged the exploration and expression of multiple voices and multiple ethno-cultural realities. In their journey to establish the truth, positivists have designed methodologies to advance more rational forms of knowing (Graff, 1979). These methodologies, however, may hinder knowledge-building by marginalizing and devaluing questions and methodologies that emphasize personal cultural experiences and embrace the narrative as a method of inquiry.

However, the postmodernist perspective is not meant to replace the search for the grand theory with the search for the grand narrative. Instead, it is an attempt to legitimize the role that personal experiences play in theory-building; as opposed to exclusive reliance upon community experiences or on the collective story of the disempowered (Richardson, 1988, p. 204). The postmodernists also seek to legitimize the role of folk lore, folk wisdom, folk legends, and popular stories that can emerge in the personal narratives of subjects (Graff, 1979). This indigenous or subjugated knowledge calls into question the politicized knowledge of gender studies or stories about black men based on the dominant discourse. Thus, black men's cultural narratives of their own lives can liberate truly indigenous ways of knowing that may have been obscured by the positivists' narrow range of research methodologies.

METHODOLOGICAL ISSUES IN
AFRICAN AMERICAN MALE RESEARCH

As rigorous methodological critiques of research on African American men emerged in the literature (Gary, 1981; Bowman, 1991), researchers began to exact more methodological rigor in research with this population. Contemporary research appears to take more care in terms of the following methods:

- in the selection of sampling frames and/or avoiding distorted overgeneralizations of data, based on skewed dyfunctional or deviant sampling frames;
- in selecting and refining data collection instruments to minimize cultural bias and/or distortions; and
- in executing a wider array of data collection methods and research designs to facilitate the examination of previously suppressed data.

The cumulative result of such methods has yielded research on African American men that is more methodologically sound and more culturally sensitive (Brown, McGregor, & Gary, 1998). However, the nature of research is that there is always a better mousetrap to be built. The kinds of methodological issues that plague today's generation of researchers on African American men are more sophisticated and complex in nature, as compared to earlier violations of elementary research principles. These issues include a need for the following research strategies:

- pre-testing actual survey research questions to determine their cognitive or construct validity, i.e., whether these questions are meaningful to African American men;
- longitudinal research to examine the unique developmental issues of African American males;
- less reliance on self-report measures as data collection instruments;
- a wider array of data collection instruments;
- more varied sources of data which have been typically underutilized, for example, ethnographic interviews, key informants, personal and public documents, artifacts, direct observation, and participant-observation;
- more complex research designs, with emphasis on including comparison or cohort groups to facilitate analysis of independent and intervening variables, as well as the analysis of intragroup differences along important structural variables, such as social class, sexual orientation, family structure, and levels of acculturation;
- a wider array of research procedures that promote the use of mixed methods, both qualitative and quantitative approaches, for example, the case study

research method to promote an emphasis on theory development, and understanding intragroup differences; and finally

- a wider array of ideographic versus nomothetic research designs, such as ethnographic research and focus groups, which have the capacity to identify strengths
and self-affirming patterns in African American men, rather than to merely cat-
alogue deficiencies. (Akbar, 1991; Bowman, 1989, 1991; Gadsden & Smith,
1994; O'Neil et al., 1995; Taylor et.al., 1990; Thompson & Pleck, 1995)

FUTURE GOALS, OBJECTIVES AND STRATEGIES FOR RESEARCH DEVELOPMENT AND DISSEMINATION

Stakeholder Involvement in Research

The foregoing review and analysis of the literature suggests four main
strategies for increasing the functional relevance, and thus, stakeholder
or community involvement in the research process. These strategies involve the need to:

- explicitly target the needs of the community;
- seek assistance from indigenous consultants and/or an advisory board with
residents from the community;
- use indigenous interviewers in the collection of data; and
- arrange for exchanges and tradeoffs, for example, provide technical assistance
to community-based organizations at the conclusion of the research project.
(Bowman, 1983)

Continued Development of Research and Dissemination Strategies

It is no small coincidence that research has greatly improved in this
area as a direct result of increasing numbers of well-trained researchers
with a genuine altruistic commitment to research on African American
men. Graduate assistantships, research fellowships, doctoral and post-
doctoral trainee and apprenticeships are critical components if this area
of research is to continue to flourish. Additionally, training seminars
and conferences that specifically target and thus promote research on
black men are other important activities that can promote networking
and mentoring among researchers and scholars. It is incumbent upon
colleges, universities, research institutes, professional organizations and

human service agencies to be active in sponsoring participants in this regard.

These institutions and organizations can also play critical roles in establishing research institutes that can serve a crucial role in nurturing future researchers, research development, and dissemination or data on African American men. These research institutes can serve important clearinghouse functions of research development and dissemination, and act as general think tanks that coordinate systematic research agendas, such as coordinating periodic annotated-interdisciplinary research bibliographies. Research centers or institutes can also function as consultants in all aspects of the research process or in assisting communities in identifying problems important to African American men and in enabling them to design their own solutions.

Finally, these research centers or institutes can perform important advocacy roles in seeking to develop funding for new and innovative lines of research for scholars. As well, these centers can play pivotal roles in impacting micro and macro systems-wide changes by helping to disseminate important research developments to key political groups, organizations, mass media, and policy makers.

CONCLUSION

Research on African American men needs to involve action-oriented, problem-solving research models that contribute not only to the study of complex social issues, but also facilitate the development of innovative solutions that help black men to empower themselves. In designing research programs on African American men, research strategies should promote community organizing, consumer involvement, and leadership development by using the principles of empowerment, advocacy, self-help, mentoring, and social support.

REFERENCES

Akbar, N. (1991). Paradigms of African American research. In R.L. Jones (Ed.) *Black psychology* (third edition) (709–726). Berkley CA: Cobb & Henry Publishers.

Alejandro-Wright, M. (1982). An intracultural perspective on research. *Child Care Quarterly 11*(1) Spring. 67–77.

Asante, M. (1988). *Afrocentricity.* Trenton, NJ: Africa World Press.

Asante, M. K. (1981). Black male and female relationships: An Afrocentric context. In L. E. Gary (Ed.), *Black men.* Beverly Hills, CA: Sage.

Austin, W. B. (1996). *National task force on African American men and boys: Repairing the breach.* Dillon, CO: Alpine Press.

Baldwin, J. A. (1981). Notes on theory of black personality. *The Western Journal of Black Studies, 5*(3). 172–179.

Banfield, E. C. (1970). The *unheavenly city: The nature and future of our urban crisis.* Boston: Little, Brown, and Company.

Banks, W. M. (1980). Theory in black psychology. Paper presented at the thirteenth annual National Convention of the Association of Black Psychologists, Cherry Hill, NJ.

Berry, J. W. (1969). On cross-cultural comparability. *International Journal of Psychology, 4,* 119–128.

Billingsley, A. (1968). *Black families in white America.* Englewood Cliffs, NJ: Prentice Hall.

Billingsley, A. (1992). *Climbing Jacob's ladder: The eduring legacy of African American families.* New York: Simon & Schuster.

Bowman, P. J. (1991). Race, class and ethics in research: Belmont principles to functional relevance. In R.L. Jones (Ed.), *Black Psychology* (third edition). (747–768). Berkeley, California: Cobb & Henry Publishers.

Bowman P. J. (1989). Research perspective on black men: Role strain and adaptation across the adult life cycle. In R.L. Jones (Ed.), *Black adult development and aging.* Berkeley: Cobb and Henry.

Bowman, P. J. (1985). Black fathers and the provider role: Role strain, informal coping resources and life happiness. In A. W. Bonken (Ed.), *Empirical research in black psychology* (pp. 9–19). Washington, DC: National Institute for Mental Health.

Bowman, P. J. (1983). Significant involvement and functional relevance: Challenges to survey research. *Social Work Research and Abstracts, 19*(4). 21–26.

Braithwaite, R.L. (2001) The health status of Black men. In R. L. Braithwaite & S.E., Taylor, (Eds.), *Health Issues in the Black community* (pp. 62–80). San Francisco, CA: Jossey Bass, Inc.

Brislin, R. W. (1970).. Black translation for cross-cultural research. *Journal of Cross-Cultural Psychology, 1,* 185–216.

Brown, D.R., McGregor, K.C. & Gary, L.E. (Spring 1998). Sex role identity and depressive symptoms among African American men. *Perspectives.* 4 (1), 4–10.

Cazenave, N. A. (1981). Black men in America: The quest for "manhood." In H. P. McAdoo (Ed.), *Black families.* Beverly Hills, CA: Sage.

Clark, K. B. (1965). *Dark ghetto.* New York: Harper & Row.

Davis, L.E. (Ed.) (1999) *Working with African American males: A guide to practice.* CA: Sage.

Etzkowitz, H. & Schaflander, G. (1969). *Ghetto crisis.* Boston: Little Brown and Company.

Evans, B. J. & Whitfield, J. R. (Eds.), (1988). Black males in the United States: An annotated bibliography from 1967 to 1987. *Bibliographies in Psychology, No. 1.* Washington, DC: American Psychological Association.

Frazier, E. F. (1939). *The Negro family in the United States.* Chicago: University of Chicago Press.

Frazier, E. F. (1932a). *The free Negro family.* Nashville, TN: Fisk University Press.

Frazier, E. F. (1932b). *The Negro family in Chicago.* Chicago: University of Chicago Press.

Gadsden, V. L. & Smith, R. R. (1994). African American males and fatherhood: Issues in research and practice. *Journal of Negro Education, 63*(4), 634–648.

Garrett, H. (1961). One psychologist's view of equality of the races. *U.S. News and World Report, 51*(4), 72–74.

Gary, L. E. (1981). *Black men.* Beverly Hills: Sage.

Gibbs, J. (Ed). (1988). *Young, black and male in American: An endangered species.* Over, MA: Auburn Publishing Co.

Glasgow, D. G. (1980). *The black underclass.* San Francisco, CA: Jossey-Bass.

Gould, S. J. (1981). *The mismeasure of man.* New York: W.W. Norton & Co., Inc.

Graff, G. (1979). *Literature against itself.* Chicago: University of Chicago Press.

Grier, W. H., & Cobbs, P. M. (1968). *Black rage.* New York: Bantam.

Herrnstein, R. J., & Murray, C. (1994). *The bell curve: Intelligence and class structure in American life.* New York: Free Press.

Hill, R. (1972). *The strengths of black families.* New York: Emerson-Hall.

Hill, R.B. (1999) *The strengths of African American families: Twenty-five years later.* Lanham, MD: Rowman & Littlefield Publishers, Inc.

Howitt, D. & Owusu-Bempah, M. (1994). *The racism of psychology.* New York: Harvester/Wheatsheaf.

Jensen, A. (1973). The differences are real. *Psychology Today, 7,* 80–86.

Jones, A. C. (1989). Psychological functioning in African American adults: Some elaborations on a model, with clinical implications. In R. Jones. (Ed), *Black adult development and aging.* Berkeley, CA: Cobb & Henry.

Kardiner, A. & Ovesey, L. (1951). *The marks of oppressions.* New York: Norton.

Kunjufu, J. (1982). *The conspiracy to destroy black boys.* Chicago: African American Images.

Lazur, R. F. & Majors, R. (1995). Men of color: Ethnocultural variations of male gender role strain. In R.F. Levant & W.S. Pollack (Eds.), *A new psychology of men* (pp. 337–358). New York: Basic Books.

Liebow, E. (1967). *Tally's corner: A study of Negro streetcorner men.* Boston, MA: Little, Brown and Company.

Lincoln, E. & Guba, E. (1989). *Naturalistic inquiry.* New York: Sage.

Logan, S. (Ed.). (2001). *The Black family: Strengths, self help, and positive change* (2nd Ed.), Boulder, CO: Westview Press.

Majors, R. & Billson, J. (1992). *Cool pose: The dilemmas of black manhood in America.* New York: Lexington.

Majors, R. G. & Gordon, J. V. (Eds.). (1994). *The American black male: His present status and his future.* Chicago: Nelson-Hall.

McAdoo, H. P. (Ed.). (1997). *Black families.* (3rd Ed.) Thousand Oaks, CA: Sage.

McAdoo, H. P. (1978). Factors related to stability in upwardly mobile black families. *Journal of Marriage and the Family, 40*(4), 761–776.

McAdoo, J. (1993). The roles of African American fathers: An ecological perspective. *Families in Society: The Journal of Contemporary Human Services, 48,* 28–35.

Mickel, E. (2001) African-Centered reality therapy: Intervention and prevention. In S. Logan & E. Freeman, (Eds.), *Health care in the Black community: Empowerment, knowledge, skills, and collectivism.* (pp. 137–162) Binghamton, NY: The Haworth Press, Inc.

Moynihan, D. (1965). *The Negro family: The case for national action.* Washington, DC: U.S. Government Printing Office.

Myers, L. J. (1985). Transpersonal psychology: The role of the Afrocentric paradigm. *Journal of Black Psychology, 12,* (1), 31–42.

Nobles, W. W. (1978). Toward an empirical and theoretical framework for defining black families. *Journal of Marriage and Family, 40,* 679–687.

Oliver, W. (1989). Black males and social problems: Prevention through Afrocentric socialization. *Journal of Black Studies, 20*(1), 15–39.

O'Neil, J., Good, G. E. & Holmes, S. (1995). Fifty years of theory and research on men's gender role conflict: New paradigms for empirical research. In R.F. Levant & W.S. Pollack (Eds.), *A new psychology of men.* New York: Basic Books.

Parham, T. A. & McDavis, R. J. (1987). Black men, an endangered species: Who's really pulling the trigger? *Journal of Counseling and Development, 66,* 220–228.

Poitier, S. (2000) *The measure of a man: A spiritual autobiography.* San Francisco: Harper and Collins.

Rainwater, L. (1966). Crucible of identity: The lower-class Negro family. *Daedalus, 95,* 172–216.

Rainwater, L. (1970). *Beyond the ghetto walls: Black families in a federal slum.* Chicago: Aldine.

Rasheed, J. M. & Johnson, W. E. (1995). Non-custodial African American fatherhood. *Journal of Community Practice, 2,* 99–116.

Richardson, L. (1988). The collective story: Postmodernism and the writing of sociology. *Sociological Focus, 21,* 199–207.

Scanzoni, J. H. (1971). The *black family in modern America.* Boston: Allyn & Bacon.

Stack, Carol B. (1974). *All our kin: Strategies for survival in a Black community.* New York: Harper & Row.

Stanfield, II, J. H. (1993). Epistemological considerations. In J.H. Stanfield II & D.M. Rutledge (Eds.), *Race and ethnicity in research methods* (pp. 16–38). Newbury Park, CA: Sage Publications.

Staples, R. (1971). Toward a sociology of the black family: A theoretical and methodological assessment. *Journal of Marriage and the Family, 33,* 119–138.

Stier, H. & Tienda, M. (1993). Are men marginal to the family? Insights from Chicago's inner city. In M. Tienda & H. Stier (Eds.), *Men, work, and family.* Newbury Park: Sage Publications.

Sudarkasa, N. (1981). Interpreting the African heritage in African family organization. In H. P. McAdoo (Ed.), *Black families.* Beverly Hills, CA: Sage.

Sudarkasa, N. (1980). African and Afro-American family structure: A comparison. The *Black Scholar, 20,* 37–60.

Taylor, R. J., Chatters, L. M., Tucker, M. B. & Lewis, E. (1990). Developments in research on black families: A decade review. *Journal of Marriage and the Family, 52,* 993-1014.

Taylor, R. L. (1995). The plight of Black men: Black males and social policy. In P. H. Collins & M. L. Anderson. (Eds.), *Race, class, gender: An anthology.* Belmont: Wadsworth.

Taylor, R. L. (1987). Black youth in crisis. *Humboldt Journal of Social Relations, 14,* 106–133.

Taylor, R. L. & Wilkinson, D. Y. (1977). *The black male in America.* Chicago: Nelson-Hall.

Thompson, E. H., Jr., & Pleck, J. H. (1995). Masculinity ideologies: A Review of research instrumentation on men and masculinities. In R.F. Levant & W.S. Pollack (Eds.), *A new psychology of men (129–163).* New York: Basic Books.

Tidwell, B. J. (1990). Research and practice issues with black families. In S. M. Logan, E. M. Freeman, & R. G. McRoy (Eds.), *Social work practice with black families (259–272).* New York: Longman.

Triandis, M. C. (1972). *The analysis of subjective culture.* New York: Wiley.

Williams, R. L. (1980). The death of white research in the black community. In R.L. Jones (ed.), *Black psychology (second edition)* New York: Harper and Row.

Willie, C. V. (1970). *The family life of black people.* New York: Free Press.

Chapter 11

RESEARCH ON THE SOCIAL SUPPORT SYSTEMS OF THE BLACK ELDERLY: INFORMAL AND FORMAL RESOURCES

BRENDA CRAWLEY

How can policy thinking and initiatives address the social support needs of elderly African Americans? Should policy thinking and initiatives address the social support needs of African Americans? Should there be a one-dimensional approach to addressing the social support needs of the elderly irrespective of ethnicity and/or race? What should be the proper mix of informal social supports and formal societal-based support? These and other questions present themselves as one reviews the literature on social support systems of the African American elderly.

Social support needs are usually conceptualized in terms of assistance needed with activities of daily living (ADL) such as personal care, basic housekeeping, meal preparation, and the like (Ralston, 1993). Some authors have also given consideration to the affiliate and emotional needs of the elderly as appropriate spheres for policy intervention, for example, friendly visitors and telephone reassurance calls. Failure to have one's social support needs met can lead to poor physical and/or emotional health as well as negatively impact/decrease the quality of life (Luckey, 1994).

Use of social services to help meet the social support needs of the African American elderly has been and continues to be the subject of research and discussions about equitable policies for this generally underserved group. As noted in the literature review section of this chapter, authors of varying persuasions emphasize that viable policies can lead to effective programs and services, including those for care-givers, along with workable service delivery structures for helping to meet the social support needs of the African American elderly. Thus, while family, relatives, and kin are essential informal sources of social support to the black elderly, it remains the case that modern, postindustrialized, and urbanized societies also require some degree of structural or formal society-based programs and services to provide care.

This chapter reviews and critically analyzes the research literature on these two areas of social support pertaining to the black elderly. The studies and conceptualizations in that review strongly indicate that the African American elderly need both informal and formal social supports. Therefore, the following question is an important context for this review: "Under what conditions and to what degree should the social support needs of the black elderly be properly met by the informal sector and by the formal sector?" The chapter also proposes a framework for enhancing this area of research, particularly for meeting challenges involved in studies on the next generation of black elderly. That generation will have considerably different historical and cultural experiences from the current one, which are summarized as part of the chapter's conclusion.

LITERATURE REVIEW

Studies Involving African American Respondents Only

The Black Church As An Informal Support. Morrison (1991) posits that the Black Church is an untapped viable community support system for offering social services. His stratified sample method was used to obtain twenty churches in West Philadelphia as research sources. He examined various contributions to the support and social service needs of black elderly who were at three levels of functioning: those who were active, infirm, or incapacitated. Overall, this author found that the size and denomination of the churches resulted in different responses to these three groups of elderly. For the active elderly, churches provided "growth and development forums" (p. 115) on a range of useful educational and informational topics, provided assistance in filling our government forms, operated food cupboard programs for the elderly, and other services. Among the infirm elderly, visitations by clergy or lay people, small cash gifts, and sometimes transportation services were available. For the incapacitated, those ". . . who needed substantial services such as home health care or actual relocation to a residential facility" (p. 112), Catholic churches were often able to use parish social ministers to provide counseling and referral assistance.

In comparison, smaller black churches lacked the internal or external resources to assist their elderly incapacitated parishioners. Some larger, mostly Baptist churches were in the process of recognizing the social service needs of their congregations in general. Morrison (1991) drew the following conclusions from his study: (1) churches need to recognize the significant contributions they can make in helping to meet the social service needs of their African American elderly, and (2) "traditional" social service providers should make better use of black churches to provide preventive as well as supportive services (p. 117).

The Black Church and Family Supports In Combination. As with Morrison, Walls and Zarit (1991) explored the potential role of the church, as well as the family, in the well-being of elderly blacks. Ninety-eight healthy subjects from local black churches in central Pennsylvania were measured on social support, religiosity, well-being, health status, and functional ability. Their findings revealed that the black elderly used family networks for support more than the church, although family and church networks often overlapped. Findings also showed that these elderly gained a considerable sense of well-being from church members, whereas those elderly with both family and church networks showed the highest levels of well-being. Walls and Zarit conclude that [some] African American aged have stronger emotional and other ties to their church(es) than they do to formal social service organizations. Because of the relationship these authors found between well-being and church connectedness, they indicate that ". . . social service agencies might work within the organizational structures of black churches to provide more services to elderly individuals living in black communities" (p. 493).

The Role of Informal Kin Network Supports. According to Luckey (1994), and as other researchers have noted, social supports in the informal sector or network of the African American elderly play a vital role in maintaining them in their communities. Luckey analyzes two frameworks from previous studies to inform her research conceptualizations of black elderly social supports among kin across generations. One framework is that of Shana, as cited in Luckey (1994), which "proposes that family members are available in serial order; in other words, if one individual is not available to help, another will step in" (p. 82). The second framework is Cantor's (as cited in Luckey, 1994) "hierarchical-compensatory model of kin and non-kin sources of support [which] suggests that the elderly prefer receiving help from close kin" (p. 82). According to Luckey (1994), neither model captures the intergenerational and complementary relations African Americans share in their relational networks.

Using historical and situational content in conjunction with case studies, Luckey (1994) draws several conclusions. First, the historical context of the African American elderly, who Luckey labels as the first generation, has generally lacked the educational and experiential bases for knowing and using social services, but it *has* been characterized by an experience of lifelong prejudice and discrimination, both of which prevent or severely restrict their use of those services. As a result, the black elderly's use of second and third generation family and kin, who are often more educated and knowledgeable about social services, becomes critical. Luckey argues that within the context of black family cohesion and the extended-family orientation, second and third generation kin are not selected in serial or hierarchical order. Communication occurs on the basis of need and is grounded in the use of fluid roles or whom can best inform and/or assist the elderly relative in securing services.

Implications for Formal Service Providers. The value of Luckey's (1994) conceptual analysis is that social service providers frequently miss opportunities to include significant kin, for example, nephews, nieces, and cousins in the communication loop of service for the elderly African American client. The challenge to providing adequate services by the formal structure is to: (1) appropriately understand the dynamics and roles in the African American elderly client's informal social support network, (2) ask the right questions of the elderly person and/or the caregiver to establish second and third generation kin involvement and relevance to care, (3) engage the relevant use of so-called distant kin, (4) identify ways in which confidentiality becomes a barrier to providing adequate care along with inducing sufficient safeguards to allow for second and third kinship generation contributions to the elder's care, and (5) rigorously examine and revise agency policies "that do not support inclusion of second- or third-generation kin as viable parts of the elder's support network. . . " (p. 88).

Richardson's (1992) study also has implications for providers who serve African American elderly clients. This researcher studied 186 urban black elders or their caregivers and key informants along with agency documents regarding actual and anticipated use of services. She used a purposeful sample, pretested interview protocols, same-race interviewers, and descriptive and multivariate analyses to draw the same conclusions and recommendations found in almost all research findings on the black elderly. Many elderly did not know about the social services available to seniors. As well, findings included the following points of need: more in-depth understanding of African American elders with caregivers by social service providers, improved community education methods for informing African American elders of services, more culturally sensitive services, greater commitment by those in the gerontology field to address economic injustice, creative outreach methods for this population of elders, and agency policies that are more attuned to African American elders.

Cross-Cultural Comparison Studies

The Role of Ethnicity and Social Supports. Cantor, Brennan, & Sainz (1994) revisit key aspects of their 1970s study of social support systems for black and white elderly in New York with the addition of Latino elder respondents in the 1990s' sample of their study. According to these researchers, a stratified representative sample of 1,570 noninstitutionalized Latino, black, and white elders, sixty-five years of age and older, was used. The basic thesis of the earlier and current studies was to discount the weight but not the importance of ethnicity in social support systems for older New Yorkers. Unsurprisingly, the 1990s' study documents that ethnicity still has some importance. They found that "Assistance between older parents and their children was moderated by ethnicity, but need, in terms of income level and functional ability, and gender emerged as more overriding factors" (p. 95).

Ethnicity and Help-Seeking Behavior. Husaini, Moore, and Cain (1994) used a sample of 1,200 black and white elderly developed from a multistage random selection process to examine the link between psychiatric symptoms and the help-seeking behavior of these respondents. Psychiatric symptoms were defined as evidence of depression and "psychiatric disorders experienced in the last six months" (American Psychiatric Association, 2000, p. 181). These researchers analyzed help-seeking behavior related to three categories: (1) professionals, (2) support networks, and (3) self-help. Their findings included the following areas: (1) black and white elderly varied slightly in regards to seeking help from family physicians and clergy; as well, neither reported high use of trained mental health professions; (2) virtually no racial differences existed in their discussions with friends, relatives and co-workers; and (3) the self-help use of prayer, hoping the problem goes away, eating more food, or going for walks showed no significant racial/ethnic differences among the respondents. As might be generally predicted, women more often sought help from those in these three categories than men. Help-seeking behavior based in psychiatric symptoms presented the most diverse help-seeking patterns between elderly blacks and whites.

Husaini et al. (1994) drew the following conclusions from these findings, that: (1) they did not find significant racial differences in a variety of help-seeking behavior except by gender and psychiatric symptoms, (2) informal supports are used more than formal ones, (3) medical services are more preferred than mental health services, (4) social workers must interface more effectively with other professionals as well as facilitate the interface between mental health and other helping professionals, and (5) social workers in clinical practice should focus on "assisting depressed and other psychologically impaired adults in finding more positive ways of dealing with emotional distress (p. 192).

Ethnicity, Family Caregiving, and Long-Term Care. Sudha and Mutran (1999) investigated informal and formal social support needs through the prism of attitudes towards adult care homes and care by families. Out of a detailed discussion of their sampling methods, the authors describe the responses of 537 elderly persons (283 African Americans and 254 whites) and 492 caregivers (265 African Americans and 227 whites). Most respondents were females living in urban localities.

Their primary finding appears to be that while ethnicity was an important indicator of unwillingness to use a rest home by the elderly, that is, African American elderly were more likely than whites to not want to use a rest home, this unwillingness did not necessarily indicate a preference for family care. Basically, the authors found that both structural barriers and cultural factors influenced ethnic differences in care choices for the black elderly respondents in the study. Interestingly, caregivers ". . . showed no ethnic difference in reluctance or unwillingness to place an elderly person in a rest home" (p. 591).

A primary value of these authors' research lies in highlighting current ethnic-based elderly attitudes toward long-term care. This is especially true for older blacks, because as Bryant and Rakowski (cited in Sudha & Multran, 1999) point out, ". . . changes in African American demographic patterns and family structures will lead to future cohorts of minority elderly having fewer and more distant family network resources on which to rely" (p. 591). This could, of course, leave such elderly without family who can care for them. Thus, their attitudes towards long-term care institutions will, undoubtedly, become even more critical (Mutran, Sudha, Desai, & Long, 2001). Any negative attitudes suggest that consumer education, information and advertising and marketing of such care facilities require a clear culturally sensitive policy response.

A CRITICAL ANALYSIS OF RESEARCH METHODOLOGY AND OUTCOMES ISSUES

Factors Affecting Common Research Outcomes

The social support needs of the African American elderly have been studied from a variety of perspectives. Those perspectives include the role of relatives and kin involvement within (siblings, cousins) and across (grandchildren, nieces, and nephews) generations, the role of race/ethnicity *and* family in meeting support needs, the needs of caregivers of the elderly, the neglected use of black community institutions such as the black church, the failure of social service delivery systems to appropriately market services to the African American elderly, the lack of sensitivity and support of service providers, and more. Regardless of the characteristics of the respondents, the research methodology, or statistical methods, conceptualizations and research on the social support needs of the African American elderly have generally led to previously noted recommendations and implications, notably that:

> Many elderly did not know about the social services available to seniors. As well, findings included the following points of need: more "in-depth" understanding of African American elders with caregivers social service, improved advertising methods for informing African American elders of services, more culturally sensitive services, greater commitment by those in gerontology to address "economic injustice," creative outreach methods for this population of elders, and agency policies that are more attuned to African American elders. (Husaini et al., 1994; Luckey, 1994; Richardson, 1992)

Several reasons can be advanced as to why studies involving black elderly respondents with differing characteristics across urban and rural locations; varying age ranges, including young old, old, and old old; and varying income levels, such as low, modest, and middle, produce generally noncompeting recommendations and implications. Two such reasons will be cited here. First, it may be that the life experiences of current black elderly, while obviously constituted of personal lifestyles, are also sufficiently similar in lifelong common historical experiences involving a lack of information about social services and/or discrimination in the use of social services. Second, there may be serious methodological flaws in the studies and conceptualizations previously reviewed. As relates to future studies and conceptualizations of the social support needs of the elderly, both explanations will be critically analyzed.

Assumptions About Common Black Historical Experiences

There can be little doubt that studies of and conceptualizations about African American elders, including the young old (65–74 years), old (75–84 years), and old-old (85 years and older), must include not only respondents' personal life courses but society's historical milieu of racially motivated discrimination, de jure and de facto segregation, and racism. Thus, it might be that regardless of any particular elderly black American respondent's personal journey, almost any study should in some way tap into these respondents' collective historical experiences of exclusion and oppression. Closely related is an assumption that during elder respondents' younger days they may have had discriminatory or racist experiences with nonelderly-related social programs and services and may be somewhat reluctant to learn about or use social services in old age. These views in no way suggest that *all* respondents had the same interpretation of discriminatory or racist experiences or that *all* service providers acted in discriminatory or racist ways. Nor should such views be construed as re-stereotyping the black elderly as victims (Ralston, 1997; Shenk, Zablotsky, & Croom, 1998). However, the corporate experience of racial discrimination has been sufficiently documented to warrant, in part, general recommendations for culturally sensitive policies and community education strategies in terms brokering services for the black elderly.

Research Methodological Limitations

Some of the studies previously reviewed used more empirical methods than other studies, but fortunately, none attempted to generalize the reported findings to *The* black elderly in the United States of America. Collectively, however, this field of studies is hampered by small sample sizes, varied age ranges among respondents, urban and non-urban milieus, individual and institutional samples, and multiple conceptual frames of reference. For example, some researchers have examined African American elderly social support needs by using concepts such as gender or a focus on older black women or black men (Conway-Turner, 1999; Crawley & Freeman, 1993; Ralston, 1997; Shenk, Zablotsky, & Croom, 1998); health status and health needs (Ralston, 1993; Yat-Sang, 1999); health and religion (Musick, 1996); mental health status (Biegel, Farkas, & Song, 1997); elderly abuse (Williams & Griffin, 1996); and even the remote population of elderly African American farm women (Carlton-LaNey, 1992). As well, it has been noted that this body of research has produced surprisingly nondivergent recommendations and implications regarding the social support systems and service needs of African American elderly, especially when compared to those of white respondents (Hudson, Leventhal, Contrada, Leventhal, & Brownlee, 2000).

A PROPOSED DUAL FRAMEWORK FOR RESEARCH
INVOLVING THE BLACK ELDERLY

A Comparative Research Paradigm

The significant societal structural changes occurring within the life-time of baby-boomer African American elderly suggest that the research framework for this group must be minimally dual in focus. First, comparative research *among* ethnic/racial elderly groups should be conducted. However, traditional comparative studies on black and white elderly should be eliminated. Modern racial/ethnic diversity in the United States is more expansive than the traditional black-white comparative research paradigm. Research from such a paradigm would likely not only reproduce negative stereotypes but perpetuate a victimhood view of black elderly and of black elderly females in particular. Hence, the proposed framework supports comparative research on all elderly groups of color such as Native Americans, Asian Americans, Latinos, African Americans, biracial individuals, and Arabs, as well as whites, and including religious, social class, location, and other significant cultural differences. Moreover, this framework emphasizes the use of multiracial/ethnic research teams and interviewers, who also represent age diversity, as appropriate (Gurnack & Johnson, 2002; Howard, Konrad, Stevens, & Porter, 2001; Levkoff, Prohaska, Weitzman, & Ory, 2000; Napoles-Springer, Grumbach, Alexander, Moreno, Forte, Rangel-Lugo, & Perez-Stable, 2000).

A NonComparative Research Paradigm

Second, Richardson (1992) makes a good case for noncomparative research on the black elderly. There is no denial that numerous baby-boomer African America elderly benefited from the major social transformations that have occurred over the past four to five decades. Nonetheless, racism as a barrier has not abated but has rather assumed modern language and garb. And while its most odious overt expressions have generally left the public space, it has been argued that modern quiet racism is just as deadly. Thus, research on future black elders should directly explore how the modern strain of racism has impacted that generation of black elderly.

Within the noncomparative research paradigm, the proposed framework encourages listening to baby-boomer black elders describe their lives, both in general and relative terms, relative to the context of current black elderly in order to identify differences. This framework further suggests that research should explore the following areas: (1) information about changes that have occurred in the identity of elderly African Americans; (2) the impact of identity as it relates to whether the black church continues to be a viable institution for informal social support networks, and (3) whether there will be a preference for Afrocentric institutional care by this group and what impact this preference could have on agency programs, services, and providers.

Common Research Topics Across the Two Paradigms

Both comparative and noncomparative research should explore respondents' definitions of social support networks, the meaning of social support to their lives, and their identification of who makes up their social support network. As well, research should hone in on whether and to what extent respondents need formal support services to supplement or substitute for their informal support systems. As mentioned previously, changes in mobility patterns along with changes in family, relative, and kinship availability may result from the social changes of the last few decades. Should the patterns of change strongly impact black family and extended family members, relative and kinship relations, and the members' proximity, it will be necessary to study this critical social support area in more depth (Bullock, Crawford, & Tennstedt, 2003).

CONCLUSION

It has always been the case that African Americans must somehow be a part of the American mainstream while facing unique group-specific challenges in U.S. society. It remains no different for future African American elderly. Research into their social support needs and networks will benefit from the two-pronged research framework discussed previously.

As these baby-boomer African Americans age, it can be reasonably assumed that they will differ somewhat from current black elderly respondents. Significantly different structural societal changes constitute key experiences for baby-boomer African American elderly. Such changes include but are not limited to the Civil Rights movement, affirmative action legislation, the women's movement, and the technological revolution. Such profound structural changes in society have affected these soon-to-be-senior citizens in education, work, financial status, and all aspects of their lives. As well, baby-boomer black American elderly, like their nonblack American counterparts, will generally have some knowledge and use of social services as well as some sense of entitlement to the programs and services which they know are funded by their tax dollars. They may well share with their counterparts across the racial/ethnic spectrum a modern conceptualization of what social welfare and social services mean. Additionally, while racism persists, unlike the current generation of elders, baby-boomer African American elderly can expect less overt discriminatory and racist social service provisions and providers.

REFERENCES

American Psychiatric Association (2000). *Diagnostic and statistical manual of mental disorders* (Fourth Edition). Washington, DC: APA.

Biegel, D.E., Farkas, K.J., & Song, L. (1997). Barriers to the use of mental health services by African American and Hispanic elderly persons. *Journal of Gerontological Social Work, 29,* 23–44.

Bullock, K., Crawford, S.L., & Tennstedt, S.L. (2003). Employment and caregiving: Exploration of African American caregivers. *Social Work, 48*(2). 150–162.

Cantor, M.H., Brennan, M., & Sainz, A. (1994). The importance of ethnicity in the social support systems of older New Yorkers: A longitudinal perspective (1970–1990). *Journal of Gerontological Social Work, 22,* 95–128.

Carlton-LaNey, I. (1992). Elderly black farm women: A population at risk. *Social Work, 37,* 517–523.

Conway-Turner, K. (1999). Older women of color: A feminist exploration of the intersections of personal, familial, and community life. In J. Dianne Garner (Ed.), *Fundamentals of feminist gerontology* (pp. 115–130). New York: The Haworth Press, Inc.

Crawley, B. & Freeman, E.M. (1993). Themes in the life views of older and younger African American males. *Journal of African American Male Studies, 1*(1), 15–29.

Gurnack, A.M. & Johnson, W.A. (2002). Elderly drug use and racial/ethnic populations. *Journal of Ethnicity in Substance Abuse, 1*(2), 55–71.

Howard, D.L., Konrad, T.R., Stevens, C., & Porter, C.Q. (2001). Physician-patient racial matching, effectiveness of care, use of service, and patient satisfaction. *Research on Aging, 23*(1), 83–108.

Hudson, S.V., Leventhal, H., Contrada, R., Leventhal, E.A., & Brownlee, S. (2000). Predicting retention for older African Americans in a community study and a clinical study: Does anything work? *Journal of Mental Health and Aging, 6*(1), 67–78.

Husaini, B.A., Moore, S.T., & Cain, V.A. (1994). Psychiatric symptoms and help-seeking behavior among the elderly: An analysis of racial and gender differences. *Journal of Gerontological Social Work, 21,* 177–195.

Levkoff, S.E., Prohaska, T.R., Weitzman, P.F., & Ory, M.G. (2000). Recruitment and retention in minority populations: Lessons learned in conducting research on health promotion and minority aging. *Journal of Mental Health and Aging, 6*(1), 5–7.

Luckey, I. (1994). African American elders: The support network of generational kin. *Families in Society: The Journal of Contemporary Human Services, 75,* 82–89.

Morrison, J.D. (1991). The black church as a support system for black elderly. *Journal of Gerontological Social Work, 17,* 105–120.

Musick, M. (1996). Religion and subjective health among black and white elders. *Journal of Health and Social Behavior, 37,* 221–237.

Mutran, E.J., Sudha, S., Desai, T., & Long, K. (2001). Satisfaction with care among elderly African American and white residents of adult care facilities. *Research on Aging, 23*(1), 61–82.

Napoles-Springer, A.M., Grumbach, K., Alexander, M., Moreno, J.G., Forte, D., Rangel-Lugo, M., & Perez-Stable, E.J. (2000). Clinical research with older African Americans and Latinos. *Research on Aging, 22*(6), 668–691.

Ralston, P. (1993). Health promotion for rural black elderly: A comprehensive review. *Journal of Gerontological Social Work, 20,* 53–78.

Ralston, P. (1997). Midlife and older black women. In J.M. Coyle (Ed.), *The Handbook on women and aging* (pp. 273–289). Westport, CT: Greenwood Press.

Richardson, V. (1992). Service use among urban African American elderly people. *Social Work, 37,* 47–54.

Shenk, D., Zablotsky, D., & Croom, M.B. (1998). Thriving older African American women: Aging after Jim Crow. *Journal of Women & Aging, 10,* 75–95.

Sudha, S. & Mutran, E.J. (1999). Ethnicity and eldercare: Comparison of attitudes toward adult care homes and care by families. *Research on Aging, 21,* 570–594.

Walls, C.T. & Zarit, S.H. (1991). Informal support from black churches and the well-being of elderly blacks. *The Gerontologist, 31,* 490–495.

Williams, O.J. & Griffin, L.W. (1996). Elderly maltreatment and cultural diversity: When laws are not enough. *Journal of Multicultural Social Work, 4,* 1–13.

Yat-Sang, L. (1999). The effects of race and ethnicity on use of health services by older Americans. *Journal of Social Service Research, 25,* 15–42.

PART THREE

MICRO-MEZZO-MACRO PRACTICE
STRATEGIES FOR BUILDING
ON THE STRENGTHS OF
BLACK FAMILIES AND COMMUNITIES
AND CHANGING LARGE SYSTEMS

Chapter 12

CULTURAL MAINTENANCE: BUILDING ON THE COMMON HERITAGE OF BLACK FAMILIES

Priscilla A. Gibson and Ruth G. McRoy

Culture is commonly viewed as a system of shared actions, values, and beliefs that guides the behavior of group members. It refers to ways of living (Pinderhughes, 1988) and to a particular social organization that are meaningful to participants in an encounter (Green, 1982). In this chapter the terms blacks and African Americans are used interchangeably to refer to people of African descent. African American families are inherently cultural beings. In the face of a history of slavery, they have maintained a distinct African culture despite efforts to eliminate it (Dill, 1988). Cultural maintenance is a world view or approach to living that places a high value on connecting with one's cultural heritage.

This chapter provides a detailed description of cultural maintenance and forms of expression related to African Americans' efforts to incorporate the concept into their daily lives. Conditions and factors that influence those efforts are included as well. That discussion is followed by a practice example of the Stamps family, a grandparent-headed household with a kinship care arrangement. Subsequently, practice strategies that incorporate the expression of cultural maintenance are applied to this case. Implications for future challenges to cultural maintenance are discussed and a summary of important points is presented in the conclusion.

CULTURAL MAINTENANCE OVERVIEW

Definition of the Concept

For black families, cultural maintenance means valuing a connection to their African heritage (Mosley-Howard & Evans, 2000), which is implied in terms and phrases such as "brother," "sister," "African American tradition," "black people," or "black culture." Cultural maintenance of black families is a world view that cherishes African American culture and its artifacts to the extent of wanting to incorporate some or all of these artifacts into those families' daily lives.

Practices and Related Beliefs

Cultural maintenance encompasses the following practices and beliefs by black families and communities:

1. Maintaining black culture through a range of overt or covert expressions that vary across individuals and subgroups: Although members of the Nation of Islam dress in suits and ties, which might convey a conservative philosophy, their ideas on black identity, self-help and personal improvement for blacks (White & Cones, 1999) indicate they strongly embrace cultural maintenance.
2. Expressing cultural maintenance as a dynamic and fluid process: From a social constructionist view, Nagel (1994) asserts that racial identities are fluid and vary across contexts and observers, while Pinderhughes (1988) describes this fluid process as the "transactional nature of culture" (p. 153).
3. Using cultural maintenance as a purposeful approach to living, which when acknowledged, appreciated, and integrated increases the quality of life for black people: Currently, blacks are forming their own definition of acceptable standards of dress, dance, language, art, music, and knowledge (White & Cones, 1999) which reflect African-centered or African American-centered themes and values (Algotsson, 2000).
4. Adopting cultural maintenance as a coping mechanism to capture pride and self-respect for being African American: Blacks are part of Africa and America–a combination that results in an emotional relationship with both and a culture that incorporates aspects of both.
5. Connecting black children to their African heritage in a positive manner (Comer & Poussaint, 1992; Boyd-Franklin & Franklin, 2000): There is a grow-

ing movement to document the achievements of African Americans that formerly lacked a presence in the literature (Kook, 1989) and for black families to use that information to instill an attitude of pride in their children (Comer & Poussaint, 1992).

In summary, cultural maintenance exists as a dynamic process that is expressed in many ways in the lives of black families. Patterns of expression vary across families and subgroups, and such patterns are influenced by both internal and external factors. Internal factors are the family's level of personal connection to its cultural heritage and how that connection is expressed. External factors reflect how others in families' environments interpret their culture and respond to the members, including the theoretical assumptions they use to explain and understand cultural maintenance within African American families and communities.

THEORETICAL CONSTRUCTS RELATED TO CULTURAL MAINTENANCE

Empowerment Theory

Cultural maintenance in African American families can best be understood by integrating the following theoretical perspectives: empowerment, strengths, and Africentric approaches. Barbara Solomon is viewed as the pioneer of empowerment theory (Simon, 1994), which espouses the elimination of the helplessness that characterizes people who are stigmatized and marginalized. Solomon (1976) emphasizes a practice approach that helps clients to attain a sense of control. Pinder-hughes (1989) links empowerment to cultural maintenance by noting: "Empowerment requires the use of strategies that enable clients to experience themselves as competent, valuable, and worthwhile both as individuals and as members of their cultural group" (p. 111).

The Strengths Perspective

The strengths perspective (Saleebey, 1997) is also intricately connected to cultural maintenance. It focuses on two factors that are salient in the lives of African American families: (a) they are perceived as having an inherent capacity in the family and in their environment to deal with their problems; and (b) they are viewed as an expert as the client (Saleebey, 1997). These two factors discount the view that African American families are deficient and dysfunctional, while supporting a belief in and value of their perspective as clients (Devore & Schlesinger, 1999). In contrast, when a professional does not embrace the strengths perspective, and there is a disagreement between him/her and the client, the professional's expert view of the situation typically takes precedence.

Logan, Freeman & McRoy (1990) noted that African American family strengths include biculturality, a nurturing extended family, support systems, and adaptability in coping. Shared values are significant as well in the lives of people of African descent. These values include (a) the importance of family and community (Wright & Anderson, 1998), (b) support for multigenerational and interdependent kinship systems (Blake & Darling, 2000), (c) valuing a helping tradition (Billingsley, 1992), (d) spiritual or religious consciousness (Harvey & Rauch, 1997; Hill, 1997; Lee, 1994), (e) an extended family and kinship system of mutual aid (Martin & Martin, 1985), (f) a strong education and work ethic (Hill, 1997), (g) interconnectedness (Harvey & Rauch, 1997), and (h) elders as keepers or maintainers of the culture (Carter, 1997).

Afrocentric Theory

Afrocentric theory identifies factors that are valued by black families and recognizes their strengths, which emerged from their ethnic traditions. Karenga (1993) describes Afrocentricity as a framework for viewing African descended people's culture in a holistic manner which includes their uniqueness, interconnectedness, and empowerment. Collins (1990) discusses the diversity in usage and meaning of Afrocentricity to African Americans. For instance, she described the concept as a way of viewing social issues confronting people of African descent with an eye toward fostering economic and social justice as well as "opposing social-scientific constructions of black culture as deviant" (p. 162).

Schiele (1996) emphasizes the collective identity derived from the Afrocentric framework which encompasses sharing, cooperation, and social responsibility. In the Afrocentric approach, group and community needs are stressed instead of individual aspirations (Akbar, 1985; Nobles, 1980). Most black families want to build strong communities that are committed to the nurturing and rearing of their children. Regardless of its use and varied meanings, clearly, Afrocentricity has a strong connection to cultural maintenance. Ruggiero and Taylor (1996) defined "heritage cultural maintenance" as an ideological position in which " ethnic groups members should maintain their heritage cultures as much as possible while adjusting to a new society" (p. 47). We use this Afrocentric theory, along with the empowerment and strengths perspectives, to understand black families living in the United States and important conditions that affect their efforts toward cultural maintenance

CONDITIONS AFFECTING CULTURAL MAINTENANCE

The Evolving Common Needs of Black families

Shared Childrearing/Socialization Traditions. Black families have some common needs that have assisted them in their cultural maintenance efforts, because such needs are often addressed in ways that reinforce their cultural traditions and values. In America, black families typically lived in communities where childrearing was the responsibility of all the adults in the neighborhood. Thus, it was common for a child to be nurtured, supervised, and disciplined by other adults in the community. Related and nonrelated adults took responsibility for overseeing the behaviors of children in their communities. Parents were informed about their children's behavior and activities without concerns about their parenting abilities being judged. This method of childrearing fits the African proverb: "it takes a village to raise a child," and it is consistent with the tradition of shared parenting within African clans. Communities took pride in this practice because it demonstrated caring. This nurturing behavior toward black children is similar to Collins' (1990) description of the ethics of caring.

Now with more integrated neighborhoods and children attending schools away from their neighborhoods, this common practice has lessened. Currently, African American families have to deal with sociopolitical issues that are negatively impacting the future of their children and communities. They express this culturally- and child-centered philosophy now through participation in community meetings that address: (a) crime rates with local politicians, the police, or the business community, (b) incidences of suspected police brutality with investigation committees, and/or (c) hazardous materials building permits with government monitoring agencies. Other examples include African American civic and socially conscious groups such as fraternities, sororities, lodges, and social clubs that sponsor activities and events to assist in the cultural development of black children and their families.

Cultural Survival Skills and Protection of Children. Another common need of black families is to prepare their children to deal with questions and issues of race (Comer & Poussaint, 1992), and to have productive lives despite the ever-present existence of racism. Blake and Darling (2000) identified the two most prevalent stressors for African American families as racism and discrimination. Preparation of children to cope with these stressors is essential due to the heightened vulnerability that confronts all African American youths, families and communities (Scannapieco & Jackson, 1996).

This preparation is directly connected to the survival of all marginalized groups (Swignoski, 1996) that are susceptible to "isms" such as racism, ageism, and sexism. What distinguishes blacks from other groups is their history of slavery and the resulting pervasive racist attitudes of the dominant society. For example, racial profiling or "driving while black" involves the experience of being stopped by the police for no apparent reason while driving. Black parents use the oral tradition for this cultural maintenance process related to cultural survival skills. They instruct their children in managing this experience by following directions regardless of the tone or words used, adopting a nondefensive attitude, limiting what they say, withholding expressions of anger, and sharing what happened with parents as soon as possible.

Helpseeking: Informal and Formal Resources. Accessing social services is another common need for many African American families, especially those in poverty who need resources from both informal and formal helping systems. Yet these often involuntary families hesitate to seek or accept help from formal systems (Rooney, 1992; McRoy, in press) in which culturally insensitive services are a barrier to cultural maintenance (McPhatter, 1997). Black families tend to seek nonstigmatized help from their informal cultural networks, which support cultural maintenance (English, 1991). In addition, the lack of attention to the sociocultural and sociopolitical context results in formal services being culturally irrelevant and unused (Wright & Anderson, 1998). The lack of knowledge and distrust of social service systems, the lack of a diverse staff (McRoy, in press), the inaccessible location of services, and negative perceptions of service delivery are also barriers (Logan, 1996).

Education as a Priority. In African American families, obtaining a good education is also a common need (Logan, 1990). Traditionally, although the black community recognized education as the best means to exit poverty (White & Cones, 1999), schools in the black community have been notoriously underfunded and understaffed, resulting in inadequate conditions that do not support learning. Therefore, low wealth black parents who are preoccupied with obtaining basic necessities to provide for their families need to be selective in how they involve themselves in the school. Comer and Poussaint (1992) stressed that "In order to take advantage of new opportunities we must raise strong, well-educated, and computer-literate black children (p. 12). African American families support education as a means to an end, which translates into increased earning power and quality of life for their children.

SocioPolitical and Other Contextual Issues

Impact of Public Policies. Public policies on the national, state, and local levels can act as a hindrance or enhancement to cultural maintenance by black families (Kook, 1989). Policies regarding discrimination in housing and employment, funding for the repair of roads to facilitate the infrastructure of a community, and the building of recreational facilities to promote the healthy development of children have a major influence on families' basic functioning, and therefore, on the time and energy they can devote to cultural maintenance. In addition, families look to the federal government to regulate policies that might be ignored at the state and local levels, especially if they are discriminatory against blacks. Currently, African American families continue to make substantial political and economic gains as well as struggle with issues that confronted previous generations. Despite the perceptions by some whites that discrimination has been eliminated by affirmative action and the voters' rights policies, African Americans continue to experience discrimination (Yetman, 1999).

Common Ethnic Traditions and Discrimination Experiences. Increasingly, new black immigrants are relocating to the United States who are similar to and different from native-born African Americans. In terms of historical commonalities, these new immigrant families are part of the African diaspora and its traditions, and like African Americans, they were either colonialized or enslaved by Europeans. Currently, they experience discrimination on the same level as African Americans. Garcia (2001) noted "Immigration and race are joined, almost inseparably, from the color line to the borderline. The majority of immigrants are considered 'people of color,' coming from Latin America, the Caribbean, Asia, Africa, and other parts of the world. And while they may 'pass' as people of color, they do not 'pass' as citizens" (p. 1). This author listed similar conditions encountered by immigrant and native-born blacks. Both groups are "undercounted, underpaid, constantly belittled by institutionalized racism, massively incarcerated, suffering astronomically high push-out rates in all levels of education, denied equal access to services and sharing similar poverty rates" (Garcia, 2001, p. 1).

Within-Group Ethnic Diversity. The population of new immigrants is very diverse in their languages, customs, religious affiliations, and reasons for relocating, as well as diverse from native-born African Americans. Unlike those who are native born, new black immigrants have chosen the United States as their new home and are voluntary residents rather than forcibly relocated. They arrive with a strong sense of cultural identity. According to Morris (1996) some black immigrants have an economic advantage over African Americans because they are successful in finding particular occupational niches. These niches then become accessible primarily to members of their subgroup and are patronized by the same ethnic subgroup consumers.

Cultural maintenance is a center stage issue for black immigrants who bring their unique perspectives to the United States. Gelfand and Fandetti (1993) listed ten factors that influence the degree of cultural allegiance and ethnic affiliation of families including: immigration experience, the language spoken at home, race and social mobility, emotional processes in the family, and political and religious ties of the ethnic group. Immigrating families must make decisions about how to negotiate their new environment and resolve questions such as: Should they be active or passive in coping with their new environment? What can they transfer from their old environment that will be cultural strengths in their new environment? What cultural artifacts are expendable and which should be maintained? Should they live in a segregated or integrated community? How much of this new culture should be incorporated into the socialization of their children? How should they handle cultural conflicts that may arise? These and other issues confront new immigrant families as they deal with the pressure to abandon their ethnic values and assimilate into a new culture (Goldenberg & Goldenberg, 2002).

Social workers who encounter these families in service agencies should take into account their culture, history, and the sociopolitical context in which they lived and currently live. Pierce and Elisme (1997), for example, list three factors to be considered when working with Haitian immigrant families, their: (1) history and culture; (2) migration patterns to the U. S.; and (3) experiences upon arrival. Where language is a barrier to communication, trained interpreters should be utilized. The focus should be on these families' experiences with discrimination as well as on issues of acculturation. As much as possible services should be located in the families' communities; people from those communities should be hired as staff; and members of the community should be involved in developing policies, programs, and services to maximize those families' options for maintaining their culture.

Influence of Ethnic Identity. In addition to diversity regarding their postdiapora countries of origin, African American families have been diverse and heterogenous historically in terms of their ethnic identities, and they remain so currently (McRoy, in press). Hence, their expressions of cultural maintenance are diverse, and are linked closely to their ethnic and cultural identities. These families may choose to be *culturally immersed* by expressing a totally black cultural framework and set of values and traditions. They may be *bicultural,* valuing and adjusting to both their black culture and the culture of the dominant society. And some of them are *acculturated,* clearly valuing the culture of the dominant society while adhering to few or no aspects of African American culture. Thus, there is not a typical African American family, cultural identity, or a wrong way to express cultural maintenance (Padilla & Perez, 2003). Consequently, a range of ideologies and behaviors exist related to cultural maintenance, which are expressed differentially by black families and communities.

Social Justice Issues

African American Males. Although black males continue to be an endangered species, there is a new, albeit slowly growing, movement to view them according to the context of their lived experiences. Black researchers and practitioners, along with scholars from other ethnic groups, have instigated this movement. This evolving view of black males incorporates the interactional effects of race and gender to explain their sociopolitical behaviors in the world (Roberts, 1994). Psychologists Nancy Boyd-Franklin and A. J. Franklin (2000) have written about the sociopolitical realities of parenting black males, including challenges faced in raising sons to successful manhood: (a) keeping them alive, (b) helping them to overcome racism, (c) getting them a good education, (d) raising them to be responsible adults, and (e) developing a positive racial identity in them. They provided ten recommendations for fostering strong racial identities and a commitment to cultural maintenance, such as displaying materials by and about prominent Africans and African Americans, talking about the legacy and history of African Americans, celebrating Kwanzaa, and countering negative media images with positives ones.

White and Cones (1999) documented current community interventions focused on the difficult task of countering these negative images of black males from external sources such as the media. Intervention efforts are targeting a wide range of needs, including provision of Afrocentric curricula by all-black male educational academies; political advocacy by the National Council of African American Men (NCAAM); and work with teen fathers on their role as responsible parents by black-helping professionals, such as social worker Charles Bellard.

Hurd and Rogers (1998) found in their study of fifty-three African American parents that men were providers of their families, positive role and cultural models for their children, and historians of African American culture. In addition, black males are slowly being seen as contributors to their children's growth and development whether or not they live with them. This increased emphasis on cultural maintenance and male involvement supports black fathers being in contact with their children as a positive influence regardless of whether they can make financial contributions to the family (O'Donnell, 1999).

Cready and Fossett (1997) stated that when they can get jobs by over-coming social justice barriers, African American males are more likely to be responsible and to live in husband and wife-headed families. Yet, little is known about the economic factors that influence African American males' employment and their ability to remain culturally centered in their parent-child relationships (Blake & Darling, 2000).

African American Children. African American children are being removed from their families by the child protection system more often than any other group nationwide (Courtney, Barth, Berrick, Needell, & Park, 1996; Morton, 1999). This situation is a social injustice and a barrier to cultural maintenance for children who are separated from their families. The problem involves racial disparity, disproportionality, or overpresentation of black children in the child welfare system. Nationally, black children constitute seventeen percent of the youth population but are estimated to be nearly fifty percent of the foster care population (Roberts, 2002; Brown, Cohon, & Wheeler, 2002).

Research has documented various reasons for this individual, family, community, and most importantly, systemic problem. Study findings on contributing factors to the problem include the following: (a) economic and social well-being of children and families (Courtney al et. 1996); (b) poverty and an array of social and structural problems (Brown & Bailey-Etta, 1997); (c) cultural- and social class-biased assessment tools (Morton, 1999); (d) racial isolation of black families within communities in which other cultural groups predominate (Garland, Ellis-MacLeod, Landsverk, Ganger, & Johnson, 1998); (e) income, mother's role in abuse, emotional abuse, race, maternal employment, and sexual abuse (Hampton & Newberger, 1985); (f) the Flemming rule, a 1960 administrative decision to prohibit AFDC benefits to homes that were immoral, or had illegitimate children or substitute fathers, which resulted in a pervading negative view of African American families (Lawrence-Webb, 1997); (g) overreporting of abused or neglected African American children versus underreporting of Caucasian children (Ards, Chung, & Myers, 1998); and (h) laws and policies such as the Adoption and Safe Families Act of 1997 (ASFA) with its time limits in foster care, and the Multiethnic Placement Act of 1994

(Kellam, 1999) and its Amendments (MEPA), which Hollingsworth (1998) noted as reducing the number of black children through unnecessary transracial adoptions and inattentiveness to cultural norms (Chand, 2000).

African American children need to be helped within the context of their families and cultural communities (Briar-Lawson, 1998). Roberts (2002) stated the overrepresentation of African American children in foster care results in the destruction of black families. To resolve this problem, she suggested systemic changes such as respecting cultural differences, increasing the staff's cultural competence, and giving parents more voice in service delivery. McRoy and Oglesby (1997) recommend increasing the adoption of African American children by revising biased policies and practices which can enhance opportunities for the group most likely to adopt them, single adults. For the social work profession, overrepresentation of African American children is an inherent social justice issue that should be addressed and resolved as such. African American families that come to the attention of the child welfare system are not provided culturally relevant services (Miller, 1997). For some families, this situation is also affected by structural or systemic inadequacies such as lack of a living wage, unemployment, and insufficient local transportation.

African American kinship care is an example of strategies for addressing this social justice and cultural maintenance issue. There are two forms of kinship care, both of which are consistent with the cultural tradition of kin keeping in black families (Brown & Bailey-Etta, 1997; Carter, 1997). One form involves informal arrangements for kinship care by a relative; this type of care enhances children's ties to their culture and cultural network. Previously, grandparents cared for grandchildren temporarily while their parents were physically absent, but psychologically present, for the purpose of relocating and obtaining better jobs. Currently, some parents are physically unavailable to care for their children because of death, or they are psychologically and physically absent due to problems with drug abuse, HIV/AIDS, homelessness, mental illness, and chronic unemployment.

Thus, a growing number of grandparents, often grandmothers, have become "new mothers again" (Gibson, 1999) when they voluntarily assume a primary caregiver role with their grandchildren. In 1992, 3.3 million children under age eighteen were living with their grandparents (Bryson & Casper, 1999). In 1997, that number increased to 3.9 million (Bryson & Casper, 1999). Of that group, 34.5 percent were African Americans. Currently, 4.5 million children live with their grandparents (American Association of Retired Persons, 2000).

The second form of kinship caregiving is foster kinship care, which is arranged by the child welfare system and is the fastest growing type of foster care (Gibbs & Muller, 2000). Legislation such as the Personal Responsibility and Work Opportunity Reconciliation Act (PRWOA) (PL 104–193), has contributed to the growth of foster kinship care with its mandated preference to adult relatives of children in need of care. Kinship care facilitates children's ties to their culture and reinforces their self- and cultural-esteem (Scannapieco & Jackson, 1996). The indigenous social support that kin-keepers provide is an example of strengths in black families (Mosley-Howard & Evans, 2000).

The African American Family. Two interacting negative views have been associated with research on black families, and consequently, with barriers to their cultural maintenance and a positive cultural identity. The first view emerged from social research which traditionally incorporated a cultural deficit model or pathological framework to describe black families by their problems while ignoring their strengths. These studies have narrowly focused on families from low-income and female-headed households (Blake & Darling, 2000). Researchers used this pathological view, combined with mass media biases (Wright & Anderson, 1998) to create negative, stereotypical views of African American family life. Cultural differences were labeled as cultural deficits, thus providing a rationale for eliminating rather than maintaining those differences.

The second view supported generalizations about black families by failing to account for the diversity within this group (Davis, 1991; Nagel, 1994). Black families were portrayed in these studies as unidimensional. The phrase "the Black family" was used to describe and stereotype every black family. Stereotyping has reinforced white prejudices about blacks and increased divisiveness across black communities regarding key issues about which they may have different perspectives. Examples of these key issues include the following: what this population wants to be called as an ethnic group; whether to maintain certain aspects of their culture, and how to do so; who should be recognized as black leaders, for what reasons, and by whom; whether particular forms of reparations are appropriate, and if so, under what circumstances and procedures should such a process be undertaken; and under what conditions is it acceptable to seek professional help and how much should be shared about cultural secrets and issues?

A PROPOSED PRACTICE APPROACH

Practice Overview

To provide culturally competent services within this practice approach, a family's expression of cultural maintenance must be taken into account. African American families inherently express the level of cultural maintenance that is valued by them and that fits with their lived experience or reality. When providing social services, it is the responsibility of social workers and other practitioners to obtain information on cultural maintenance related to the family's life, its needs and strengths, and how these factors are influencing its approach and responses to the helping process. Securing such information begins the process of relationship building with the family and provides an understanding of its situation. When helping professionals use this approach, the process of being culturally competent with a particular family begins. As cultural maintenance information is incorporated into the interaction between family and social worker, the cultural competence approach continues to develop (Dunn, 2002).

To summarize, culturally competent services for African Americans, based on the proposed approach, include the following interrelated components: (a) creation of an emotionally welcoming environment, (b) understanding the sociopolitical context of families of African descent, (c) a view of families as experts on their lives and solutions, (d) involvement of extended family members and others in the cultural network or community, (e) the importance of community, (f) identification of cultural and other strengths, (g) and exploration of the families' cultural maintenance practices and beliefs. Thus, culturally competent services require cultural maintenance as their key ingredient. The following illustration depicts this view:

Family	+	**Social worker**	=	**Cultural competent approach**
[Expression of cultural maintenance] into every aspect of service delivery]		*[Obtaining information about and using cultural maintenance]*		*[Infusion of the family's expression of cultural maintenance into the work]*

Practice Example: The Stamps Family

The Stamps, a couple in their 60s, have raised five children who are adults and are currently caring for their youngest daughter Kwanna's three children, ages 7, 4, and 2. Mrs. Stamps is a caregiver for her husband who is convalescing from a serious ailment and is trying to remain active in her church. She is a retired elementary school teacher who completed college after all of her children were in school. Mr. Stamps is also retired, and although recovering from an ailment, interacts with his grandchildren daily.

Prior to becoming primary caregivers, the Stamps allowed Kwanna and her children to live with them until stable housing could be obtained. The Stamps reported having a very close relationship with their grandchildren. Child Protection Services initially took the children from Kwanna and placed them in an emergency center, after she began neglecting them while abusing drugs. The Stamps were very upset about the removal of their grandchildren, felt the children should have been placed with them, and took action promptly to get custody of the children. Mrs. Stamps said her only consolation during that time was the fact that she knew some of the workers at the emergency placement center.

After obtaining custody of their grandchildren, the Stamps had them evaluated, which resulted in the two youngest, both males, being diagnosed with developmental delays. While Mrs. Stamps did not completely agree with the diagnosis, she followed through with the re-ferral for early intervention services at a local center. She believes her grandchildren are not retarded but lacked exposure to and sup-port for learning because Kwanna did not read to them or allow them to play with toys. Kwanna told her mother that she made the youngest children sit quietly most of the time when she was high on drugs.

After Mr. Stamps became ill, Mrs. Stamps was forced to apply for public assistance. They receive a monthly cash allotment for the three grandchildren but the food stamps allotment is dependent on their monthly income and expenditures. They are in a much worse financial situation because of caring for their grandchildren. Mrs. Stamps described her relationships with various social workers from the child welfare system as "okay." However, some of her workers have been rude and discourteous. Currently, there is a social worker from child protection assigned to them.

Although the case plan requires Mrs. Stamps to supervise Kwanna's visits with the children, Mrs. Stamps thinks this is unnecessary, because although Kwanna was neglectful, she did not physically abuse them. Mrs. Stamps stated that Kwanna is very involved in every decision made about the children, but there is no contact with their father. Mrs. Stamps plans to return her grandchildren to Kwanna's care after the latter successfully completes all requirements of child protection's case plan. Mrs. Stamps stated that her other adult children as well as many friends at church and relatives provide informal social support. Despite problems with some social service providers, Mrs. Stamps reportedly feels blessed by the Lord because she has her health, can care for her husband and grandchildren, and receives help from members of her cultural community.

Principles for Direct Practice

The following six practice principles are consistent with the general approach described in the practice overview section. Each principle is described in terms of its use by social workers and other helping professionals with African American families. This discussion also demonstrates how the principles apply specifically to the Stamps family from the previous section.

Practice Principle I: Begin interaction with the family by obtaining information on its expression of cultural maintenance. Be aware that cultural maintenance is an approach to living that depicts what is valued from the family's cultural heritage. The Stamps clearly value the family and having a close connection with family members. They do not want strangers caring for their grandchildren, regardless of the financial hardship incurred by their household. They also value Kwanna's opinion (the mother of their grandchildren) about her children and plan to return them to her when appropriate. Mrs. Stamps wants to be treated with dignity, and in a culturally respectful manner by service providers. She also values educational development services for her grandchildren as long as they are not stigmatized or labeled as "retarded." Religion and attending church services are important to Mrs. Stamps; she also involves her grandchildren in these activities. Community and informal social and cultural supports have been helpful to the Stamps.

To obtain related information on the Stamps' or other families' expressions of cultural maintenance, practitioners should ask the following questions:

1. Please tell me what is important to you about your present situation?
2. Tell me more about your family's values related to the present situation?
3. How is this situation affecting you and your family? What cultural or other practices and activities have you used to cope with the situation? What happened as a result?
4. Who do you turn to most often when you want help? What happens when you do? Who do you want to be involved as we discuss your situation here?
5. What has been your experience with other professionals regarding your situation?
6. What has been helpful to you and your family? What has not been helpful to you and your family?
7. How do people you are close to in your family or cultural group handle similar situations? What can you use from their experiences?
8. What do you see as the best solution or outcome in this situation for you and your family?
9. What else in this situation or outside of it needs to change, whether or not you're in control of those things?
10. How do you identify yourself racially or culturally? What does that mean to you in your present situation?

Practice Principle II: Increase knowledge about and respect for people of African descent. To work effectively, it is essential to develop an understanding of the dynamic interrelationship between privilege and oppression, cultural maintenance practices, and the client family's history (Hines, Garcia-Preto, McGoldrick, Almeida, & Weltman, 1992). Relationship building with a family of African decent demands respectful communication and treatment. To have survived the vicissitudes of oppression, bond as a community, and strive to achieve success, black families have to possess tremendous emotional and psychosocial strengths. A first step in the assessment of cultural maintenance and other factors involves identifying and acknowledging strengths in the family, environment, community, social network, extended family, and cultural group (Johnson, 1997; Jarrett & Burton, 1999). For example, the Stamps should be treated with the same dignity and respect accorded them within the African American community for their strengths and status.

Social workers should be respectful by referring to the couple as "Mr. Stamps" or "Mrs. Stamps," unless instructed otherwise by them. Their cultural status as African American elders dictates this kind of respect. As such, it can be assumed that the Stamps have survived many ethnic indignities in the dominant society, while in African American communities, they and other elders are valued for the experience and wisdom they have gained from living (White & Cones, 1999). Cultures that value their older members generally do not accept their wise elders being called by their first names. Calling these elders by their first names or asking them how they want to be called implies a familiarity that does not exist, and exposes a serious gap in knowledge about and respect for the group's cultural traditions (McRoy, in press).

There seems to be an unwritten policy equating the presence of black men as negating the need for social services. They have been placed at the margins of social work practice (O'Donnell, 1999), based on a European view that, without financial resources men are not useful. This view stigmatizes black men because it defines them only in terms of financial power and ignores socioeconomic and cultural biases that limit them in gaining such power (White & Cones, 1999). Therefore, despite his medical condition, Mr. Stamps should be included in the collaborative relationship building process along with Mrs. Stamps. Clearly, he provides an important source of cultural maintenance based on his knowledge of African American traditions and experience as a male role model for his grandchildren. Including him and other black males in services can help to improve their relationships with social service providers which have not been positive in the past (Leashore, 1997).

Practice Principle III: Be inclusive of family members and significant others in service delivery. It is important for social workers and other practitioners to acknowledge and support exchanges of resources among black families and between these families and their communities. This principle also includes supporting the expression of affection among black family members as a culturally meaningful resource. Blake and Darling (2000) discovered that the resource with highest level of exchange within African American families was love, among the many types of resources exchanged by these families. Thus, African American families' caring and support clearly impact positively upon their quality of life.

Social services with the Stamps family, regardless of agency setting or practice field, should begin by involving extended family and other community members that they want included. The Stamps, their grandchildren, Kwanna, their other adult children, and other supports should be included based on the Stamps' preferences. This principle supports the strengths that each cultural subsystem provides to the total family system and the reverse, by acknowledging and encouraging the use of the community as a resource to families. It also supports cultural maintenance practices and community building. Generally, social work services are provided to the immediate family only, with all others being excluded. Flexibility in including all interested and significant others as defined by the family adds cultural resources to the problem-solving process. For example, Mrs. Stamps is very active in her church and feels supported by the church community. Exploring this connection for informal resources such as respite care or activities for the grandchildren is consistent with the family's cultural maintenance priorities.

Practice Principle IV: Service needs should be assessed from a black family's view itself within the influence of their sociopolitical context. The lives of black families are influenced by the context of their lived experience. Social workers must conduct holistic assessments that include a view of a family's sociopolitical and cultural contexts (Wright & Anderson, 1998). Helping professionals should follow each family's lead by viewing them as experts and forming collaborative partnerships with them. To be effective kinship care providers, the Stamps may request numerous services for themselves, their grandchildren, and Kwanna. While their prior kin-keeping experience when their daughter and grandchildren lived with them did not lead them to seek formal services, their financial circumstances require that step currently. Yet, as African Americans, they may be seen by the child welfare system as just another black family that cannot care for its members. In fact, the Stamps are acting as a resource for the child welfare system which is saving money by providing funds to the grandparents rather than providing the more expensive foster care payments to strangers. The Stamps are also supporting their grandchildren's development in the culturally supportive environment of the black community (Gibson, 1999). All options for social services should be presented and explained to the couple. Where there are limits in terms of child welfare services, these need to be acknowledged to the Stamps and subsequently advocated for within that system or other appropriate systems.

Practice Principle V: Tackle social justice issues that emerge from oppression of and power differentials between African American families and the dominant society, regardless of the source. African Americans encounter a power differential when interacting with the dominant society that hinders them from obtaining equitable supports and services. Assisting African American families to interact more effectively with powerful systems and their representatives, including helping professionals and other organizational staff, is essential. Social workers might find themselves at odds with bureaucrats and other service providers who do not ascribe to the cultural maintenance practice approach.

For example, the Stamps value early intervention services for their two youngest grandchildren to enhance their developmental and educational progress. However, they do not want them to be labeled as having cognitive deficits. Assisting Mr. And Mrs. Stamps to prevent labeling and to empower themselves requires the provision of information from special education legislation about parental involvement and due process. This type of advocacy is important, considering that young black males are overrepresented in special education programs and in high school dropout rates (White & Cones, 1999). These grandparents may need a similar type of advocacy to deal with social workers in the child welfare system who continue to respond to them in an unprofessional and disrespectful manner. Finally, advocacy may also be needed to support their requests for resources that enhance the grandchildren's cultural maintenance, such as participation in rites of passage programs sponsored by all-black academies and becoming members' of children's divisions of black lodges.

Principles for Community Building or Mezzo Practice

Locating Services in Black Communities. Social workers must be aware of the importance of community and community building for black families in terms of practice. Consultants and agency-based practitioners should encourage such communities to allow services to be located within their boundaries to increase the likelihood that the residents will accept those services. When professionals invite representatives from the community to participate in the development of the mission, services, policies, and procedures of service agencies and other organizations, the possibility of congruency between the needs of that community and the organizational infrastructure is increased. Thus, at all levels of social service agencies, community practitioners and consultants can help assess, plan for, and address the needs of black families as they are articulated by the families themselves, within the cultural context of their communities and cultural maintenance priorities.

Using a Broad Lens for Focusing Community Interventions. Community practitioners' and consultants' efforts to support African American's community building should also focus on the sociopolitical context of these communities. The sociopolitical realities of these families must be addressed, for example, helping community members to develop and/or increase their affordable housing stock, seek funding for youth and family recreational facilities, improve the staffing and funding of school systems, increase employment and full economic development opportunities, locate resources for leadership and political activism development, support intergenerational cultural maintenance programs, and help to build the capacities of public transportation systems that are connected to the well-being and mobility of black communities. Such resources can help professionals to support African American families from a more holistic perspective, while at the same time, supporting their broader efforts toward community building and collective sufficiency

IMPLICATIONS FOR FUTURE CHALLENGES
TO CULTURAL MAINTENANCE

Challenges to cultural maintenance will continue as society struggles with the acceptance of ethnic and racial group differences. Yet a foundation has been laid with the growing acceptance and use of empowerment theory and the strengths perspective. The Afrocentric approach is less known, and therefore has not gained as much acceptance as the other two perspectives within dominant society or in research/

academic areas. Challenges to cultural maintenance overall include research issues, policy barriers, and assimilation/social class demands.

Research Documentation of the Practice Approach's Effectiveness

The lack of research to document the effectiveness of a cultural maintenance approach with black families is challenging, but this is not surprising due to the newness of this practice framework. Documentation does exist, however, for exploring experiences of African American families from the strengths and empowerment perspectives. Fine, Schwebel, and James-Myers (1987) described three models, which have been used to conduct research on African Americans: (a) emergent, (b) structural-functional, and (c) pathological. The emergent model clearly fits with cultural maintenance in that it emphasizes cultural aspects that stem from the African heritage of black families in a positive way.

The structural-functional model emphasizes the strengths of African American families, but from the standpoint of comparing them and their cultural differences with white families. Comparing such differences based on this research model, without attention to the sociopolitical context or realities of African Americans, could encourage victim blaming and biased interpretations by researchers. This possibility lessens the cultural appropriateness of the structural-functional model. Lastly, the pathological model is unacceptable because it labels African Americans as psychologically unstable and as suffering from the legacy of slavery. Use of the pathological model, largely by white researchers, has fueled African American communities' historical concerns and mistrust of social science research and the intentions of social scientists.

To address this and other research challenges, in social work and other studies to evaluate the effectiveness of this cultural maintenance approach with traditionally oppressed groups such as African Americans, methodology should be a primary consideration. First, qualitative research methods should be used to capture the unique experiences of these families during service delivery. Ideally, the assumptions framing the study, specific questions, and accompanying research procedures should incorporate a focus on aspects of cultural maintenance. Second, black family consumers need to be active partners in the development of these research questions and procedures. In addition, pertinent definitions need to be constructed that are acceptable to both the families and the researchers, as well as the inclusion of member-checking procedures in which consumers help to plan and monitor the entire research process. Third, African American families and their communities need to participate in identifying the benefits of the particular research for each party involved including the researchers, families, and community. Fourth, findings need to be disseminated locally, with the input of consumers and the inclusion of recommended steps that will be implemented as a result of the research to improve social work practice to African American families.

Social Policy Barriers

Currently, family-blaming social policies continue to challenge dominant society's acceptance and valuing of ethnic differences, and therefore, support for cultural maintenance practices and beliefs by black families. Clearly, the best support for the cultural maintenance practice approach and for these practices and beliefs is family-friendly social policies. Wilson (2000) described such policies as providing opportunity-enhancing resources and increasing supports for economic self- and collective sufficiency. When African American wage earners cannot obtain jobs that provide a living wage and necessary family health benefits, that barrier can successfully challenge productivity, ethnic-esteem, and efforts to maintain cultural traditions that make them different. To meet this challenge, clinical, community, and policy practice social workers should advocate for policies that provide resources for culturally related needs (Briar-Lawson, 1998), rather than blame those cultural differences for complex structural problems.

Assimilation or Social Class Demands on Black Families

Mosley-Howard and Evans (2000) aptly stated, to fully understand African American families, "the degree to which African Americans adhere to an Africentric world view and the degree of acculturation within the majority culture are critical in any examination of the African American family" (p. 430).

Cultural maintenance is considered one end of a cultural adaptation continuum, which involves two opposing ideological positions. At the opposite end is cultural assimilation (Ruggiero et al., 1996). Ethnic groups of color living in a dominant society make choices about their cultural adaptation by maintaining aspects of their cultural heritage or by assimilating into the dominant culture. Park and Burgess (1921) concluded that assimilation is a product of social contact interaction with those of the dominant culture.

Economic and political barriers can lead to devastatingly hopeless attitudes, encouraging some African Americans to adapt closer to the assimilation end of this continuum, for example, to a middle-class non-culturally centered lifestyle and identity (as opposed to a middle-class bicultural lifestyle and identity). Cultural maintenance is ideologically inconsistent with adaptation at the assimilation end of the continuum, making it less desirable or possible for African Americans who choose assimilation. To address this challenge, culturally competent social workers or cultural coaches can help black families to articulate their concerns about these issues, whether or not they have been able to identify them previously. Families may need assistance in weighing the potential positive and negative consequences of different adaptation options, and help in acknowledging the sociopolitical reality that complete assimilation by most African Americans is impossible. Moreover, assimilation may not be preferred or acceptable to individuals and families who are committed to cultural maintenance (Freeman, 1990).

CONCLUSION

Cultural maintenance is inextricably connected to African Americans' existence in contemporary America and to their interactions with social systems. To use this approach requires a valuing of both their African and African American heritage. Their dual or bicultural skills are strengths, as they can enhance functioning in both the sustaining and nurturing communities.

Social workers have an obligation to support the range of practices African American families engage in to express their philosophy and beliefs about cultural maintenance. While the profession clearly emphasizes valuing culturally competent services, social workers must continue to understand how exploring a family's cultural maintenance practices and philosophy related to the situation of concern is an essential part of such practice. Incorporation of cultural maintenance needs and concerns especially requires the inclusion of males, extended family members, and significant others who act as cultural resources.

This process also acknowledges that black children are best cared for within the nurturing environment of their families, communities and culture, whenever that is possible. Finally, the approach emphasizes that African American families, regardless of their presenting situations, have many unique strengths that practitioners should acknowledge and incorporate into the service delivery process.

REFERENCES

Akbar, N. (1985). Our destiny: Authors of a scientific revolution. In H. P. McAdoo & J. L. McAdoo (Eds.), *Black children: Social, educational, and parental involvements* (pp. 17–31). Beverly Hills, CA: Sage.

Algotsson, S. (2000). *African styles down to the details.* New York: Random House, Inc.

American Association of Retired Persons (2000). Census number and percentage change since 1990: Children under 18 living in grandparent-headed households. (www.aarp.org/grandparents/)

Ards, S., Chung, C. S., & Myers, S. L. (1998). The effects of sample selection bias on racial differences in child abuse reporting. *Child Abuse & Neglect, 22*(2), 103–115.

Billingsley, A. (1992). *Climbing Jacob's ladder: The enduring legacy of African-American families.* New York: Simon & Schuster.

Blake, W. M., & Darling, C. A. (2000). Quality of life perception of African Americans. *Journal of Black Studies, 30*(3), 411–427.

Boyd-Franklin, N. & Franklin, A. J. (2000). *Boys into men: Raising our African American teenage sons.* New York: Penguin.

Briar-Lawson, K. (1998). Capacity building for integrated family-centered practice. *Social Work, 43*(6), 539–550.

Brown, A.W., & Bailey-Etta, B. (1997). An out-of-home care system in crisis: Implications for African American children in the child welfare system. *Child Welfare, 76*(1), 65–83.

Brown, S., Cohon, D., & Wheeler, R. (2002). African American extended families and kinship care: How relevant is the foster care model for kinship care? *Children and Youth Services Review, 24*(2), 53–77.

Bryson, K., & Casper, L. M. (1999, May). *Co-resident grandparents and grandchildren.* U. S. Bureau of the Census, Current Population Reports, Special Studies, Series P23–198. Washington, DC: U.S. Government Printing Office.

Carter, C. S. (1997). Using African-centered principles in family-preservation services. *Families in Society, 78,* 531–538.

Chand, A. (2000). The Over-presentation of Black children in the child protection system: Possible causes, consequences and solutions. *Child and Family Social Work, 5*(1), 67–77.

Collins, P. H. (1990). *Black feminist thought: Knowledge, consciousness, and the politics of empowerment.* London: Harper Collins.

Comer, J. P., & Poussaint, A. F. (1992). *Raising black children*. NY: Plume.

Courtney, M.E., Barth, R.P., Berrick, J.D., Needell, B., & Park, L. (1996). Race and child welfare services: Past research and future directions. *Child Welfare, 75*(2), 99–137.

Cready, C. M., & Fossett, M. A. (1997). Mate availability and African American family structure in the U. S. nonmetropolitan South, 1960–1990. *Journal of Marriage and the Family, 59,* 192–203.

Davis, R. J. (1991). *Who is Black?: One nation's definition*. University Park, PA: Pennsylvania State University Press.

Dill, B. T. (1988). Our mothers' grief: Racial ethnic women and the maintenance of families. *Journal of Family History, 13,* 415–431.

Devore, W., & Schlesinger, E. (1999). *Ethnic sensitive social work practice* (5th ed.). Boston: Allyn and Bacon.

Dunn, C. (2002). The importance of cultural competence for social workers. *The New Social Worker, 9*(2), 4–5.

English, R. A. (1991). Diversity of world views among African American families. In J. E. Everette, S. Chipungu, & B. Leashore (Eds.), *Child welfare: An Africentric perspective* (pp. 19–35). New Brunswick, NJ: Rutgers University Press.

Fine, M., Schwebel, A. I., & James-Myers, L. (1987). Family stability in Black families: Values underlying three different perspectives. *Journal of Comparative Family Studies, 1,* 1–23.

Freeman, E.M. (1990). The black family's life cycle: Operationalizing a strengths perspective. In S.M.L. Logan, E.M. Freeman, & R.G. McRoy (Eds.), *Social work practice with black families: A culturally specific perspective* (pp. 55–72). White Plains, NY: Longman.

Garcia, A. Racism, immigrants, and their discontent (2001). http://www.nnirr.org/archived-netnews/spring.

Garland, A.F., Ellis-MacLeod, E., Landsverk, J. A., Ganger, W., & Johnson, I. (1998). Minority populations in the child welfare system: The visibility hypothesis reexamined. *American Journal of Orthopsychiatry, 68*(1), 142–146.

Gelfand, D. E., & Fandetti, D. V. (1993). The emergent nature of ethnicity: Dilemmas in assessment. In J. B. Rauch (Ed.), *Assessment: A sourcebook for social work practice* (pp. 357–369). Milwaukee, WI: Families International.

Gibbs, P., & Muller, U. (2000). Kinship foster care moving to the mainstream: Controversy, policy, and outcome. *Adoption Quarterly, 4,* 57–87.

Gibson, P.A. (1999). African American grandmothers: New mothers again. *Affilia, 14*(3), 329–343.

Goldenberg, H., & Goldenberg, I. (2002). *Counseling today's families* (4th ed.) Pacific Grove, CA: Brooks/Cole.

Green, J. W. (1982). *Cultural awareness in human services*. Englewood Cliffs, NJ: Prentice–Hall.

Hampton, R.L., & Newberger, E. H. (1985). Child abuse incidence and reporting by hospitals: Significance of severity, class, and race. *American Journal of Public Health, 75*(1), 56–60.

Harvey, A. R., & Rauch, J. B. (1997). A comprehensive Afrocentric rites of passage program for Black male adolescents. *Social Work, 42,* 30–37.

Hill, R. B. (1997). *Research on the African-American family: A holistic perspective.* Westport, CT: Auburn House.

Hines, P. M., Garcia-Preto, N., McGoldrick, M., Almeida, R., & Weltman, S. (1992). Intergenerational relationships across cultures. *Families in Society, 73,* 323–338.

Hollingsworth, L. D. (1998). Promoting same-race adoption for children of color. *Social Work, 43*(2), 104–115.

Hurd, E. P., & Rogers, R. (1998). A friend and a brother: Understanding the role of African American men in child-rearing. *Journal of Family Social Work, 3*(1), 5–23.

Jarrett, R. L., & Burton, L. M. (1999). Dynamic dimensions of family structure in low-income African American families: Emergent themes in qualitative research. *Journal of Comparative Family Studies,* 177–187.

Johnson, L. B. (1997). Three decades of Black family empirical research. In H. P. McAdoo (Ed.), *Black families,* (pp. 94–114). Thousand Oaks, CA: Sage.

Karenga, M. (1993). *Introduction to black studies.* Los Angeles: University of Sankore Press.

Kellam, S. (1999). The color of care: Connect for kids website. http://www.connectforkids.org.

Kook, R. (1989). The shifting status of African Americans in the American collective identity. *Journal of Black Studies, 29*(2), 154–178.

Lawrence-Webb, C. (1997). African American children in the modern child welfare system: A legacy of the Fleming Rule. *Child Welfare, 76*(1), 9–13.

Leashore, B. R. (1997). African American men, child welfare, and permanency planning. *Journal of Multicultural Social Work, 5*(1/2), 39–48.

Lee, J. (1994). *The empowerment approach to social work practice.* New York: Columbia University Press.

Logan, S. M. L. (1990). Black families: Race, ethnicity, culture, social class, and gender issues. In S.M.L. Logan, E. M. Freeman, & R. G. McRoy (Eds.), *Social work practice with Black families: A culturally specific perspective* (pp. 18–37). White Plains, NY: Longman.

Logan, S. (1996). Epilogue: Understanding help-seeking behavior and empowerment issues for Black families. In S. L. Logan (Ed.), *Black family strengths, self-help and positive change* (pp. 193–206). Boulder, CO: Westview Press.

Logan, S. M. L., Freeman, E. M., & McRoy, R. G. (1990). *Social work practice with Black families: A culturally specific perspective.* White Plains, NY: Longman.

Martin, J.M., & Martin, E. P. (1985). *The helping tradition in the Black family and community.* Silver Spring, MD: National Association of Social Workers.

McPhatter, A. R. (1997). Cultural competence in child welfare: What is it? How do we achieve it? What happens without it? *Child Welfare, 76*(1), 255–277.

McRoy, R. G. (in press). Cultural Competency with African Americans. In D. Lum (Ed.), *Culturally competent practice: A framework for growth and action.* Washington, DC: CSWE.

McRoy, R. G., & Oglesby, Z. (1997). Achieving same-race adoptive placements for African American children: Culturally sensitive practice approaches. *Child Welfare, 76*(1), 85.

Miller, D. B. (1997). Parenting against the odds: African American parents in the child welfare system-A group approach. *Social Work with Groups, 20*(1), 5–17.

Morris, F. L. (1996). *Urban labor markets: Immigrants vs. African Americans.* Cambridge, MA: Harvard University Press.

Morton, T.D. (1999). The increasing colorization of America's child welfare system: The overrepresentation of African-American children. *Policy & Practice, 57*(4), 23–30.

Mosley-Howard, G. S., & Evans, S. B. (2000). Relationships and contemporary experiences of the African American family: An ethnographic case study. *Journal of Black Studies, 30,* 428–452.

Nagel, J. (1994). Constructing ethnicity: Creating and recreating ethnic identity and culture. *Social Problems, 41,* 152–176.

Nobles, W. (1980). African philosophy: Foundations for Black psychology. In R. L. Jones (Ed.), *Black psychology* (pp. 23–36). New York: Harper & Row.

O'Donnell, J. M. (1999). Involvement of African American fathers in kinship foster care services. *Social Work, 44,* 428–441.

Padilla, A.M. & Perez, W. (2003). Acculturation, social identity, and social cognition: A new perspective. *Hispanic Journal of Behavioral Sciences, 25*(1), 35–55.

Park, R. E., & Burgess, E. W. (1921). *Introduction to the science of sociology.* Chicago, IL: University of Chicago Press.

Pierce, W. J., & Elisme, E. (1997). Understanding and working with Haitian immigrant families. *Journal of Family Social Work, 2*(1), 49–65.

Pinderhughes, E. (1989). Empowerment for our clients and for ourselves. *Social Casework, 64,* 331–338.

Pinderhughes, E. (1988). Significance of culture and power in human behavior curriculum. In C. Jacobs & D. Bowles (Eds.), *Ethnicity and race* (pp. 152–184), Washington: DC: NASW Press.

Roberts, D. (2002). *Shattered bonds: The color of child welfare.* New York: Basic Books.

Roberts, G. W. (1994). Bother to brother: African American modes of relating among men. *Journal of Black Studies, 24*(4), 379–390.

Rooney, R. (1992). *Strategies for working with involuntary clients.* New York: Columbia University Press.

Ruggiero, K. M., & Taylor, D. M. (1996). Why minority group members perceive or do not perceive the discrimination that confronts them: The role of self-esteem and perceived control. *Journal of Personality and Social Psychology, 72*(2), 373–389.

Saleebey, D (1997). *The strengths perspective in social work,* (2nd ed.). New York: Macmillan.

Scannapieco, M., & Jackson, S. (1996). Kinship care: The response to family preservation. *Social Work, 41*(2), 190–196.

Schiele, J. H. (1996). Afrocentricity: An emerging paradigm in social work practice. *Social Work, 41,* 284–294.

Simon, B. L. (1994). *The empowerment tradition in American social work: A history.* New York: Columbia University Press.

Solomon, B.B. (1976). *Black empowerment: Social work in oppressed communities.* New York: Columbia.

Swigonski, M. E. (1996). Challenging privilege through Afrocentric social work practice. *Social Work, 41*(2), 153–161.

White, J.L., & Cones, J.H. (1999). *Black man emerging: Facing the past and seizing a future in America.* New York: Routledge.

Wilson, G. (2000). Race, class, and support for egalitarian statism among the African American middle class. *Journal of Sociology and Social Welfare, 27,* (3), 75–91.

Wright, O. L., & Anderson, J. P. (1998). Clinical social work practices with urban African American families. *Families in Society, 79,* 197–205.

Yetman, N. R. (1999). Introduction: Definitions and perspectives. In N. R. Yetman (Ed.), *Majority and minority: The dynamics of race and ethnicity in American life* (6th ed., pp. 1–38). Boston: Allyn and Bacon.

Chapter 13

SOCIAL JUSTICE, POLITICAL ACTIVISM AND SYSTEMS CHANGE RELATED TO BLACK FAMILIES AND COMMUNITIES

SADYE L. LOGAN

*In few periods of our history has the whole fabric of
America life been altered so drastically as during the
Civil War and the period immediately following it.*

John Hope Franklin

When one thinks of social and economic justice, political activism, and systems change with respect to black families and communities, it is natural to think first about the impact of colonialism, imperialism, slavery, apartheid, and other systems of domination and oppression that created and sustained blighted communities and families in poverty. However, it is equally important to consider the triumphs, resilience, and courage of African Americans in the face of such daunting circumstances. Therefore, this chapter discusses the evolution of black families and communities from a sociopolitical or social justice framework, while also emphasizing family and community rebuilding strategies for system changes and maintenance of their strengths and other cultural resources during reconstruction and later periods.

THE INITIAL REBUILDING PROCESS IN THE SOUTH

Reconstruction and Post-Slavery Oppression Throughout the South

After more than two hundred years of enslavement, the idea of being free was intoxicating for African Americans. They were envisioning a life in which their families would be together, the basic necessities of life would be available, and above all, they would have ownership of a piece of land and their own homes. A formal education for their children was a major priority. Recognizing the need for education, sympathetic northern white missionary associations and freedmen's aid societies built schools all over the South. However, schoolteachers of color and African American ministers who owned many of the buildings where the schools were located supported some of the schools entirely or in part.

Access to education was not the only change that many of the freed slaves anticipated. They also believed that all forms of abuse would end with emancipation (Billingsley, 1992; Sterling 1997). However, this was not the case. Despite the thirteenth, fourteenth, and fifteenth amendments of the U. S. Constitution which ensured their rights as freed people and government programs such as the Freedmen's Bureau and charitable organizations from the North, violent responses from southern whites were overwhelming. The passage of the Reconstruction Act in March 1867 made it possible for black men to vote and to hold political office. Although they made up a majority of the electorate in five southern states, blacks did not control the Reconstruction south. Only in South Carolina did they make up a majority of those elected to the state legislative. However, this political development in South Carolina and the potential for black political power in other parts of the South motivated whites to shift from random acts of violence to organized terror tactics. Accordingly:

> Leading southerners met in a Nashville hotel to draw up a contribution for "an institution of Chivalry, Humanity, Mercy and Patriotism" the Ku Klux Klan. Operating outside the law, bands of armed men, including doctors, lawyers, storekeepers, and poor whites roamed at night. Their officers had names like Grand Giant, Grand Titan, Grand Wizard; their uniforms consisted of grotesque capes and masks and long black, red, and white gowns. The intent was to strike terror in the hearts of superstitious freed (black) people and to disguise the wearers so that they could commit murder, arson, and rape with impunity. (Sterling, 1997)

Klansmen shot both black and white political leaders, whipped voters, and intimidated working people to keep them from voting. Although the U.S. Congress passed the Ku Klux Klan Act of 1871 which imposed fines and imprisonment on Klansmen found committing acts of violence and mass murder, it was to little avail. The violent acts of the Klan and other related groups continued into the next century and beyond. Along with physical acts of violence, violence was also perpetuated in the form of oppressive economic, social, and political conditions similar to slavery.

The reconstruction or rebuilding of the South lasted for six years. The Reconstruction Act provided guidelines for southern states to form new governments and support for assisting families and communities in the building and rebuilding process. The end of Reconstruction, however, signaled the beginning of a national crisis for the four million newly-freed African Americans. At that time, eleven of every twelve blacks lived in the South. In response to overwhelming oppression in the South, blacks began the "Great Exodus" north and westward to Kansas, Missouri, Oklahoma, and Ohio (Painter, 1977). They later moved to all parts of the United States. By 1940 more than one million blacks had moved and settled in the northeast and north central regions of the country (Ruiz, 1990).

Although vestiges of this national crisis which followed emancipation still manifest themselves today in the lives of poor families and children, African Americans on the whole survived the oppressive conditions of the South and the discrimination they encountered in the North (Hochschild & Rogers, 2000). During the postcivil war period the lifestyles of the blacks living in the South were very diverse. In the rural south blacks were basically illiterate tenant farmers who had large families to support. Despite the challenges of an oppressive economic and social system, these rural families sacrificed much to educate their children. They worked hard, and built lodges, schools, churches, and other institutions that reflected a self-help orientation to family and community life (Franklin, 1969 & Logan, 2001).

South Carolina as an Example of State Level Reconstruction

Economic, Education, and Lifestyle Issues. Some blacks living in southern cities like Charleston, South Carolina and Hampton, Virginia were exposed to a more progressive and privileged lifestyle than those in other Southern states. In Charleston, for example, prosperity lasted from approximately 1866 to 1877, and in Virginia from 1870 to 1890 (Edgar, 2000; Engs, 1979). In these cities blacks had capital in banks, and owned property and businesses. They held jobs as laborers, skilled craftsmen, and professionals. Many sent their children to private schools.

Some private South Carolina schools for blacks were well-known, such as the Avery Normal Institute in Charleston, Howard School in Columbia, Mather Academy in Camden, Penn Normal and Industrial Schools on St. Helena Island, and Brainard Institute in Chester. During and after Reconstruction, these schools provided education and training for the state's black leadership. However, for more advanced education blacks had to leave the state and attend schools in Europe as well as American schools, including Oberlin, Yale, Harvard, Bowdin, and Amherst.

One of the major successes of the Reconstruction government in South Carolina was the establishment of a universal, public-funded system of education. According to the 1868 state constitution, educational institutions funded by the state were "open to all the children and youths of the state, without regard to race and color" (Edgar, 2000 p. 392). Black as well as white children were given an opportunity for schooling for the first time. The University of South Carolina became the only southern state university open to black students during that period. In 1875, its student body was ninety percent black. White Carolinians considered the integration of the university at all levels (students, faculty, and tutors) as one of the most heinous acts of Reconstruction.

Political Progress and Challenges. In the political arena, South Carolina blacks achieved greater political power than blacks in any other southern state. According to Edgar (2000), between 1867 and 1876, of the 487 elections for state and federal offices, black Carolinians won 255 of them. Furthermore, in the South Carolina General Assembly from 1872–1876, black Carolinians were elected to the position of Speaker of the House, and from 1872–1877, to the position of president pro tempore of the senate. They also chaired two-thirds of the most influential committees in the state General Assembly. During Reconstruction, six of fifteen black Americans serving in the U.S. Congress were from South Carolina. Persons of color were elected to the positions of lieutenant governor, adjutant general, secretary of state, and

treasurer between 1872–1877. Of the three members of the state supreme court, one was a black man who served from 1870–1877. Blacks
were not very successful in county level elections, as whites continued
to be elected sheriffs, court clerks, and county treasurers (Edgar, 2000).

Generally, white Carolinians were horrified by these political advances and dismissed all black office holders as "illiterate, venal,
rogues" (Edgar, p. 388). In truth, Edgar (2000), notes that eighty-seven
percent of the black legislators were literate, more than three-fourths
were property owners and taxpayers, and at least one in four had been
free persons of color before the Civil War. Most of them were middle-
income artisans, shopkeepers, and farmers. Despite these facts, during
that period whites and their descendants distorted the accomplishments
of South Carolina's black leaders. Edgar (2000) further acknowledges
that, for the most part, South Carolina's 1868 constitution was a model
document, despite the refusal by white citizens to acknowledge it as
their own, since primarily blacks had written the document.

For most whites, political and public equality meant social equality,
and social equality was synonymous with racial intermarriage in their
minds. These sentiments are reflected in a document entitled: the
Respectful Reconstruction of White People of South Carolina, which
was written in 1868:

> We do not mean to threaten resistance by arms. But the white people of our state
> will never submit to Negro rule. We may have to pass under the yoke you have
> authorized but by moral agencies, by political organizations, by every peaceful
> means left us; we will keep up this contest until we have regained *the heritage of
> political control handed down to us by our honored ancestry.* (Edgar, 2000, p. 377 (italics
> added))

However, resistance by whites to sharing the political process was
anything but peaceful. Native whites, in alliance with northern white
immigrants, launched a brutal onslaught against black officeholders,
successfully removing them from office eventually. This period in history has shown that when blacks had political power it was shared with
whites and all benefited. However, when whites regained the political
power through intimidation and brute force, they removed all elected
blacks officials from office and systematically worked to completely dis-
enfranchise all blacks. It took South Carolina another century to elect
a black to the state senate through a special election. Within the next

decade after that milestone, the number of black elected officials in South Carolina continued to increase. However, not unlike the current political process in South Carolina, inequality in the American political process remains an issue for Americans of color in all parts of the country (Hochschild, 2003).

Impact on Social Indices for Black South Carolinians. In spite of such political progress, what has remained a constant is the restricted quality of life experienced by South Carolina's large African American population. According to recent data, African Americans in South Carolina are more likely to live in poverty than are whites. Black women of children-bearing age have nearly eight times the HIV infection rate of white women, experience nearly twice the rate of low birth weight babies and infant deaths as do whites, and are almost twice as likely not to have graduated from high school. African Americans represent 69.5 percent of the state's male prison population, but only eight percent of its male college enrollees.

These South Carolina statistics for black adults seem high when compared to national rates on African American juvenile crime. Nationally, African American youth comprise fifteen percent of the population from ages ten to seventeen; however, they account for twenty-six percent of all arrests among that population, forty-four percent of arrests for violent crimes by juveniles, and forty percent of juveniles in residential placement or custody (S.C. Kids Count, 2001). Almost one half of South Carolina residents, aged sixty-and-over, live in rural areas and have difficulties accessing health and mental health care because they lack transportation. African Americans make up twenty-four percent of this age sixty-and-over population.

CONTEMPORARY SOCIAL JUSTICE
CONDITIONS AND FACTORS

Effects of Racial Isolation and Marginalization

Differences in the life expectancy rates between whites and blacks nationwide are a good indicator of the effects of racial isolation and other social justice barriers over the years since Reconstruction. For example, there is over a five-year difference in the life expectancy rates for South Carolina whites and African Americans, primarily as a result of low income, poor nutrition, and inadequate health and preventive care (Ibid, 2001). These conditions are similar to those of poor blacks in other parts of rural America and in most large urban areas. Generally these urban areas are described as ghettos, defined here as a group of contiguous neighborhoods that are almost exclusively inhabited by the members of one cultural and/or social class group. People live in these ghettos as a result of racial isolation policies practiced by larger society, related to housing, education, and employment injustices, which predetermine where and how they will live (Freeman, 2001).

For black Americans, the ghetto has been a pattern of residential and social segregation since the postemancipation period. Massey and Denton (1993) believe the emergence of the black ghetto resulted from a series of deliberate decisions by white Americans to deny black people access to urban housing markets and to reinforce their residential segregation. Decades of segregation, economic deprivation, racial and social isolation, and psychosocial alienation resulted in a series of violent urban riots during the 1960s.

Federally-Sponsored Responses

As a result of the violence, destruction, and economic and social inequities, President Johnson appointed a national commission of elected officials and public figures that was chaired by Governor Otto Kerner of Illinois. The commission's report concluded that the riots stemmed from the underlying problem of segregation, the persistence of racial isolation and discrimination, and a historical legacy of disadvantages in employment, education, and public welfare. Despite the commission's recommendations that federal housing programs be given a new thrust aimed at overcoming the prevailing pattern of racial segregation, and whites expressed new support for the principle of open housing, the existing pattern of residential segregation continued across the country (U.S. National Advisory Commission on Civil Disorders, The Kerner Report, 1988, pp. 35–108). Racial discrimination persisted not only in real estate transactions, but also in the home loan industry where blacks' loan applications were rejected at rates considerably higher than those of whites (Massey & Denton, 1993; Dedman, 1990).

Responses by Public-Private Partnerships

Although the fight for fair housing seems never ending, the case of Chicago's North Lawndale community is a sign that some progress has occurred. The North Lawndale community was once described as a desolate area, incinerated by the riots that broke out during 1968 following Dr. Martin Luther King's assassination. More than half the community's population moved out between 1960 and 1990. Beginning in 1999, new construction of homes began within the area, with many selling for as much as $275,000. A confluence of many events, including the support of the city's government to provide grants to first-time homeowners in partnership with a private development company, made this experiment in urban reclamation a community-wide success. For an illustration, see E. Cose, June 7, 1999 article in *Newsweek Magazine:* "The Good News About Black Americans." In contrast, the reclamation of blighted communities in other cities has been community-based, for example, in Oakland CA, New York, Chattanooga TN, and Savannah, GA. Allen Temple Baptist Church in California has generated more than twenty million dollars worth of new construction projects. These projects include a 60,500 square foot Family Living Center, which the church opened in 1999. The center provides activities for various age groups in the community, ranging from young children to the elderly. It also has a 24-unit complex for treating HIV/AIDS patients.

SUMMARY OF SOCIAL JUSTICE CONDITIONS AND FACTORS

The evolution of black families and communities is reflected in the following life-altering events over time: slavery, emancipation, reconstruction, segregation and racial isolation, and varying levels of integration. The question is what do these interrelated events suggest for systems change and maintenance of cultural strengths regarding black families and communities? First, these events show that African Americans are a strong resilient people with a vision for a multicultural society where everyone has equal influence in shaping the larger society's values. Secondly, it is evident that African Americans are highly intelligent, sophisticated in business affairs and politics, as well as very tuned into the nuances of living in a race conscious world. Thirdly, these events show that the quality of life and overall well-being of black families and communities are inextricably linked to the political, economic, education, and social systems of the larger society. But most importantly, these events underscore the need for major black economic development, which includes diversified employment or jobs at every level of the occupational spectrum; the accumulation of assets or wealth by African Americans; constructive national domestic policies; strong self-help programs that are integrated into black churches, clubs, and lodges; and supportive nurturing families and communities.

STRATEGIES FOR SYSTEMS CHANGE AND MAINTENANCE

Deconstructing Racist Media Distortions and Creating New Visions

Nearly two years ago, the popular press ran numerous cover stories on the good news about black America. According to one of those articles by Cose (1999), this was the best time ever to be black in America. Crime rates were down; jobs and income levels were up. Given that more black men than ever were in prisons; black suicide rates had risen; HIV/AIDS continued to ravish black men, women, and children; and youth academic achievement remained elusive, not everyone was celebrating. Furthermore, many feared that the tenuous gains that had occurred could easily be eradicated by an economic downturn or by the legal-political assault on affirmative action policies and programs. Both fears were realized.

The challenges, therefore, remain the same for African American families and communities, including the importance of understanding how media distortions reinforce racial myths about blacks and the prejudices of white America. It is also imperative that African Americans take control of their own stories, rather than allowing the media to decide which stories will be marginalized or silenced and which will be broadcast for self-serving purposes (Raines, 2002). This means African Americans should wake up to their greatness as a people and become aware of their responsibility to help eradicate the poverty and oppression that are destroying the very souls of black Americans (Kilson, 2002; Jackson, 2000). A new vision is needed for what is possible and for what must occur.

Using Strategic Planning and Other Community-Wide Strategies

Although the following recommendations were made by the Joint Center for Political and Economic Studies more than a decade ago, they continue to serve as useful guidelines for systems charge and maintenance and for social justice in black communities (Franklin & Norton, 1987): The crafters of this report, entitled Black Initiative and Governmental Responsibilities, believe that African American families and communities should:

1. Incorporate more consciously into their lives the rich and vibrant traditions of black values.
2. Devise a blueprint for action that spells out the roles and responsibilities of the government, in a stable economy, for its poor and oppressed citizens.
3. Plan and work more consistently to mobilize or redirect its strong self-help traditions.

Taken together, these recommendations parallel the National Urban Leagues' current call to reconstruct Black Civil Society. According to Hugh B. Price, president of the National Urban League (2001), black civil society is the aggregate of all voluntary agencies and organizations, the people who staff these agencies and organizations, the people who live in predominately black communities and/or have relatives who do, and the people who attend black churches. This cadre of stakeholders constitutes the strengths of African American communal life; therefore, it must move the rebuilding process forward. This call to action may take many forms of collaboration, advocacy, and partnering in building new systems and reforming unresponsive and unsupportive systems.

An example of such responses is the Urban League's national education initiative: the Campaign for Africa American Achievement. This campaign's purpose is to mobilize local communities through the Urban League's national network of affiliates to support and encourage high scholastic achievement in black children. The campaign is a prototype for the kind of networking and linkages that must be accomplished between, across, and within black community groups. It will be a challenge to make these communities into places where all people are supported in growing toward their fullest potential.

Shaping Future Research, Policy, and Program Initiatives

Research Initiatives. Coupled with the above community-wide initiatives, there is a need for ongoing research, policy, and program initiatives to address racial inequities in all spheres of life–health, education, politics, public welfare, housing, criminal and juvenile justice, the military, transportation, communication, religion and spirituality, and recreation. Despite a popular belief in this country that race is not a significant factor in determining the quality of life of most African Americans, the latter's daily experiences as well as research have corroborated the tenacious, though often insidious, impact of racism. Researchers point out that racial discrimination continues to be a major barrier in the labor market, and in the education, health care, housing, and political systems. Hence, racial discrimination continues to impact the overall well-being of society in ethnic-, class-, and gender-specific ways. In this context, Williams (1999) states:

> Racial discrimination is more than the irrational manifestation of individual prejudice. It becomes a form of competitive domination, a racialized economic action that simultaneously reproduces white privilege and denies opportunities and rewards to people of color. (p. 145)

Therefore, ongoing research must address this type of institutional or structural racism. It should explore how structural racism leads to inequitable practices and treatment in all spheres of life, and the specific consequences for African Americans from their perspectives and in their own voices. All systems should be the focus of such research–the economy, law and justice, and education–including other areas that stigmatize or exclude blacks from a desirable quality of life.

Social Policy Initiatives. Those in positions to develop social policies have a pattern of reinforcing conflicts between low wealth individuals and families from different ethnic groups. Williams (1999) clarifies the sources of those conflicts: this country's narratives about race, wealth, and work. Those narratives perpetuate white economic privilege and an aversion to race-based policies designed to reduce income inequities. Policy makers "repeatedly tell working-class white men (that) it is ill-gotten, colored gains that have kicked them to the economic curb," or that "poor black women were robbing state coffers and had to be stopped" (Williams, 1999, p. 147).

These socially sanctioned biases require a renewed and expanded focus with respect to policy development in areas that perpetuate oppressive and inflexible systems. Those areas include the economy, criminal justice, health care and health insurance coverage, housing, education, entrepreneurship and wealth building, and racial discrimination. For example, policies regarding Earned Income Tax Credit, a living wage, and family-friendly employment benefits should be the focus of political activist efforts. These policies not only enhance the economic structure of all low-wealth families, but especially the economic situations of the black working poor. Increased racial profiling and incarceration rates for a disproportionate number of black youths and adults and other people of color must also be addressed in terms of policy reforms.

Program Initiatives. Additionally, program initiatives must be implemented to effectively support families and children, and to support the educational aspirations of college students. Furthermore, given the increasing numbers of African Americans being imprisoned, more effective programs must be developed to successfully reintegrate those released from prison back into the community and into their families. Examples of such programs are the National Urban League Early Literacy Programs (Reid, 2002; Cox & Spriggs, 2002) and the Fair Housing Initiatives Program sponsored by the Housing and Urban Development Department (HUD), which was designed to prevent or identify and resolve discriminatory housing practices.

Such programs must be continued. Discriminatory practices in the home loan industry and in governmental loan programs must also be combated. Because of rapid technological advances, it is imperative that current and future African American workers' skills be enhanced through ongoing education and training programs (Mason, 1999). Increasing opportunities for the creation, maintenance, and support of small business programs is another must. This program strategy can allow working and middle-income families, especially blacks and other people of color, to secure assets and build wealth.

Maintaining a Spiritual and Africentric Orientation

Finally as a people, African Americans should consciously embrace a spiritual orientation to guide the way they think, act, and live their lives on a daily basis. It is obvious from the foregoing discussion that a great deal of unfinished business exists with respect to economic and social justice issues for black families and their communities. Their spiritual orientation and the Africentric paradigm are an organizing framework for addressing social and economic injustices, discriminatory practices, policy reforms, spiritual development, program development, and research initiatives. These proposed strategies for systems change and maintenance are essential for the survival of African Americans, in the spiritual and cultural domains, and in all other areas.

CONCLUSION

Research, policy and program development must be ongoing and used in combination to create effective and sustainable communities and services in order to address social justice issues of importance to African Americans. This approach, coupled with consistent individual and collective advocacy, can make a significant difference. Working together, this society can create a world in which no one is left behind—a world in which all systems work together to eradicate poverty, eliminate racism, and create a just society.

Richard H. Cain, an African American congressman from South Carolina, in speaking for the passage of a federal civil rights act, described the type of environment a just society will create for all people:

> We do not want any discrimination to be made. I do not ask for any legislation for colored people of this country that is not applied to the white people of this country. All that we seek is equal laws, equal legislation, and equal rights throughout the length and breath of this land. (Edgar, 2000, p. 43)

REFERENCES

Billingsley, A. (1992). *Climbing Jacobs ladder: The enduring legacy of African American families*. New York: Simon and Schuster.

Cose, E. (1999, June 7). The good news about black America. *Newsweek, vol. CXXX III,* no. 23, 28–40.

Cox, L.C. & Spriggs, W. (Eds.) (2002). Special research report: Negative effects of TANF on college enrollment. In D. Lee (Ed.), *The state of black America*. (pp. 223–251). Washington, DC: National Urban League.

Dedman, B. (1990, January 22). Blacks denied S & L loans twice as often as whites. *Atlanta Journal and Constitution,* p.1.

Edgar, W. (2000). *South Carolina: A history of Columbia, SC.* Columbia, SC: University of South Carolina Press.

Engs, R.F. (1979). *Freedom's first generation of Blacks: Hampton, VA 1861–1890.* Philadelphia, PA: University of Pennsylvania Press.

Franklin, J.H. (1969). *From slavery to freedom: A history of Negro Americans* (3rd cd.) New York: Vintage Books.

Franklin, J.H., & Norton, E.H. (1987). *Black initiatives and governmental responsibility: A policy framework for racial justice.* Washington, DC: Joint Center for Political Studies.

Franklin, J.H., & Moss, A.A. (1988). *From slavery to freedom: A history of Negro Americans.* New York: Knopf.

Freeman, E.M. (2001). *Substance abuse intervention, prevention, rehabilitation, and systems change strategies: Helping individuals, families, and groups to empower themselves.* NY: Columbia University Press.

Hochschild, J. and Rogers R. (2000). Race relations in a diversifying nation. In J. Jackson (Ed.), *New directions: African Americans in a diversifying nation.* (pp. 45–85). New York: National Planning Association.

Hochschild, J. (2003). The future of inequality in American politics. In G. Pamper & M. Weiner (Eds), *The future of democratic politics.* NJ: Rutgers University Press.

Jackson, J. (Ed.) (2000). *New directions: African Americans in a diversifying nation.* New York: National Planning Association.

Kilson, M.L. (2002). African Americans and American politics 2002: The motivation phase. In D. Lee (Ed.), *The state of black America 2002.* (pp. 149–180). Washington, DC: National Urban League.

Logan, S.L. (2001). *The black family: Strength, self-help and positive change* (2nd Ed.). Boulder, CO: Westview Press.

Mason, P.L. (1999). Family environment and intergenerational well-being: Some preliminary results. In W. Spriggs. (Ed.), *The state of black America: National Urban League (45–90).* Washington, DC: National Urban League.

Massey, D.S., & Denton, N.A. (1993). *American apartheid: Segregation and the making of the underclass.* Cambridge, MA: Harvard University Press.

Painter, N. (1977). *Exodusters: Black migration to Kansas after reconstruction.* New York: Knopf.

Price, H.B. (2001). Black America's challenge: The reconstruction of black civil society. In L.A. Daniels (Ed.), *The state of black America: National Urban League, (13–18).* Washington, DC: Urban League.

Raines, F.D. (2002). What equality would look like: Reflections on the past, present and future. In D.A. Lee (Ed.), *The state of black America 2002.* (pp. 13–28) Washington, DC: The National Urban league.

Reid, K. S. (December 13, 2002). Early literacy focus of Urban League efforts. *Education Week,* 25–28.

Ruiz, D.S. (1990). Social and economic profile of black Americans, 1989. In D.S. Ruiz (Ed.), *Handbook of mental health and mental disorders among black Americans* (pp. 3–15). New York: Greenwood Press.

South Carolina Kids Count. (2001). *Children at risk: State trends.* Columbia, SC: Department of Public Health.

Sterling, D. (1997) (Ed.). *We are sisters: Black women in the nineteenth century.* New York: W.W. Norton.

U.S. National Advisory Commission on Civil Disorders (1988). *The Kerner report.* New York: Pantheon Books.

Williams, R.M. (1999). Unfinished business: African American political economy during the age of "color-blind" politics. In W. Spriggs (Ed.), *The state of black America: National Urban League (pp. 137–152).* Washington, DC: National Urban League.

Chapter 14

ECONOMIC AND SOCIAL DEVELOPMENT WITHIN BLACK FAMILIES AND COMMUNITIES

EDITH M. FREEMAN

Social and economic development in black communities is strongly linked to the residents' collective use of social and economic empowerment strategies. Burwell (1995) noted that the best example of such strategies is the black philanthropic tradition, or a sustained history of giving, which is a critical aspect of this group's African heritage, often constrained historically by social and economic factors. "Empowerment arises from victorious group experiences . . . in every city, town and hamlet" in which "actions of givers are at the center of analysis," highlighting African American ". . . qualities like self-development, self-determination, protest, and resourcefulness" (Burwell, 1995, pp. 28, 33). The informal economy within black communities, as reflected in the trading of basic goods and services among the residents, is another example of unique social and economic empowerment strategies. These strategies are cultural strengths when viewed through an African American lens. When a European rather than African American lens is used, however, such strategies often are ignored or labeled as cultural deficits (Cowger, 1994).

The current economic downturn, caused by global terrorist acts and other social-economic factors, along with the present conservative political climate, have disadvantaged families in general. Moreover, these changes have undermined the effectiveness of empowerment strategies used by black families and communities to address the current drug abuse crisis, chronic health problems amidst shrinking public sector health resources, homelessness, and high unemployment. While these systemic barriers and community problems have affected many black families, those in the working class and those living in poverty have been especially vulnerable; because they often lack social and economic reserves beyond their immediate cultural network resources (Barry, 2001; Barusch, 2002).

This chapter highlights these resources and other strengths of black families and communities that exist in spite of such impediments to economic and social development, through a discussion about empowerment in general and historical aspects of black empowerment strategies in particular. The rebuilding or enhancing of black communities is also discussed, including a range of poverty reduction and social equity strategies that are consistent with black empowerment, mutual aid, and philanthropic traditions. Burwell's (1995) concept of collecting economic empowerment stories is utilized to present examples from which social work practice implications are summarized related to economic and social development in black communities.

EMPOWERMENT AS THE CORE OF SOCIAL AND ECONOMIC DEVELOPMENT

The Concept of Empowerment in General

A clear definition of empowerment is essential for understanding the economic and social development needs of black families and communities. "Yeich and Levine (1992) believe empowerment involves oppressed people mobilizing themselves and others to cause changes in society that provide them with more power over their lives. Related to this definition is the concept of self-efficacy, . . . a feeling that often results when individuals understand and own the process of change in which they are involved. Furthermore, the definition implies that empowerment has important social, political, and economic aspects.

The Social Component. Based on the above definition, social empowerment occurs when people feel mastery and competence in managing their multiple social roles and environments (Burwell, 1995). The helping process is an example of a key social environment in which African Americans and other clients should not only explore their choices, but also should have the power, competencies, authority, and active roles necessary for exercising those choices (Cox, 1991; Hartman, 1993). In addition, other key social environments in which empowerment is crucial are the family, social/cultural networks, school, work, civic organizations, and the spiritual and religious domains. An individual's self-efficacy or accomplishment is often heightened when successful action and empowerment occur in a venue where they can be observed and valued by significant others, for example, within the family or social-cultural network.

The Political Component. In contrast, the goal of political empowerment is greater collective control over decisions and processes that affect a community's quality of life and sufficiency (Freeman, 1996). This type of empowerment addresses community concerns about racial and ethnic oppression and the resulting political and economic inequities, as well as other constraints against a community's self-definition and control. Political empowerment results in a transfer of power from external institutions to people within their communities (Freeman, 2001; Gutierrez, 1995). Essentially political empowerment expands the vertical or hierarchical linkages between former sole decision makers, who are often external to a community, and community members, through political action and community development (Zippay, 1995).

The Economic Component. Many authors view political and economic development, and the underlying empowerment process, as inseparable because each lays a foundation and acts as a catalyst for the other (Burwell, 1995). Economic empowerment is defined as expanding people's options for economic self-sufficiency or generating economic opportunities at a level beyond improving individual incomes (Colton, 2002; Gueron & Pauly, 1991). It involves simultaneous changes at the community and policy or institutional level (McGregory, 1991), through power sharing (participation in economic decisions), opportunities for building assets and other resources (support from economic equity policies), and capacity building (skill development in economic areas). In contrast to these general economic empowerment supports, it is important to identify some of the more culture-specific empowerment resources that Black communities have drawn upon over time.

Historical Aspects of Black Empowerment

African Helping Traditions Prior to and During Slavery. Prior to the diaspora, which forcefully relocated black people to many other parts of the world, a common healing tradition existed across different tribes and geographic areas on the African continent. This cultural healing tradition became the basis for empowerment during black slavery in the Americas, England, and the Caribbean, and during the European colonization of Africa. Table 14.1 includes some of these healing specialists and techniques as sources of individual and collective empowerment, which were maintained in various forms by blacks during slavery and colonization. For example, mentoring circles for girls and boys were one of several cultural maintenance institutions in Africa. Those circles involved the teaching of essential agrarian, domestic, and hunting skills to youths, and tribal rites of passage that signaled the movement of individuals from childhood into an adult status, or from adulthood to the status of elder.

Slavery policies/laws prohibited the maintenance of such child- and elder-centered cultural traditions, as a systemic mechanism for eliminating unity among slaves in order to isolate them from their culture and each other. Other cultural-economic traditions were eliminated in this process, such as gender- and age-related divisions of labor for agrarian and hunting activities, and dances/chants used for celebrating harvests from which everyone benefited and felt healed. In spite of these and similar prohibitions, orphaned or dislocated black children were integrated into family structures present on the same plantations, and then were mentored individually through the development of essential skills and involvement in cultural rites. In this manner, the healing tradition was maintained in a different form, yet it created new opportunities for culturally meaningful empowerment and self-efficacy for black people.

In comparison, the griot role that elders traditionally assumed in Africa was maintained during slavery through other creative means. Culturally-centered religious services conducted by black preachers helped to maintain griot traditions such as call and answer, talking

Table 14.1 African Healing Traditions

Healing Specialists	Healing-Empowerment Strategies
The Herbalist (First defense role)	Pharma-therapy, natural or folk medicine
The Fetish Man (Male priest role)	Divining, foretelling, fetish prescriptions
The Medium (Female caretaker role)	Possession dances, music as therapeutic accomplishment
The Healer (Holistic role)	Shock therapy, dream interpretations, sacrifices and religious offerings, exorcisms
The Sorcerer (Evil power role)	Charms, manipulations, spells, hexes
The Griot (Cultural wisdom role)	Oral tradition: narratives, stories, proverbs, parables, hero/heroine making
Mentoring Circles (Cultural maintenance role)	Teaching agrarian, domestic, and hunting skills; rites of passage and social roles

drums, and inspirational narratives, which nevertheless had to be disguised to resemble European rituals. McRoy (1990) notes that, "Creating their own means of worship which reflected a combination of West African beliefs and Christianity, slaves used metaphors, rhythmic chants and music, clapping, prayers and sermons, shouting, and stomping of feet as a means of religious expression and emotional uplift" (p. 6), and as a form of empowerment.

Another example of the griot role involved informal storytelling events in black quarters by other elders on a given plantation or group of plantations. Empowerment occurred most often when these griots extolled the heroic exploits of African forebears, those who jumped ship and died during the middle passage, and those involved in a persistent resistance to slavery through the underground railroad. While this and other African healing traditions provided a culturally unique religious-social empowerment experience during slavery, significant efforts toward black economic development and empowerment were not possible in such oppressive circumstances.

Black-Helping Traditions During Post-Slavery and Current Periods. During the post-slavery period up to current times, black-helping traditions have more effectively integrated social, economic, and political empowerment strategies and development. For the immediate post-slavery period, assistance consisted of family reunification and relocation efforts by black individuals and by the Freedman's Bureau, which the federal government established from 1865 to 1871 but severely underfunded (McRoy, 1990). Black philanthropy also involved individuals helping other blacks to participate in local farming and business economies, through small farm ownership, sharecropping, small businesses, and craft guilds (Martin & Martin, 1985). Some blacks migrated to large urban centers in the north or to all black towns in Oklahoma, Kansas, Florida, and other states where family members and individual black community residents provided economic, political, and social supports.

Black collective helping, in contrast to these individual and family supports, often involved more long-term and systemic mutual aid and philanthropy. Those long-term efforts provided empowerment and development opportunities for black people during the post-slavery period, and many efforts continued during the early years of the twentieth century. There were disagreements, however, about the preferred type of leadership development such efforts should be used to achieve:

i.e., W.E.B. Dubois' political activist leadership or Booker T. Washington's self-education and vocational training leadership (Kilson, 2000; O'Donnell, 1995). This conflict about leadership strategies and resource allocations has continued into the present period, in various forms, although there may be increased consensus among blacks that both approaches are viable and necessary.

Black churches assumed an even greater role immediately after black emancipation and during the early part of the twentieth century, by founding various benevolent societies for sick benefits, burial services, food, work, and other economic and social development opportunities (DuBois, 1909). In addition, black lodges for masons or odd fellows were developed to provide assistance in economic, social, and political development, along with community-based savings clubs/ credit unions, food cooperatives, social clubs, professional associations, and social action organizations.

Black people formed private relief groups that established black orphanages, hospitals, juvenile detention facilities, and institutions for the disabled and elderly, once it became apparent that white social service organizations would not provide those services to blacks (Burwell, 1995; McGregory, 1991; Ross, 1976). While these formal and informal cultural supports helped to maintain many of the African healing traditions and empowerment strategies shown in Table 14.1, other cultural roles, once available, have been constrained by ongoing economic, social, and political oppression against blacks. Examples of currently constrained roles in that table include the herbalist, medium, and mentoring roles. The latter role in particular, by its decreased presence in black communities across the country, implies that black economic and social empowerment opportunities today may be greatly diminished.

REBUILDING BLACK COMMUNITIES: FROM POVERTY REDUCTION TO SOCIAL AND ECONOMIC EQUITY APPROACHES

Overview of Approaches

Over time a continuum of poverty reduction and social/economic development approaches has been established to address the needs of African Americans and other impoverished or working-class groups.

Figure 14.1 indicates that those approaches, for the most part, are either primarily focused on individuals or groups or on entire neighborhoods and communities. Those approaches on the local development end of the continuum are more focused on human and social capital mobilization, while those on the individual development end are focused on consumptive or poverty reduction approaches.

Poverty Reduction Approaches

As noted in Figure 14.1, poverty reduction approaches have become synonymous with the maintenance of poverty for many low wealth black families, although some families have clearly benefited from such programs (Kim, 2000). Those public sector programs include income maintenance, job training programs, and site- or voucher-based rental housing. The most recent welfare reform was the Personal Responsibility and Work Opportunity Reconciliation Act of 1995 (NASW, 1996). It requires able-bodied individuals to work, and attempts to link more clearly time-limited subsidies with building families' self-sufficiency, but it ignores systemic causes of poverty.

For example, as some researchers point out, the depressed job market, employment discrimination against blacks, and loss of health benefits that are linked directly to welfare eligibility are systemic factors that have blocked blacks' and poor people's opportunities for self-sufficiency (Hartmann, Spalter-Roth, Sills, & Yi, 2003; Kim, 2000; Midgley, 1999). Other nonsystemic changes, such as the use of income transfer vouchers, tend to benefit the elderly, Caucasians, and married-couple families rather than blacks and female-headed families (Kim, 2000; Ozawa, 1994). Those strategies and systemic conditions severely limit the latter's voluntary movement off welfare and/or restrict them to the lowest rungs of the working-class ladder.

Social Responsibility and Opportunity Approaches

Most of these approaches are funded by organizations in the private sector, including mainstream and cultural organizations. Over the years, private foundations have funded many individually focused programs for mentoring youths and providing leadership development, access to higher education and related resources, prevention of substance

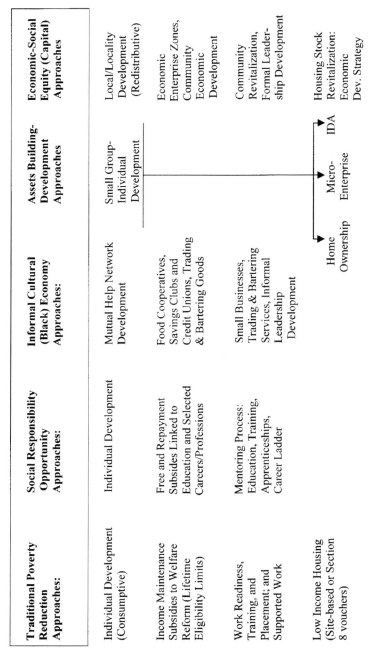

Figure 14.1   Black Families: Continuum of Poverty Reduction to Social & Economic Equity Approaches

abuse and gang involvement, development of youth entrepreneurs as a form of economic development, and provision of other career ladder supports (Freeman, 1996). While individual empowerment is implicit in such programs, an underlying assumption is that recipients will repay those supports by helping to change and empower their communities economically and socially. Generally, there is little provision in these programs for more direct efforts toward community development in these areas.

Similarly, some black organizations including sororities, fraternities, clubs, church groups, social activist centers, political alliances, businesses, and special college funds (e.g., the United Negro College Fund) have provided funding for mentoring black youths, adults who are starting new businesses, and single parents in need of educational and employment resources. These individual-centered approaches often are more culturally sensitive than some mainstream programs. For example, they may provide cultural coaches or an orientation period that prepares recipients for culturally unique demands in higher education or in particular career fields such as the need to become bicultural (Freeman, 1990). These approaches also have an implicit social responsibility assumption regarding black recipients who are expected to "give back" to their communities, sometimes in specified or unspecified ways.

Informal Black Economy Approaches

Figure 14.1 highlights how informal economy approaches focus on the development of black self- and mutual-help networks rather than individuals, in contrast to poverty reduction and social responsibility approaches. With informal approaches, goods and services are provided to community or network members, often in exchange for other goods and services and/or for small amounts of money. The exchanged goods and services include child care, barber and beauty shop services, catering, auto repair, odd jobs, small electronics repair, fruits and vegetables, and advice about relationship or business conflicts. These systems' formats are often unique to the black communities in which they develop, but there are some similarities. Three common formats are:

1. *Human Development:* The system involves fund raising to obtain part of the formal economy's charity dollar (public or private) to further support a black community's internal and informal exchange of goods and services for economic development (Burwell 1995; Rodgers & Tartaglia, 1990).
2. *Street Entrepreneurship:* The system is supported solely by internal and informal exchanges of goods and services by individuals/small networks with expertise/skills in key areas, on an as-needed basis, but who do not generally have access to business supports from the formal economy (McFadden & Walz, 1998; McInnis-Dittrich, 1995; Voydanoff, 1984).
3. *Community Transformation:* This system involves more ongoing internal and informal exchanges based on interconnected mutual help projects such as a farmers' market or urban gardens, food cooperatives, money lending, an odd jobs bank, child care matches, or clothing exchanges (Johnson, 1980; O'Donnell & Osirim, 1992).

Voydanoff (1984) points out that residents establish these exchange systems in order to cope with various forms of economic distress. For example, systems may be established when communities become chronically depressed economically; cities withdraw basic resources from a community (community divestiture); businesses go through downsizings, creating job losses and diminished incomes that may differentially affect particular communities; or large numbers of new immigrants who lack an economic base move into a community.

While informal economy approaches often develop in response to these external economic conditions, their development is also strongly influenced by black people's cultural history in African, where village life was guided by concepts of shared work and collective sufficency (Johnson, 1980). Research has documented that these concepts guided the development of informal economies and mutual-help projects during the post-slavery and progressive eras within many black communities, for example, in South Carolina (Burwell, 1995), Georgia (Ross, 1976), and Chicago (Johnson, 1980; O'Donnell, 1995). These and other examples of informal economies demonstrate the cultural strengths and mutual respect that are the heart of economic empowerment experiences within black communities (Burwell, 1995).

These approaches are also known as black philanthropy, the street economy, the informal sector, and racial self-help (Burwell, 1995; Mc-Fadden & Walz, 1998; Osirim, 1992; Weems, 1993). Such concepts have not only been applied to informal exchange systems within black communities but also to blacks in Africa (Osirim, 1992), Latinos in

Mexico (McFadden & Walz, 1998), and to poor white communities in this country such as Appalachia (McInnis-Dittrich, 1995). To be effective, these informal systems often require the help of indigenous leaders who act as informal coordinators for exchanges. This role seems to combine the healer and griot empowerment roles shown in Table 14.1, because it involves sharing advice and cultural history along with providing information about how the identified range of goods and services can be exchanged.

Many advantages of informal economy approaches are apparent from this discussion, but there are disadvantages as well, in terms of black communities' economic and social development. These systems can become institutionalized, especially street entrepreneurship and community transformation systems, but they do not change the long-term structural problems, such as community divestiture, that partially influence their development. Because some systems may involve unreported income by residents, those individuals may be at risk for prosecution from punitive public welfare and internal revenue policies about such income (McInnis-Dittrich, 1995; McFadden & Walz, 1998). Finally, because some informal systems are not connected to the formal economy, in contrast to human development systems, they cannot provide pathways into that economy. Many black and Hispanic women, often called "the poorest of the poor," are helped by informal economies, nevertheless, they may continue to have fewer economic and social development opportunities by remaining cut off from the formal economy.

Assets Building Approaches

Assets building, according to Page-Adams and Sherraden (1997), involves helping low wealth families save for a range of goals, including education, microenterprise, home ownership, and other economic and social development purposes. It focuses on building communities from within on a small scale (Raheim, 1996), and generates multiple opportunities for community members to enhance their self-reliance and well-being. This approach is shown near the social capital end of the continuum in Figure 14.1, particularly because it shifts the focus from income alone or consumption to building assets from saving and investing, and from work with individuals alone to skill building within small community networks (Sherraden & Sherraden, 2000). Approaches to assets building generally consist of three main areas: self-employment or microenterprise, individual development accounts (IDAs), and home ownership, with IDAs serving as the pathway for subsidizing these other two areas (Alisultanov, Klein, & Zandniapour, 2002; Page-Adams & Sherraden, 1997).

Ideas about IDAs and self-employment emerged out of social and economic development research in other countries. For example, studies on informal economies established by women in African have provided important lessons (Raheim, 1996), along with studies on the Grameen Bank approach with women in Bangladesh involving microenterprise and individual development accounts (Jansen & Pippard, 1998). This early focus on women's self-employment and savings opportunities in other countries has helped to create programs that are social class- and gender-sensitive in this country, often established by women's organizations, refugee centers, and community action agencies. Examples include programs for black and other low-income women, Native Americans, AFDC recipients, displaced homemakers, dislocated workers, and Southeast Asian refugees (Banerjee, 2001; Clark, Huston, & Meister (1994; Raheim & Bolden, 1995).

Programs often involve lending money to participants or providing them access to credit for decreasing ethnic, gender, and social class discrimination barriers; and providing credit repair education, consumer education for home purchase/maintenance, coaching for home loan applications, business training, saving and investment education, and technical assistance (Banerjee, 1998; Page-Adams & Sherraden, 1997; Shobe, 2001). While these positive aspects make assets building approaches useful for helping black communities to economically revitalize and develop themselves, there are some disadvantages to these approaches as well.

As an example, poverty and unemployment rates for blacks in this country are disproportionately high. Assets building approaches to social/economic development from within are at too small a scale to effect the real changes necessary for eliminating these structural problems. Schreiner (1999) points out that microenterprise projects, for instance, only increase participants' movement from welfare to self-employment at a ratio of less than one in 100, and that they tend to attract those with the most assets among the poor. Participants tend to be self-selected individuals with the most years of education, highest skills, broadest experience, and strongest support networks, i.e., these programs tend to not attract individuals with fewer assets from among the poor or working poor. Also the effectiveness of these approaches is frequently undermined by policy barriers (Edwards & Mason, 2003; Raheim, 1997), such as inadequate numbers of substance abuse treatment beds for AFDC mothers who are addicted and who are expected to develop microenterprise projects and to recover simultaneously.

Social and Economic Equity Approaches

Economic and social development has been defined as an approach that involves community reinvestment by and collaboration with external funders. A major goal is to retain the profits of development within the target community, and to ensure a high degree of community determination in this process (Weil & Gamble, 1995). Another goal is to institutionalize procedures that go beyond responding to situational opportunities and crises, and that establish a process of long-term community planning to assess and resolve development needs. Midgley (1996) concludes that this approach can effectively involve three different but related strategies: human capital mobilization, social capital formation, and the promotion of productive employment and self-employment. Regardless of the strategies involved within a community, some common sources of funding have been identified, including a combination of city and county governments, federal agencies, banks, foundations, consortiums, external developers, and political activist organizations.

What makes these approaches different from other examples on the continuum in Figure 14.1 is their emphasis on social and human capital and on social and economic equity. The life circumstances of socially disadvantaged groups such as African Americans and the poor are not improved by general economic progress. In fact, social equity and justice for those groups can only be established by social and economic development approaches that include redistributive mechanisms, such as reforms in policies and institutions that help to maintain such disadvantages (Hartmann et al., 2003; Linhorst, 2002. Other equity aspects involve building the capacities of community residents to enhance their social and economic well-being, and providing both economic development opportunities as well as basic services that help to build a community's infrastructure and its economic sustainability (Weil & Gamble, 1995).

The emphasis on social *and* human capital is equally important for black community development. The concept of social capital focuses on promoting the material well-being of local people through sustainable forms of economic development (Midgley & Simbi, 1993; Jansen & Pippard, 1998). For example, improving a community's available housing stock in quantity and quality provides a significant form of social captital that can be a catalyst for wider economic and social development. Social capital efforts should be combined with human capital methods. The latter concept refers to supporting substantial improvements in community members' life quality, hopes, motivation, and meaning (Midgley & Simbi, 1993), in recognition that building social capital within black communities does not automatically lead to social well-being or human capital development.

A number of other concepts have been used to refer to social and economic equity approaches, for example, locality or local development, sustainable community development, globalization, redistributive growth, social investment, community reconstruction, mainstreaming strategies, and community enterprise zones (Banerjee 2001; Edwards & Mason 2003). These concepts have two common implications, first, that social and economic development efforts require empowerment and institutionalization. For example, it is noted that such efforts rely heavily on political, social, and psychological empowerment techniques in order to achieve capacity building at macro, mezzo, and micro-levels. Secondly, these concepts indicate that sustainable communities can only be established in the presence of two factors: A visible form of political and economic support from the government (based on economic equity policies), and inclusion/acceptance of a third party support mechanism by the community (such as a credible private foundation or existing cultural organization) (Linhorst, 2002).

SOCIAL WORK PRACTICE IMPLICATIONS

Black People's Lived Experiences as Viable Reources

The social and economic development approaches illustrated in the previous discussion and in Figure 14.1 are related to important practice guidelines, which to be effective, must be grounded in the African cultural and empowerment healing practices in Table 14.1. Utilizing this cultural context and current realities, two examples of African American empowerment stories or healing experiences (Burwell, 1995) are presented in the next section, from which some essential practice implications are summarized.

African American Empowerment Stories

Example #1: Background Information. Kyle was a 14-year-old African American high school student when he was invited by his counselor to apply for an economic development program that involved a combined social opportunity and assets building approach (see Figure 14.1). He lived in an urban impoverished, multicultural community. The program included three main components: (1) Assets building/college preparatory services, (2) Teen-age pregnancy and gang involvement prevention, and (3) Leadership and self-esteem development. This high school program was a bridge to a related pre-college orientation program designed to help youth of color adapt to college during the summer preceding their freshman year. Part of the course required class members to participate in an exercise over several sessions that was designed to help them develop oral histories about their paths to social, economic, and educational opportunity. It was assumed that once their oral histories were formulated and shared in a peer-supported environment, they could use the stories to enhance their handling of future cultural and social challenges during their college years.

Example #1: Kyle's Empowerment Story. Kyle began his empowerment story by stating:

> I guess I was supposed to be in college, or I wouldn't be here; I had plenty of troubles on the way. I joined this savings club in high school. It was supposed to help me save money for college. I could

just save and invest the money or start a small business with the help of the program. We had this group of students and we met together twice a week about our savings accounts; IDAs they called them. I decided to save and invest; see, the program matched your savings. My parents got involved in coaching me, cheering me on, and they convinced me to start a small business. So I, I mean we, started a catering business with my families' help and my peers in the club. You know, black clubs, churches, community centers, students' birthday parties, football and basketball games. We had some setbacks, but after a while, things got better. I had a coach from the program, a white retired guy who'd had his own business. He helped a lot, I thought he was a little strange at first, but I got so I trusted him, and he believed in me.

In my senior year, my parents were trying to buy a house, their first house in twenty years of marriage, and they wanted to borrow money out of my account because they were short on the down payment. The program director said absolutely not, it was my account, for my college, and that was that. My parents were so upset, they wanted me to leave the program. Other family got involved, took sides, so before I knew it I was staying with my grandmother and my parents were mad at me and half our relatives. We got this humongous family. They stayed mad all last year. It was hard, but I just hung on. When I got ready to come here for the summer orientation, I didn't think they'd come to the family get together, but they did. I should've known they'd come through. It all worked out in the end, but I learned something. For black people, family is everything. The program just didn't dig it, I mean what its like to be black. They said I needed to stay focused on my goals.

Example #1: Practice Implications. A number of practice implications are apparent from this empowerment story. First, practitioners and planners involved in social and economic development approaches in black communities should be knowledgeable about and respectful of the cultural values of the residents. These approaches should be designed with those value priorities in mind, so that the needs of the family unit and extended family network can be addressed, and the supports they provide are enhanced. In Kyle's program, the focus was on providing social and economic opportunities for black youths individually, within small networks with their peers, but in isolation of the complete cultural context that surrounded them. That cultural context is based on many African traditions: Interdependence, collectiveness versus an individual-orientation, mutual healing and empowerment, and human capital (cultural well-being) as the guide to social capital (material well-being) as shown in Table 14.1.

The program's inflexible response to the parents' needs contributed to a major family crisis and threatened the program's goal of college completion and leadership development for Kyle and other youths. Even if the program decided that the youths' IDA funds could not be used as loans to other family members, it could have developed procedures for linking parents to other sources of funding and for brokering those resources.

A second practice implication is the importance of using culturally-centered procedures, such as cultural coaches, rites of passage, mentoring circles, and oral histories/narratives to help black families and other community members clarify cultural lessons for future coping. In this example, the social and economic opportunity-assets building program linked its participants to a pre-college summer orientation seminar for youth of color, which helped them to anticipate the demands of college and their new multicultural environments. The use of the oral history method to assist these youths in identifying and sharing their empowerment narratives was an excellent bridge for teaching them about the importance of biculturality and creative uses of economic and social development opportunities.

Example #2: Background Information. A church-sponsored housing development within a predominantly black and low-income community was the site where the need for social and economic development was first identified. The west coast city in which this community was located had gradually divested its resources from it, having decided that the residents lacked interest in available programs and would continue the high rate of vandalism and property damage in the area. The community itself was concerned about the violence, drug abuse, school dropout rates, high unemployment, inadequate housing, and lack of recreational resources that had plagued the area over the years.

These chronic conditions helped the community to mobilize and involve itself in a planned sustained effort toward economic and social development, beyond the crisis of the day, as it had tended to do in the past. The community was able to establish a combined approach to its problems (see Figure 14.1), which consisted of the following components: (1) A youth social and economic opportunity component involving Afrocentric antidrug/antigang services (mentoring circles, rites of passage, and a youth entrepreneurial/assets building program); (2) A holistic cultural health promotion component (culturally-centered nutrition; exercise; health education regarding racial stress, drugs, HIV, health risks for particular diseases for African Americans, and herb/vegetable gardening; and outpatient crisis and well-patient clinic services; (3) An informal economy component (with an indigenous coordinator who operated a food cooperative, urban gardens, clothing exchange, savings/investment clubs, and child care exchanges; and (4) A social and economic equity component, which included economic, social, and political development projects such as a trash collection business, creating new private/public housing stock, and supporting/educating candidates from the community to run for relevant public offices; and policy reforms/systems changes focused on getting the city to reinvest in the community regarding human and basic services and securing external investors for the community's development projects.

Years after this combined development approach was initiated, one of the community residents was nominated for a leadership award and was asked to write a brief story, for the award presentation, about her role in helping the community to transform itself.

Example #2: The Empowerment Story. Ms. Dunkin wrote the following empowerment story:

> They said, you write the story, Ms. Dunkin. You know the story of what happened better than anyone else. I guess it all started with us wanting to do something about the young people in the housing development. They were getting killed, no jobs, kicked out of school, nothing to look forward to, just hanging out in the development every day. Hope had come and gone for them. The city had pulled the bus service out; they said there wasn't enough riders and their drivers were getting robbed and mugged. Long story short: that signaled the end for this community, we knew then no one believed we were worth helping. So, the kids that wanted to work couldn't get to their jobs; and those that didn't, had an excuse.
>
> We asked the community's health center to help us get the bus ser-

vice back. They said no at first, until we reminded them that their new health education initiative wouldn't work if people couldn't get there. They helped us start a letter-writing campaign to the bus company. The company agreed to provide two new routes within the community on a sixty-day trial basis to see if there'd be enough riders and the drivers would be safe. We organized a bus-riding campaign; even got residents who had cars to park them and ride the buses. We had to set up a volunteer patrol on the buses to prevent robberies or any violence. It worked and the bus company caved in. Then we thought, we need more than just band-aids like this, we need a whole plan of economic projects; so we contacted a foundation and they said, "We don't fund ideas, send us a full proposal." They did agree to send a representative to one of our meetings when we said we're not talking about one project but a whole economic redevelopment plan. He came to the meeting, and then introduced us to a professor at the university, who helped us create a community economic and social development plan, along with a funding proposal.

The professor said we needed a symbol of the community's commitment to the plan before submitting the proposal to the foundation. I told him about the bus riding campaign; how several of us noticed a group of dope dealers camped in the park across from one of the bus stops. They kept threatening bus riders and selling their dope, so the young kids were afraid to go to the park. They had pulled an old couch up to the curb where they sat day after day. These drug dealers were always there, but one morning for some reason the couch was empty. Two of the volunteer patrols burned it. People in the neighborhood came to the park all through the day and cheered. We left the burned-out couch there for two days and then hauled it away.

The professor, Dr. Estes, agreed what happened *was* a symbol that the community was ready to move forward. The foundation approved our planning grant, and later gave us an implementation grant that the city matched with government funds. It wasn't that we never had problems after that, but we became a real community, and we've never looked back. I was just one of many, we all helped.

Example #2: Practice Implications.   In addition to the two practice implications discussed regarding the first empowerment story, the above example is useful for identifying a number of other implications. Essentially, practitioners and planners need to shift from using poverty reduction approaches in black communities to the use of combined social and economic development approaches (Midgley, 1995). In this second example, a black community used such a combined approach effectively, including youth opportunity, informal economy, assets building, and social and economic equity components. Most importantly, the target community should determine the combination of approaches selected, as it did in the above example; in consideration of the community's unique needs, strengths, and cultural values. Another caveat to this practice implication is the need to educate policy makers regarding community determination and social equity requirements, and to significantly influence their future policy initiatives and reforms in those areas (Zhan, Sherraden, & Schreiner, 2002).

A second implication is the importance of helping black communities to assess their readiness to undertake social and economic development efforts. Assessments should include special attention to the need for sustainability in terms of those efforts, or long-term commitment by residents, and the need for empowerment because often oppression may cause residents to feel hopeless (Hartmann, Spalter-Roth, Sills, & Yi, 2003). In the example involving Ms. Dunkin and her community, it was clear that residents no longer wanted to respond with Band-Aid© approaches, and that they were ready for a larger, more comprehensive approach to location development (see Figure 14.1).

Third, this same example highlights the importance of helping black communities to establish multiple and diverse sources of funding, including reinvestiture steps by local government, leveraged or matched funding from diverse sources, planning grants from private resources that allow for a community's unique learning curve, implementation funding, and funding for ongoing technical assistance and brokering services by community and external experts. The community leader's empowerment story also documents how this practice principle can be operationalized, and how a community's credibility and legitimacy are automatically enhanced by the support implied from multiple funding sources (Weil & Gamble, 1995).

A final practice implication involves the importance of creating intergenerational components for social and economic development within black communities (McRoy, 1990). Child- and elder-centered African traditions clearly support a cultural village approach, as shown in Table 14.1, which is focused on a range of intergenerational healing and empowerment traditions. The first empowerment story reflects a youth only focus, whereas in contrast, the second example employs intergenerational components in order to build upon the cultural values of youth-centered cultural traditions, eldership, interdependence, and collectiveness.

CONCLUSION

This discussion about African traditions and practice implications helps to identify other implications related to social work education and research. For example, including university faculty to provide technical assistance, whether to draw upon their strengths in cultural knowledge about African Americans, community practice, or social/economic equity issues, provides opportunities for them to influence related curriculum reforms. Such reforms can enhance the preparation of social workers and other helping professionals for culturally competent practice within black communities. Many practitioners assume that black social and economic development refers to job readiness and employment and training programs, which maintains their narrow focus on poverty reduction approaches. Curriculum changes, such as the introduction of courses on social and economic development within black communities, can help to broaden the focus of social workers' education, and hence broaden their practice to include social/economic equity issues and systems changes.

From a research perspective, a focus on social and economic equity and empowerment in social work education requires that more attention be directed to the voices and meanings of oppressed residents in black communities. The focus of such research may be on documenting the needs of those residents or on exploring their process of culturally-centered location development and other strengths. Attention at that level requires philosophical and methodological changes in research being conducted within those communities to examine their use of redistributive approaches and the effects. For example, philosophical changes such as viewing residents as experts and understanding/

respecting African traditions that influence their responses to development efforts are important. Finally, the use of oral histories, empowerment narratives, griots, cultural coaches, and other black healers to shape the research data collection and analysis process is equally important in terms of essential methodological changes.

REFERENCES

Alisultanov, I., Klein, J., & Zandniapour, L. (2002). *Microenterprise as a welfare to work strategy: One year findings.* NY: Field: The Aspen Institute.

Banerjee, M. (2001). Micro-Enterprise training (MET) program: An innovative response to welfare reform. *Journal of Community Practice, 9*(4), 87–107.

Bannerjee, M.M. (1998). Microenterprise development: A response to poverty. *Journal of Community Practice, 5,* 63–83.

Barry, B. (2001). *Culture and equality.* Cambridge, MA: Harvard University.

Barusch, A.S. (2002). *Foundations of social policy: Social justice, public programs, and the social work profession.* Itasca, IL: F.E. Peacock Publishers.

Burwell, N.Y. (1995). Shifting the historical liens: Early economic empowerment among African Americans. *The Journal of Baccalaureate Social Work, 1,* 25–37.

Clark, P., Huston, T., & Meister, B. (1994). *1994 directory of microenterprise programs.* Washington, DC: Aspen Institute for Humanistic Studies.

Colton, M. (2002). Editorial. Special issue on social work and social justice. *British Journal of Social Work, 32*(6), 659–667.

Cowger, C.D. (1994). Assessing client strengths: Clinical assessment for client empowerment. *Social Work, 39,* 262–268.

Cox, E.O. (1991). The critical role or social action in empowerment oriented groups. *Social Work with Groups, 14,* 77–90.

DuBois, W.E.B. (1909). *Efforts for social betterment among Negro Americans.* Atlanta, GA: Atlanta University Press.

Edwards, K., & Mason, L. (2003). State policy for individual development accounts in the United States: 1993–2003. Working paper. St. Louis, MO: Center for Social Development, Washington University.

Freeman, E.M. (2001). Conceptual, theoretical, and research issues related to empowerment practice. In E. M Freeman (Ed.), *Substance abuse intervention, prevention, rehabilitation, and systems change strategies: Helping individuals, families, and groups to empower themselves* (3–32). New York: Columbia University Press.

Freeman, E.M. (1996). Welfare reforms and services for children and families: Setting a new practice, research, and policy agenda. *Social Work, 41,* 421–432.

Freeman, E.M. (1990). The black family's life cycle: Operationalizing a strengths perspective. In S.M.L. Logan, E.M. Freeman, R.G. McRoy (Eds.), *Social work practice with black families: A culturally specific perspective* (pg. 55–72). N.Y.: Longman.

Gueron, J.M., and Pauly, E. (1991). *From welfare to work.* NY: Russell Sage Foundation.

Gutierrez, L.M. (1995). Understanding the empowerment process: Does consciousness make a difference? *Social Work Research, 19,* 229–237.

Hartman, A. (1993). The professional is political. *Social Work, 38,* 365–366.

Hartmann, H., Spalter-Roth, R., Sills, E. & Yi, H. (2003). *Survival at the bottom: The income packages of low-income families with children.* Washington, DC: Institute for Women's Policy Research.

Jansen, G.G., and Pippard, J.L. (1998). The Grameen Bank in Bangladesh: Helping poor women with credit for self-employment. *Journal of Community Practice, 5,* 103–123.

Johnson, L.O. (1980). The role of education in Western culture history: Tanzania as a model of education for self-reliance. Doctoral Dissertation. NY: Brandeis University.

Kilson, M. (2000). The Washington and DuBois leadership paradigms revisited. *The Annals, 568,* 298–313.

Kim, H. (2000). Poverty in welfare states: A comparative study of antipoverty effectiveness of taxes and income transfers. Doctoral Dissertation. Madison, WI: University of Wisconsin-Madison.

Linhorst, D. M. (2002). Federalism and social justice: Implications for social work. *Social Work, 47*(3), 201–208.

Martin, J., & Martin, E. (1985). *The helping tradition in the black family.* Chicago: University of Chicago Press.

McFadden, J. & Walz, T. (1998). The informal economy in a post-capitalist society: The Mexican experience. *Social Development Issues, 20,* 67–76.

McGregory, J. (1991). *May the work I've done speak for me: The migration text of the lucky ten social club* (10–14). Thousand Oaks, CA: Sage Publications.

McInnis-Dittrich, K. (1995). Women of the shadows: Appalachian women's participation in the informal economy. *Affilia, 10,* 398–412.

McRoy, R.G. (1990). "A historical overview of black families." In S.M.L. Logan, E.M. Freeman, & R.G. McRoy (Eds.), *Social work practice with black families* (3–17). White Plains, NY: Longman.

Midgley, J. (1999). Growth, redistribution, and welfare: Toward social investment. *Social Service Review, 73,* 3–21.

Midgley, J. (1995). *Social development: The development perspective in social welfare.* Thousand Oaks, CA: Sage.

Midgley, J., & Simbi, P. (1993). Promoting a development focus in the community organization curriculum: Relevance of the African experience. *Journal of Social Work Education, 29,* 269–278.

National Association of Social Workers (1996). Policy statement: the Personal Responsibility and Work Opportunity Reconciliation Act of 1995. Washington, DC: NASW.

O'Donnell, S.M. (1995). Urban African American community development in the Progressive Era. *Journal of Community Practice, 2,* 7–26.

O'Donnell, S.M. & Karanja, S.T. (2000). Transformative community practice: Building a model for developing extremely low-income African American communities. *Journal of Community Practice, 7,* 67–84.

Osirim, M.J. (1992). The state of women in the Third World: The informal sector and development in Africa and the Caribbean. *Social Development Issues, 14,* 74–87.

Ozawa, M.N. (1994). Distribute effects of benefits and taxes. *Social Work Research, 18,* 7–13.

Page-Adams, D. & Sherraden, M. (1997). Asset building as a community revitalization strategy. *Social Work, 42,* 423–434.

Raheim, S. (1997). Problems and prospects of self-employment as an economic independence option for welfare recipients. *Social Work, 42,* 44–53.

Raheim, S. (1996). Microenterprise as an approach for promoting economic development in social work: Lessons from the self-employment investment demonstration. *International Social Work, 39,* 69–82.

Raheim, S., & Bolden, J. (1995). Economic empowerment of low-income women through self-employment programs. *Affilia, 10,* 128–154.

Rodgers, A. & Tartaglia, L.J. (1990). Constricting resources: A black self-help initiative. *Administration in Social Work, 14,* 125–137.

Ross, E.L. (1976). Black heritage in social welfare: A case study in Atlanta. *Phylon, 37,* 297–307.

Schreiner, M. (1999). Self-employment, microenterprise, and the poorest Americans. *Social Service Review, 73,* 496–523.

Sherraden, Mi., and Sherraden, Ma. (2000). Asset building: Integrating research, education, and practice. *Advances in Social Work, 1,* 61–77.

Shobe, M.A. (2001). Relationships between assets and personal, social, and economic well-being. Doctoral Dissertation. Lawrence, KS: University of Kansas.

Voydanoff, P. (1984). Economic distress and families: Policy issues. *Journal of Family Issues, 5,* 273–288.

Weems, R.E. (1993). A blueprint for African American economic development. *Western Journal of Black Studies, 17,* 96–100.

Weil, M.O., and Gamble, D.N. (1995). Community practice models. In R.L. Edwards (Ed.), *Encyclopedia of Social Work, 19th Edition* (577–593). Washington, DC: National Association of Social Workers.

Yeich, S., and Levine, R. (1992). Participatory research's contribution to a conceptualization of empowerment. *Journal of Applied Social Psychology, 22,* 1894–1908.

Zhan, M., Sherraden, M., & Schreiner, M. (2002). *Welfare recipiency and savings accounts in individual development accounts.* St. Louis, MO: Center for Social Development. Washington University.

Zippay, A. (1995). The politics of empowerment: Empowerment of low-income populations as a component of social work and community development practice. *Social Work, 40,* 263–267.

Epilogue

THE DUAL PERSPECTIVE REVISITED: AN INTEGRATED APPROACH TO PRACTICE, RESEARCH, AND POLICY WITH BLACK FAMILIES

Edith M. Freeman

Epilogues are characterized by a common effort to grapple with compelling past issues and by a look forward toward exciting new opportunities and possibilities. This indeed is the purpose of epilogues. Focusing on both past and future, rather than on one or the other, whether in terms of epilogues *or* cultural issues, underscores the importance of the dual perspective. Leon Chestang (1979) reminds us that meeting the expectations of both one's ethnic group and those of dominant society, which are often in conflict, requires the adoption of such a perspective. In essence, use of the dual perspective reveals an underlying no-win cultural dilemma that confronts African Americans, as well as other marginalized groups: whether to assimilate or remain at the margins of dominant society.

The dual perspective not only reveals this typically devalued cultural dilemma, but in addition, it is a tool for rephrasing the dilemma and for providing new possibilities for resolving it. This perspective shifts the discussion from whether African Americans should assimilate or remain marginalized (either-or), to an exploration of the different adaptation options that are available to them (both, neither, other new combinations). Consequently, this and other benefits make it useful to

306

revisit the dual perspective in this epilogue, by reviewing how it has been applied to understanding African American families in the past. The chapter then analyzes new possibilities for using this perspective to understand future challenges for black families and helping professionals. Finally, the implications from this analysis are described in terms of an integrated practice, research, and policy development approach with these families.

REVISITING PAST CONCEPTUALIZATIONS OF THE DUAL PERSPECTIVE

Conceptual and Ecological Clarity

The dual perspective was first conceptualized by Norton (1978), who indicated that it is:

> The conscious and systematic process of perceiving, understanding, and comparing simultaneously the values, attitudes, and behavior of the larger societal system with those of the client's immediate family and community system. It is the conscious awareness of the cognitive and attitudinal levels of similarities and differences in the two systems. (p. 3)

This seminal concept helped other scholars to identify potential opportunities and risks involved in applying the dual perspective to African Americans. Chestang (1979), for example, recognized that when African Americans adopt a dual perspective, it provides a foundation for strengths such as biculturality and cultural maintenance (see Chapter 12). It also reveals risks such as the surfacing of cultural conflicts and ethnic stress that demand resolution for good social/cultural health. He conceptualized the existence of a nurturing environment, based on this perspective, which provides a normative cultural context for African Americans, and a task environment, from which they and other marginalized groups obtain tangible resources and experience barriers to their power and well-being.

Chestang noted that practitioners must be knowledgeable about the ecology of African Americans' lives, about their nurturing environment and its cultural supports, in order to effectively intervene with these families. On the other hand, practitioners must also be aware of risks that the task environment poses for such families, and be prepared, as individuals with often-unacknowledged professional power, to advocate for systems and institutional changes when necessary (Freeman, in press; Linhorst, 2002).

Social Work's Historical Mission

In addition to its support of systems and individual changes, the dual perspective is also consistent with social work values and methods in its rejection of the positivist scientific paradigm as the only or best view of reality. Thus, the dual perspective has made the exploration of alternative theoretical paradigms more feasible, paradigms that are more supportive of the profession's historical mission to serve disadvantaged groups. For instance, social construction theory has provided social work with an alternative way of understanding dominant society's relationship with marginalized groups such as ethnic groups of color, women, the disabled, and the elderly.

This theory assumes the existence of multiple realities, which are determined by people's different positions in society, rather than the existence of only one reality from the standpoint of the dominant discourse. It rejects rigid either-or categories like good or bad and right or wrong, and replaces them with nonhierarchical rubrics such as similarities and differences. Furthermore, the theory values local knowledge while warning against the corrupt use of power, including professionals who use their knowledge to support some client groups and to blame/reject others (Saleebey, 1999).

Other alternative paradigms have been useful as well to social work in this regard. The Africentric approach supports the dual perspective; based on the former's dualistic philosophy that values harmony between people and nature, individual identity as a collective identity, and the union of the material with the spiritual self. Schiele (1997) asserts that: ". . . every individual is a composite and a reflection of the spiritual world of ancestors and the material world of the living" (p. 25). This approach rejects the Eurocentric belief that some people are inherently more special than others, and that based on their status, should be entitled to more value and privileges than others. "Instead of punishing people who may have less resources and talents, the Afrocentric viewpoint ensures that those with less resources and talents can have equal access to the benefits and technology of the entire community or society" (Schiele, 1997, p. 27). Clearly, the Africentric viewpoint is an example of how the dual perspective has been operationalized in African thought and philosophy. Similarly, the Africentric philosophy has lent support to the profession's historical mission by providing an alternative discourse on the diametrical relationship between those with privilege and those who are oppressed and marginalized (Beverly, 2001; Hartmann, Spalter-Roth, Sills, & Yi, 2003).

NEW POSSIBILITIES REGARDING THE DUAL PERSPECTIVE

This above exploration of past experiences in conceptualizing and applying the dual perspective helps in considering new possibilities for its use. As to the future, the dual perspective can be useful in helping African Americans to meet a number of ongoing and emerging challenges. The following challenges are included: (1) efforts to make culture the problem, (2) increased sociopolitical barriers in the task environment that can increase the risk status of black families, (3) trends away from cultural maintenance that have been bolstered by threats to our national security, and (4) related greater demands on black-helping professionals.

A View of Culture as "The Problem"

There are two important aspects of African Americans' cultural experiences that are relevant to this challenge. First, African Americans have a unique and rich culture that reflects who they are and what they believe, value, and practice in terms of cultural traditions, apart from their experiences of oppression. Although they were captured and forcefully removed from their mother country to other countries during the African diaspora, they took many of their cultural traditions and ways of being with them, some of which exist today as strengths, in spite of efforts by Europeans to physically and psychologically restrain manifestations of those traditions, including clothing, language, food, art, religion, music, and family life (Freeman, in press).

A second aspect of African Americans' cultural history has been their experience of slavery and oppression in this country (Butler, Lewis, & Sunderland, 1998), which was designed to destroy the above manifestations of their culture. African Americans developed various ways of responding to and coping with this long-term tyranny, and in the process developed significant strengths and social problems, as well as experienced barriers to formal resources necessary for their survival.

In the current sociopolitical climate, it has become fashionable to label African American culture as the basis for these social problems, by confusing their culture with some of the unsuccessful ways they have responded to and coped with oppression. Hence, as Chapin (1995) explains, dominant society has confused black people and their culture with the social problems they have experienced, and has blamed them for systemic factors that are at the root of those problems. To view African Americans only in terms of those oppression experiences and how they have coped is to miss the essence of who they are as a cultural group.

The dual perspective can be useful in addressing this challenge, that only black people and their culture are responsible for their problems. This perspective supports the assumption that the personal is political, and that problems encountered by all marginalized groups involve both individual and family contributing factors *as well as* systemic or structural roots (Hagen, 1992). Therefore, the perspective can help African Americans to refute this victim-blaming challenge by recognizing the dual sources of their social problems.

Increased Risk Factors in the Task Environment

Increased risk factors for black families related to the social problems identified in the previous section have contributed to the flight of middle-income families from urban ghettos across the country. An ever-widening divide has developed between poor and working class blacks who remain in these ghettos, and many middle-income African Americans who no longer live within the central cities. Many black Americans who no longer live in inner cities continue to have emotional ties, and contacts with relatives, businesses, and service organizations there, as well as attend cultural/social events in inner city areas. In spite of these cultural supports, the loss of financial and leadership resources from those areas has made it easier for local governments and businesses to withdraw basic resources and services from them, contributing to increased risk conditions for the remaining mostly low-income residents.

Again, the dual perspective is useful for addressing this challenge to

African Americans. This perspective can reinforce the dual responsibility of black families to work toward improving their personal well-being *and* that of blacks as a whole simultaneously, instead of viewing this responsibility as an either-or proposition. African Americans will need to join across the widening socioeconomic divide in order to continue efforts to strengthen the nurturing environment and advocate against barriers in the task environment. Oliver (1989) highlights this dual responsibility in his definition of Afrocentricity as:

> The internatization of values that emphasize love of self, awareness of traditional African heritage, and personal commitment to the economic and political power of African Americans and other people of African descent. (p. 26)

Trends Toward Diminishing The Importance of Culture

Threats to this country's national security, such as the September 11th terrorist attack and the possibility of nuclear and/or biological war, have led to increased calls for national patriotism and loyalty. Many believe that the most effective way to handle external threats is for Americas to forget their cultural differences and view themselves as one unified, strong culture. This belief implies the need to return to old approaches to differences such as the melting pot, circle the wagons, assimilation, and colorblind perspectives, hence, diminishing the importance of various ethnic group cultures. This belief seems most tenable when you consider that it has been the rallying cry that led Americans to survival and victory in other perilous times.

However, in the past, African Americans have used the dual perspective as a foundation for their biculturalism, and as an important survival strategy that does not exclude a strong sense of patriotism toward this country. Biculturality and the dual perspective will need new emphasis in the face of this new challenge for national patriotism. Those concepts can clarify for African Americans how they can be *both* patriotic Americans and maintainers of their culture simultaneously, and perhaps serve as models for other ethnic groups in this regard (Taylor-Brown, Garcia, & Kingson, 2001).

Greater Demands on African American Professionals

Practitioners and researchers as a general group have been admonished to maintain a professional and scientific perspective, in accordance with the ethics and procedures within their disciplines. Practitioners and researchers of color, however, typically face additional demands and pressures to assimilate from an individual cultural perspective, and to assume a colorblind or race-neutral stance in their professional work. These pressures have been fed, in part, by this society's melting pot approach to cultural differences and by the positivist research paradigm, which emphasizes scientific objectivity and an antistandpoint theory perspective. Hence, to interject political and social justice issues into practice and research has been considered unprofessional and unscientific by some scholars.

The challenge for all helping professionals of color, and for African American professionals in particular, is to develop alternative models of professionalism that are both culturally centered *and* that take into consideration these conflicting demands from dominant society and their professional cultures. The dual perspective encourages such professionals to wear several hats or to be bicultural or even multicultural. Thus, this perspective can support black professionals in maintaining their indigenous local knowledge about the ethnic cultural world or nurturing environment, and in actively pursuing personal cultural maintenance activities that make assimilation culturally irrelevant. The perspective can also support them in simultaneously integrating their indigenous local knowledge and experiences with their professional knowledge and competence from the task environment, leading to more ethical, professional, and culturally-centered work with black families and communities.

This dual approach by African American professionals implies that they have special stewardship and social responsibility roles with their ethnic communities that, no doubt in the future, will become even more challenging. Professional organizations such as the National Black Psychologists Association and the National Black Social Workers Association can provide resources for meeting this challenge in the form of conferences, published articles, policy analyses and other sponsored research on the topic, and joint practice projects. Local discussion groups and networks can provide additional supports to African American helping professionals by using these and other group approaches. Finally, university departments/schools of social work, psychology, and community development can help address this challenge through curriculum reforms in graduate courses, sponsored forums on the topic, integrated research projects involving African American researchers and practitioners, and culturally sensitive dissemination of information from these efforts.

PRACTICE, RESEARCH, AND POLICY IMPLICATIONS

A number of changes in practice, research, and policy areas are implied from the above discussion of future challenges in services to African American families and their communities. Because these three areas overlap in significant ways, they can also be related to the four challenges in a similar manner. This synergy or integration between the three areas is important because, for too long, rigid divisions have been made between them, making collaboration between research, policy, and direct practice professionals difficult. This pattern may also have made it evident to African American families and communities that such professional issues are more important than the realities of coping with day-to-day life in those communities.

Practice Implications

To address increased sociopolitical barriers in the task environment (Challenge #2), effective practice approaches with black families and communities will need to include both family support and community development/capacity building components. Family supports include resources that help these families to meet their basic needs, both tangible and intangible needs, such as housing, health care, adequate food and clothing, safety, education, and employment and training, as well as general well-being, cultural esteem, and quality of life (Freeman, 2000). These social and economic supports for black families should be provided simultaneously with community capacity building resources in order for families to maintain and enhance the positive qualities of their nurturing environments. Furthermore, those supports can help the residents to address barriers in that environment along with increasing barriers/risks in the task environment, for example, existing violence within their communities and the institutional racism often reflected in the large systems that they encounter (Freeman, 1996).

Another implication is that programs should not use community capacity-building/development approaches in isolation of these family support components. Doing so can reinforce a belief by black families and communities that the related programs and community practitioners are not sufficiently knowledgeable about African American culture as separate from, but related to, the effects of oppression on this population (Challenge #1). It will be clear to these families, for instance, that the practice approach being used is based on assumptions about a lack of individual responsibility and the black culture itself as "the problem."

A third practice implication is the importance of integrating culturally specific components with mainstream or traditional components in programs that serve African American families, based on trends away from cultural maintenance related to national security threats (Challenge #3) (Dunn, 2002). Families and communities may be struggling with cultural conflicts that affect how they practice their traditions (cultural maintenance), environmental barriers to needed resources, low cultural esteem from negative ethnic images in the media and other experiences, and inadequate problem-solving skills. Culturally specific components such as teaching skills for deconstructing negative media messages and facilitating social activism to resolve policy barriers to resources can help to address these and other issues.

Black families also experience universal problems such as loss and grief and role transitions for which some solution focused approaches in mainstream programs can be useful. However, practitioners should consider how the cultural context of black families and communities influences those issues and their responses to these mainstream approaches. This integrated use of culturally specific and mainstream practice approaches with this population will, of course, need to be supported by related curriculum reforms in university graduate programs in social work, psychology, sociology, public health, community development, and the like.

Research Implications

Related to the above practice implications are issues and challenges that arise when conducting research with African American families and communities. These stakeholders are local experts on their rich culture apart from the effects of their oppression experiences on that culture (Challenge #1). Consequently, they should be involved as active partners, collaborators, and participants in the research process. Moreover, based on Challenge #4, regarding the special demands/ unique responsibilities of African American researchers and practitioners, those stakeholders should also be involved as researcher-practitioner collaborators who can effectively integrate their local knowledge about culture with their professional competencies (Galinsky, Turnbull, Meglin, & Wilner (1993). As stakeholders they can ensure that qualitative ethnographic procedures, which are useful for capturing local knowledge and unacknowledged voices, are included in the research process (Bogdan & Taylor, 1990; Freeman, 2000).

African American researcher-practitioner collaborators can direct the focus of studies to how the nurturing environment affects cultural maintenance, esteem, and problem solving, as well as the role of cultural supports and barriers within that environment (Challenge #1 regarding culture as a strength rather than "the problem" and Challenge #3 in terms of trends away from cultural maintenance). These collaborators can also facilitate research on risk factors and supports in the task environment, which are affected so seriously by the increased sociopolitical barriers implied by Challenge #2. The focus on needed systems changes that are identified by such research can inform political action practice approaches that are used with black families and communities, as well as policy reform implications (Chapin, 1995; Freeman, 2000).

Implications for Social Policy Analyses/Reforms

The previous focus on culture as a strength and solution rather than a problem (Challenge #1), has definite implications for social policies. Policy analyses should be a politically motivated research strategy used by research-practice partners in studies conducted in collaboration with black families and communities. Policy reforms that surface from the findings of such research can become the basis for helping professionals' mezzo-macro practice approaches aimed at the systems changes that African American families and communities identify as important for their quality of life, access to needed resources, and opportunities for capacity building (Butless & Smeeding, 2001). In this way, it becomes clear that the potential effectiveness of this three-pronged approach depends on the extent to which helping professionals can integrate their practice, research, and policy efforts. Chapin (1995) indicates that the development of strengths focused policies is dependent on whether marginalized groups are an active part of the policy-making team and whether their local knowledge about cultural issues is valued and acted upon as part of the change process.

CONCLUSION

Clearly, the future of practice, research, and policy on areas of interest to African Americans is both promising and challenging from this discussion. An integrated approach is needed, rather than current fragmented efforts driven by professional issues, as the landscape or task environment confronting black Americans worsens. The dual perspective is useful for countering society's tendency to polarize issues related to culture in a hierarchal manner, from which marginalized groups such as African Americans suffer dire consequences. African American helping professionals and their like-minded white counterparts must use past, current, and future challenges to proactively learn from the past *and* anticipate the future. Only then can they help black Americans to strengthen their nurturing environments in culturally meaningful ways, while simultaneously facilitating their active efforts to address barriers in that environment and within the task environment, using the integrated practice, research, and policy strategies recommended in this epilogue.

REFERENCES

Beverly, S.G. (2001). Material hardship in the United States: Evidence from the survey of income and program participation. *Social Work Research, 25,* 143–151.

Bogdan, R., & Taylor, S. (1990). Looking at the bright side: A positive approach to qualitative policy and evaluation research. *Qualitative Sociology, 13,* 183–192.

Butler, R.N., Lewis, M.I., Sunderland, T. (1998). Special concerns: Race and ethnicity, older women and gender issues, crime, alcoholism, deafness, blindness, and sexuality. In *Aging and mental health: Positive psychosocial and biomedical approaches* (157–200). Boston: Allyn & Bacon.

Butless, G., & Smeeding, T. (2001). The level, trend, and composition of poverty. In S. Danziger & R. Haveman (Eds.), *Understanding poverty* (pp. 320–333). New York: Russell Sage Foundation.

Chapin, R.K. (1995). Social policy development: The strengths perspective. *Social Work, 40,* 483–495.

Chestang, L. (1979). Competencies and knowledge in clinical social work: A dual perspective. In P.L. Ewalt (Ed.), *Toward a definition of clinical social work* (pp. 1–12). Washington, DC: National Association of Social Workers.

Dunn, C. (2002). The importance of cultural competence for social workers. *The New Social Worker, 9,* 4–5.

Freeman, E.M. (In press). African American family violence and substance abuse: A systems perspective. In R.G. McRoy & R. Fong (Eds.), *The intersection of culture, violence, and substance abuse.* Washington, DC: The Council on Social Work Education.

Freeman, E.M. (2000). The use of qualitative social inquiry research to evaluate a multicultural family support-community development program. Paper presented at the International Conference on Evaluation for Practice. Huddersfield, England: University of Huddersfield, School of Human and Health Services.

Freeman, E.M. (1996). Welfare reforms and services for children and families: Setting a new practice, research, and policy agenda. *Social Work, 41,* 521–532.

Galinsky, M.M., Turnbull, J.E., Meglin, D.E., & Wilner, M.E. (1993). Confronting the reality of collaborative practice research: Issues of practice, design, measurement, and team development. *Social Work, 38,* 440–450.

Hagen, J.L. (1992). Women, work, and welfare: Is there a role for social work? *Social Work, 37,* 9–14.

Hartmann, H., Spalter-Roth, R., Sills, M., & Yi, H. (2003). *Survival at the bottom: The income packages of low-income families with children.* Washington, DC: Institute for Women's Policy Research.

Linhorst, D.M. (2002). Federalism and social justice: Implications for social work. *Social Work, 47,* 201–208.

Norton, D. (1978). *The dual perspective.* New York: Council on Social Work Education.

Oliver, W. (1989). Black males and social problems: Prevention through Africentric socialization. *Journal of Black Studies, 20,* 15–39.

Saleebey, D. (1999). *The strengths perspective in social work* (Second Edition). New York: Macmillan.

Schiele, J. (1997). An Afrocentric perspective on social welfare philosophy and policy. *Journal of Sociology and Social Welfare, 44,* 21–39.

Taylor-Brown, S., Garcia, A., & Kingson, E. (2001). Cultural competence versus cultural chauvinism: Implications for social work. *Health and Social Work, 26,* 185–187.

AUTHOR INDEX

A

Adams, J.A., 98
Ager, J., 171
Ager, R., 66
Akbar, N., 208, 211, 215, 241
Alejandro-Wright, M., 201
Alexander, A., 184, 192
Alexander, M., 230
Algotsson, S., 238
Alisultanov, I., 293
Allen, J.A., 14, 15
Allen, W., 17
Allen-Meares, P., 25, 158
Almeida, R., 253
American Association of Retired Persons,
    author, 249
Amuleru-Marshall, 136,
Anderson, J.P., 240, 243, 249, 254
Anderson, K.L., 107
Anderson, M.R., 178
Anderson, N.B., 72, 76, 77, 78
Anderson, S.C., 140
Angelou, M., 184
Apraku, K.K., 15
Ards, S., 247
Asante, M., 9, 13, 193, 208, 210
Astin, M., 98
Austin, W.B., 204

B

Bachman, J.G., 138, 141
Bailey-Etta, B., 247, 248
Baker, F.M., 73, 140, 141

Baker, S., 144
Baldwin, J.A., 11, 208
Banerjee, M.M., 293, 295
Banfield, E.C., 206
Banks, R., 137
Banks, W.M., 202
Barnes, S.L., 5
Barry, B., 282
Barth, R.P., 247
Barusch, A.S., 282
Baughman, J.T., 76
Beckerman, A., 141, 145
Beckett, J.O., 125
Behl, L.E., 97
Bell, C.C., 111, 140, 141
Belton, W.J., 78
Bennett, E.C., 119, 120
Bennice, J.A., 98
Benokraitis, N.V., 98
Berg, I.K., 124
Berger, R.L., 147
Berla, N., 175
Berrick, J.D., 247
Berry, J.W., 210
Berry, M.F., 186
Beverly, S.G., 44, 309
Biegel, D.E., 229
Billig, S., 175
Billingsley, A., 17, 74, 78, 119, 131, 185, 202,
    207, 240, 267
Billson, J., 203
Biordi, D.L., 14
Bischoff, U.M., 123
Blake, W.M., 240, 247, 249, 254
Blassingame, J.C., 186

SUBJECT INDEX

A

African continuity or survival perspective, assumptions about, 7–8; effects on adaptation of Africans to slavery, 8; foundation for a common heritage framework, 8

African discontinuity perspective, assumptions about, 6–7; cultural limitations of programs based on, 7

Africentric/Afrocentric practice approaches, application to practice cases/situations, 31–37; components of, 9–15, figure 1.1; culturally relevant ecomaps and genograms for, 33–37, figures 2.2 and 2.3; practice framework for, 29–31, table 2.1; relevance to cultural maintenance for black families, 250–257

Africentricity/Afrocentricity, definition of related to African descended people, 9, 210; research framework for studies on African American men, 210–211; research framework for studies on black women, 192–194; support provided for addressing social justice issues, 277–278; underlying theory for, 240–241

Assets building approaches, for economic development in black communities, 292–294

B

Black Church, as an important social support for the elderly, 222–223; its role in black family and community housing production, 58–60; spirituality related to, 27–29; traditional helping role during slavery, 284, 286

C

Challenges and risks, common to African Americans, 13–14; 26–27; focused on substance abuse problems, 136–137; involving environmental factors relevant to educational achievement, 159–163; linked to future social-political conditions, 309–313; of importance to the black elderly, 222; related to mental health of African Americans, 72–73; relevant to cultural maintenance goals, 243; role demands on black researchers and practitioners, 311–313; significant to black men, 204–205

Common heritage framework, of African descended people, components of, 9–13, figure 1.1; focused on work and employment, 119; implications for social work practice with, 9; overview of, 8–9; within-group differences related to, 14–15

Community building approaches, addressing work and employment needs of black families, 126–127; effects of deficit research on communities' efforts to address substance abuse issues, 146–147; focus on cultural maintenance needs, 256–257; importance in increasing housing accessibility, 57–61; relevance to social justice issues, 275; significance